Hercules
of the
Revolution
a novel based on the life of Peter Francisco

by

Travis S. Bowman
a 6th Generation Descendant of Peter Francisco

with James Warder

Copyright © 2009 by Travis S. Bowman

Published in the United States by Bequest Publishing and printed at Lightening Source Incorporated in Tennessee.

Library of Congress Control Number: 2009905525
Bowman, Travis S.
Hercules of the Revolution : a novel based on the Life of Peter Francisco / Travis S. Bowman. – 2nd Edition

---

Cover designed by Comfort Publishing.

Photos provided by:
Stephen Wilfong Photography
District Design Studio
Out of the Darkroom – Film Photography

Editing by:
Linda-Lee Bowman
Kim Cassell

ISBN: 978-0-615-29635-7

Printed in the United States of America

Second paperback edition.

Bequest Publishing
PO Box 1239
Davidson, NC 28036
(877) 783-8380
HerculesoftheRevolution.com

HISTORIC SITES AND FACTS ABOUT PETER FRANCISCO

Peter Francisco's home in Dillwyn, Virginia called Locust Grove was listed on the National Register of Historic Places in 1972.

This historic marker in Hopewell, Virginia quotes George Washington's famous saying that Peter was his "One Man Army".

This Peter Francisco monument stands downtown Newark, New Jersey across from Penn Station.

This Peter Francisco monument stands at the Guilford Courthouse National Military Park in Greensboro, North Carolina.

HISTORIC SITES AND FACTS ABOUT PETER FRANCISCO

This Peter Francisco monument stands in Hopewell, Virginia close to where he was found abandoned on a dock in 1765.

This Peter Francisco monument stands in New Bedford, Massachusetts recognizing him as a patriot of Portuguese descent. The plaque quotes George Washington's famous saying about Peter.

The United States Post Service issued this bicentennial stamp in honor of Peter Francisco in 1976.

This portrait of Peter Francisco was painted in 1828 and hangs in the hall of the Virginia State Capitol building.

CONTENTS

About the Author..6

Acknowledgements...7

Preface...9

1) Give Me Liberty or Give Me Death.................................11

2) Life in the Azores Islands...25

3) Kidnapped by Pirates...37

4) Alone and Abandoned...49

5) Slavery not School..65

6) From Boyhood to Manhood...83

7) A Call to Arms, March 1775.......................................103

8) Preparing to Leave...123

9) Off to War..135

10) A Battle and a Friend for Life...................................149

11) New Battles and a Winter of Distress............................163

12) Another Battle, Another Musketball.............................189

13) The Hercules of the Revolution.................................201

14) A Return to Virginia...217

15) Peter and Susannah..237

16) Colonel Mayo and the Cannon..................................255

17) Burying a Friend...271

18) A Gift from Washington...285

19) Left for Dead...301

20) The End is Near..317

Epilogue..327

ABOUT THE AUTHOR

 Travis Bowman is a 6th generation descendant of Peter Francisco. He is of similar stature standing 6'6" tall just like Peter and is featured on the front cover. As an actor he enjoys telling Peter's story through dramatic impersonations with a 6' broadsword similar to the one George Washington had made for Peter. Travis' family is originally from Virginia where Peter was raised and resided most of his life. Coincidently, Travis was born the day after Virginia declared March 15th, Peter Francisco Day.

Travis's grandfather was stationed in London during WWII, and his father served the US for forty years at the Department of Defense. He was born and raised in Baltimore, Maryland, lived in Europe as a kid for three years, and spent eight years in the beautiful Pacific Northwest. Today, he resides in Charlotte, North Carolina with his wife and two boys.

ACKNOWLEDGEMENTS

There are many people in my life that I want to thank for assisting directly or indirectly with this book. Please forgive me if I forget to acknowledge the part that you played in this literary work, but know that I am thankful for all the friends and family that have helped over the years.

In memory of Rosalie Francisco Barret, my great-grandmother and great-granddaughter of Peter Francisco, I am ever indebted to the phenomenal heritage that she passed down to me. I appreciate her lovingly caring for my mother when she was a young girl and for raising a great son.

To Bill and Mildred Barret, Rosalie's first born son and daughter-in-law and my grandparents, I am so thankful that you shared Peter Francisco's story with me when I was a little boy. Granddaddy, who passed away in 2003, was a hard working man and always provided for his family. Grandmother, you're very sweet and I love to hear you share about life events from years gone by. You have an amazing memory! Thank you for raising my mother, Linda-Lee, to be a nurturing and loving mother.

I want to thank my parents; Paul and Linda-Lee Bowman, for teaching me to appreciate the freedom that we enjoy in this country.

Mom, I am especially thankful for the countless hours that you spent editing and revising this book. Thank you, Dad, for teaching me Godly character and what it means to be a real hero.

Thank you, Michelle – my love and best friend, for your support as I spent so many hours researching Peter's story, and then countless more hours behind a computer putting it into a book. Thank you for always loving me and believing in me despite my failures.

To Austin and Josh, my boys, thank you for understanding when I missed a game or time with you so that I could work on this book. You guys are the best sons a father could ask for. Always remember to be grateful for the freedom you have in the United States of America because of those who fought with bravery and honor, just as Peter Francisco did.

Last but not least, thank you, James Warder and Bruce Nemet, for working with me to put this epic legend onto paper and into a novel. Without you this story would have never come to life, and my great-grandfather's story might have never been told.

PREFACE

Have you ever thought about all the things that you enjoy on a daily basis? The average American owns a home, a car, a computer, a cell phone, a television with over one hundred channels to watch at any given time, and many other things that are considered luxuries in other countries. We shuffle our kids around to different sporting events, and we so easily forget that everything we enjoy came at a price...a high price.

When I was nine years old, my father was stationed in Germany with the Department of Defense, and we lived in a small village for three years. It didn't take long for me to realize that many people from other countries could only dream of living in the United States. That experience began a journey in my own life of understanding how blessed I am to live in the United States of America.

When I was young, my grandmother - Mildred Barret, told me that I was related to a giant from the Revolutionary War, but I was well into my thirties before I began to research the stories of my ancestor. It wasn't until I visited one of the four Peter Francisco monuments on the east coast that I found out the whole story.

I really connected with Peter's story on two levels. First, I realized that I stood the same height as Peter, which put me in his shoes and helped me to see life from his perspective. Secondly, I have always despised racism, and this story shows the atrocity of determining a person's worth by the color of his skin. But, Peter doesn't let that ruin his life and, ultimately, he triumphs over racial discrimination.

I hope that you find this story of bravery, strength, romance, and honor about my great-grandfather just as inspiring as I did. But more importantly, I hope that you become more appreciative of the freedom you enjoy and inspired by the blood that was shed for your happiness.

1

GIVE ME LIBERTY OR GIVE ME DEATH

Arising with dawn on that mild morning, he readied himself to head for the nearby livery stable where he would prepare for the short carriage ride from the inn where he and Judge Winston had stayed to St. John's Church. It was the largest building in Richmond, and that March 23, 1775 would put the otherwise ordinary place of worship on the map of American history in a way that Peter Francisco could not have imagined.

As he exited the inn, Peter looked up and down the main street of the largest town he had ever visited. It would appear that the entire population of nearly 600 was still fast asleep. The lone figure of this giant teenager -- six-feet, six inches tall nearing his 15th birthday -- strode almost silently toward the livery, save for the crunching sound of dirt clods beneath his 240-pound body. He was happy to see that he really wasn't the only person awake in town. The stable owner was there preparing for another busy day, expecting large crowds of people again from all over the Virginia colony like those who had descended the last few days on Richmond, the seat of the Second Virginia Convention.

"Good morning, sir," spoke Peter respectfully to the man whose back was turned while gathering oats for his equestrian guests to breakfast on.

Startled, the man turned around to see Peter's immense figure standing in the doorway. "Good morning to you, too. I was just getting ready to feed your two American Cream Drafts…beautiful creatures they are."

"Yes, they are beautiful," Peter responded. "But you look like you've got lots of horses to feed today, so I'll take care of mine." The fact that the two horses actually belonged to the judge and not to Peter was of little consequence. From the very first day Peter had laid eyes on these two equines, he had adored them as if they were indeed his own.

He took a bucket of oats in each of his oversized hands and walked over to the huge beasts. At his height, Peter could look them in the eye. "There, there, now, I've brung you something to eat." Almost in unison, the horses seemed to nod a greeting to Peter as he approached. Each, in turn, nuzzled his face before dipping his massive head in the bucket. "We've a big day before us," he said softly to the horses. "The judge says we'll be hearing great and powerful things at the church today. Then later in the week the judge says we'll be headin' back home to Hunting Tower. Do you miss Hunting Tower? Of course you do."

12

After they had finished eating, Peter entered their stall and began brushing and rubbing their ivory-colored coats. He loved feeling their well-defined muscles twitching under his deft hand. This closeness of feelings between man and beast was unusual to say the least. Having finished their rubdown, Peter then gathered their collars, bits and bridals and prepared them to be hitched to the carriage that he and Judge Winston had ridden from Hunting Tower Plantation in Buckingham County. The judge was the local representative to this convention, a convention that would ultimately go far in deciding the fate of the colonies in their disagreements with England.

Now, most carriage drivers would simply take their horses around to the back of the stable where all the visitor carriages were kept, but Peter decided to wheel the carriage around to the front himself. He grabbed the tongue of the carriage and, as big as he was, easily guided it through the massive doors on the front side of the stable, then returned for the horses. As he began to hitch them up, he noticed Judge Winston walking down the street.

"Good morning, Peter. I trust you slept well," he greeted.

"Yes, sir, and good morning to you," Peter replied.

"Have you had your breakfast?"

"No, sir. I had the innkeeper's wife fix me some biscuits last night, and I'll eat them later. I just thought it best to be ready to go whenever you wanted, seein' as how you don't like to never be late for meetings and things."

"You know me well, Peter, you know me well."

During the course of the conversation, Peter had been finishing the job of hitching the horses to the carriage, which now stood ready to take the judge to his destination.

"Excellent, Peter," said Winston. "Then we should be getting on to the church. I have a feeling in my bones that we are about to make history today." With the demeanor of a dedicated servant, Peter opened the door to the carriage and the judge took his seat. Then Peter climbed onto the driver's station. Before giving the signal, he reached down beneath his feet to feel where he had placed the sword and pistol the judge had asked him to bring on this trip. They were still there, right where he had placed them only a few minutes before.

"Gidup," Peter prodded the horses in his gentle voice, and the Creams obeyed his command instantly.

As they rode to the outskirts of town in silence, they passed many fine homes belonging to some of the wealthier residents of Richmond. Soon St. John's Church came into view, sitting almost majestically on a hill overlooking the James River. It was an imposing structure, adorned in white with a massive spire rising out of the center front of the church and encasing the large front doors. Completed in 1741, the church was a part of Henrico Parish, a parish that had been established by early settlers in 1611.

A few other folks had arrived early, as well. Patrick Henry, the judge's nephew, was talking to two other men who appeared to be of equal substance and stature as he. Peter couldn't know it at the time, but they were Thomas Jefferson and George Washington. At six-feet-two, Washington was an especially imposing figure, though he seemed less

14

imposing by remaining quiet, just nodding in agreement as Jefferson and Henry engaged in animated conversation.

Indeed, today history would be made and would set a course that would change the destiny of the New World; but no one here could possibly imagine that. At least not yet.

Among those arriving at the church to occupy seats in the visitor's gallery were Susannah Anderson and her father. Peter noticed their arrival, and just a single look at Susannah made his heart skip a beat; at least it felt that way to Peter. Even though they lived in totally different social strata, his previous encounters with both the young lady and her father emboldened Peter. Although his knees felt like the jelly he had often spread on a Sunday morning biscuit, he ambled over to their carriage. When he had covered the twenty or so yards' distance, Peter reached up to take hold of Susannah's hand as she stepped down from the fully enclosed carriage. That touch sent chills down Peter's spine.

"Why, Peter," she said, "you are always such a gentleman. And how are you today?"

"Seeing you has made me much better already." Peter was almost shocked to even say such bold words.

Susannah's father had departed the opposite side of the carriage and walked around the back to where Peter and Susannah stood. He noticed that their eyes seemed locked on each other as he tapped Peter on the shoulder. He wasn't entirely sure he liked that, but after all, Peter had saved his daughter's life. "Peter, my boy, it's good to see you again. And I see you're wearing the hat I gave you…wonderful, wonderful."

"Yes, sir," said Peter. "I save wearin' it for special occasions like this."

"Indeed, today should be very special. It will be good to get all this nonsense out of the way at last. Come now, Susannah, we want to find good seats in the church."

As her father grabbed her arm, Susannah glanced back. "Bye, Peter, I'll see you later."

"Good day, Miss Susannah." Peter's mouth felt like he had been crossing the desert.

He rejoined the judge, regaining his senses and remembering his duties as bodyguard.

Other dignitaries also began to arrive, and soon they were all filing into the church. Judge Winston looked at Peter and said, "You might want to take station near one of the windows today. My nephew intends to address the body with words I think important for you to hear."

During the previous days of the convention, Peter had lingered around the open windows, due to unseasonably mild temperatures, but most of the speeches he had heard had not been very inspiring, and most seemed to favor keeping relations with Great Britain as they were. But Peter knew the position that the judge's nephew would take, and he wanted to hear every persuasive word. At his size, Peter was able to easily make his way to one of the windows. Through it he could see the judge, Patrick Henry and the two men that Henry had been speaking to earlier. He could also see Susannah Anderson and her father, and his heart skipped a beat again, for this young lady had truly captured his fancy.

Different people rose, spoke and sat. Some of them inspired mild clapping or audible "Here, here's." None of them was very noteworthy until Patrick Henry rose from seat number forty-seven, strode purposefully and confidently to the center of the room, and turned to address the delegates.

"No man, Mr. President, thinks more highly than I do of the patriotism, as well as abilities, of the very honorable gentlemen who have just addressed this House," Henry began, his tone almost apologetic. "But different men often see the same subject in different lights; and, therefore, I hope it will not be thought disrespectful of those worthy gentlemen if, entertaining as I do opinions of a character very opposite to theirs, I shall speak forth my sentiments freely and without reserve."

Henry's voice began to rise. "This is no time for ceremony. The question before this House is one awful moment to the country. For my own part, I consider it as nothing less than a question of freedom or slavery; and in proportion to the magnitude of the subject ought to be the freedom of the debate...." Peter watched as Henry began to circle the room, making eye contact with as many delegates as possible, while not speaking a word.

"Mr. President," Henry began again, "it is natural to man to indulge in the illusions of hope. We are apt to shut our eyes against a painful truth, and listen to the song of that siren till she transforms us into beasts. Is this the part of wise men, engaged in a great and arduous struggle for liberty?" With that utterance, the young patriot held out his arms from his sides as if asking the question of all there assembled.

"Are we disposed to be of the number of those who, having eyes, see not, and, having ears, hear not, the things which so nearly concern their temporal salvation? For my part, whatever anguish of spirit it may

17

cost, I am willing to know the whole truth; to know the worst, and to provide for it." Henry let his arms drop to his sides and his shoulders slump. He stood silent for several moments, and Peter wondered if he was finished. Then with arms raised and hands above his head, he looked toward the ceiling and continued, "I know no way of judging the future but by the past. And judging by the past, I should wish to know what there has been in the conduct of the British ministry for the last ten years to justify those hopes with which gentlemen have been pleased to solace themselves and the members of this House."

Peter scanned the room. While some of the listeners just sat impassively, others were nodding in agreement, including Judge Winston, Thomas Jefferson and George Washington. As for Jefferson, a small smile crept across his face. Peter took a moment to further survey the visitor's gallery until his eyes rested on Susannah. She was shaking her head, and Peter was a bit disheartened, for he was drawing his own conclusions, and they were much different from what hers appeared to be. Nevertheless, at that moment, she looked toward the window where Peter was standing, and when her eyes met his, she couldn't help but smile demurely. "Suffer not yourselves to be betrayed with a kiss. Ask yourselves how this gracious reception of our petition comports with those warlike preparations, which cover our water and darken our land," the young orator pleaded.

Henry was again moving around the room with arms waving, the tone of his voice imploring for answers to his questions. Peter, too, was being swept up in the emotional pleadings. "Let us not deceive ourselves, sir. These are the implements of war and subjugation; the last arguments to which kings resort." Fatigued, Henry dropped his arms once again to his side. He looked as though he had been beaten, but he had not been, for when he spoke again, his voice crescendoed. "They are meant for us; they can be meant for no other. They are sent over to bind and rivet upon us those chains which the British ministry have been so long forging. And what do we have to oppose them?"

More of the delegates were nodding in agreement now, and Peter could sense his own head doing the same. "Shall we resort to entreaty and humble supplication? Let us not, I beseech you, sir, deceive ourselves. Sir, we have done everything that could be done to avert the storm which is now coming on. We have petitioned; we have remonstrated; we have supplicated; we have prostrated ourselves before the throne, and we have implored its interposition to arrest the tyrannical hands of the ministry and Parliament." Henry's voice grew louder, his gestures more exaggerated. "Our petitions have been slighted; our remonstrances have produced additional violence and insult; our supplications have been disregarded; and we have been spurned, with contempt, from the foot of the throne!"

Henry allowed himself a moment to turn completely around and cast his eyes across the sea of delegates. Then his eyes glanced out the window where Peter was standing, and a look of acknowledgement was exchanged between them. Henry began to speak more rapidly. "If we wish to be free -- if we mean to preserve inviolate those inestimable privileges for which we have been so long contending, if we mean not basely to abandon the noble struggle in which we have been so long engaged, and which we have pledged ourselves never to abandon until the glorious object of our contest shall be obtained -- we must fight! I repeat it, sir, we must fight." Henry had grabbed a nearby banister that

19

separated him from some of the delegates. He gazed at the men he knew to be in favor of appeasement and lowered his face to theirs, his eyes fierce with passion. "An appeal to arms and to the God of hosts is all that is left us!" Henry turned to face the rest of the body there assembled. "They tell us, sir, that we are weak; unable to cope with so formidable an adversary." Everyone knew that he was referring to those men he had just personally addressed. "But when shall we be stronger? Will it be the next week, or the next year? Will it be when we are totally disarmed, and when a British guard shall be stationed in every house?"

Some of the delegates began straining to hear every word of the orator's now moderated tone. Peter cocked his head further into the window as well, with the added benefit of seeing Susannah more easily. "Shall we acquire the means of effectual resistance by lying supinely on our backs and hugging the delusive phantom of hope, until our enemies shall have bound us hand and foot?"

Beginning a gradual rise in voice, Henry further entreated his audience, "The battle, sir, is not to the strong alone; it is to the vigilant, the active, the brave. Besides, sir, we have no election. If we were base enough to desire it, it is now too late to retire from the contest. There is no retreat but in submission and slavery! Our chains are forged! Their clanking may be heard on the plains of Boston! The war is inevitable…and let it come! I repeat, sir, let it come!"

It was all Peter could do to contain himself. He so dearly wanted to cheer, yet he knew it was not his place to demonstrate in such a manner. Some shouts of affirmation issued from within the church. Other delegates yelled in the negative. Patrick Henry just stood silent, waiting for their voices to be stilled. When he spoke again, his voice was

20

measured. "It is in vain, sir, to extenuate the matter. Gentlemen may cry, "Peace, Peace," but there is no peace. The war is actually begun!" His voice intensified now. "The next gale that sweeps from the north will bring to our ears the clash of resounding arms." With continued crescendo, Henry's voice was now louder than at any other time. "Our brethren are already in the field! Why stand we here idle? What is it that gentlemen wish? What would they have?"

Henry once again circled the room. "Is life so dear, or peace so sweet, as to be purchased at the price of chains and slavery?" He returned to the center of the room, his eyes raised skyward. "Forbid it, Almighty God!"

With arms raised above his head, Patrick Henry made his final declaration. "I know not what course others may take; but as for me, give me liberty or give me death." These last words were delivered as thunder, while he remained in his pose.

Many of the delegates were on their feet cheering and applauding, among whom were Washington, Jefferson and Judge Winston. Some of the people remained seated. Peter had never felt such emotion. His very soul had been swept away. Out of the corner of his eye, he saw the Andersons rise and make their way to the front door. Peter pushed through the crowd of men gathered around him, pressing toward the window so that they, too, could hear. He ran around to the front of the church just in time for the Andersons to exit. "Wasn't that speech compelling?" Peter commented to the Andersons. "But do you not agree with it all?"

Susannah's father brusquely brushed past Peter, preferring not to engage conversation. His daughter turned, and the eyes with which Peter

21

had been so enchanted glared back at him. "If that foolishness is truly what you think, Peter Francisco, then you are also a fool -- a fool on a fool's errand. So go back to your foolish friends. But I warn you, this course will render nothing but heartache and despair. Good day." Watching Susannah enter the carriage with her father, Peter stood feeling crushed, as though someone had hit him in the chest with a twenty-pound blacksmith's hammer.

As her carriage pulled out of sight, leaving only a dusty trail, Peter thought about the words of Patrick Henry, and one word stood out more than any of the others. Freedom. What did it really mean? What would it mean to him? If he were free, could he come and go as he pleased? Could he one day own property? Could he marry a young lady like Susannah Anderson?

Slumping down pensively on a nearby tree stump, propping his head with those huge hands, the dejected teenager focused his eyes on the road ahead. Yet he continued to ponder Patrick Henry's words. They seemed to reverberate in his head like waves crashing against a boat, their ebb and flow much like the emotional tide Peter found himself experiencing at this very moment. He looked down at the James River. It was that river on which Portuguese pirates had abandoned a young boy at City Point nearly ten years ago. He wondered where his family was now and what they were doing. He had been just five-years-old, such an innocent age, when the precious gift of freedom had been stripped away from him. Peter thought about the long road behind him and the journey he had taken since that time when he was so young…and so afraid.

Now putting fear aside and discounting how the Andersons had reacted, Peter knew -- he knew deep in his very soul -- that freedom was well worth fighting for. More than that, he now knew it was well worth dying for.

2

LIFE IN THE AZORES ISLANDS

Life in the Azores Islands was nearly idyllic in 1765, especially for a five-year-old boy whose family was comparatively wealthy relative to many others on the island of Terceira. Little Pedro Francisco was a bundle of energy, and he loved exploring near the family home, a home that by the standards of the day and place would be considered a mansion.

Pedro could not recall all the details of his family's arrival from Portugal. He barely remembered the day when they had set sail from the mainland to these islands discovered by Portuguese explorers in the early 1400's. Located about 950 miles from Portugal, the island of Terceira, one of several making up the Azores, was originally known as the Island of Jesus Cristo and was later known as the Phantom Island of Brazil. But none of that mattered to Pedro.

The island, by any name, was the best place to live in the whole world, at least for this noble boy. Sometimes Pedro just stood in the front yard and watch the entertainment on the ocean. From there, on the hills overlooking the harbor of Porto Judeu, he could make out dolphins and whales cavorting in the ocean, including the mammoth Sperm Whale and distinctively marked Orcas. Though very young, Pedro was saddened that whaling ships from all over the world could be seen harpooning these magnificent creatures, dragging them to shore and harvesting anything in the least bit worthwhile, then dragging the carcass back out to sea for an inglorious burial. However, that didn't dampen the boy's love for the ocean, and he could almost imagine himself as a seafarer one day. At other times, he and his sister wandered down to the port itself. The harbor always seemed to be teeming with all types of ships and sloops, and there was a buzz of activity with these vessels offloading riches from the Americas and India, then taking on cargo of grain and woad, a local plant that yielded rich, deep dyes.

Terceira Island was actually the culmination of four overlapping stratovolcanoes, whose combined mass was a mere 148 square miles. The youngest of those volcanoes had erupted only a couple of years before the family had arrived, and since it was due west of Porto Judeu, and the winds seemed to prevail from that direction, the faint smell of sulphur, -- or rotten eggs -- would occasionally wafted over the coastal waters where Pedro roamed; and on clear days, some smoke could still be seen billowing from the now- resting volcanic dome.

As with all tropically-influenced weather systems, the winds frequently interrupted a day of exploring by the sudden onset of a rain shower or thunderstorm. Nevertheless, that didn't stop Pedro -- and occasionally his sister -- from exploring nearby grottos with their stalactites and stalagmites. From time to time, family and friends spent the day at Mata da Serreta, a forest on the volcano's slope that featured such lush vegetation that a soul could easily become lost in contemplation surrounded by such beauty of paradise.

Pedro was especially fond of watching the islands' variety of bird life, including all types of shearwaters and petrels. He was particularly taken by the Azorean buzzards, for which the group of islands had been named, as these birds were so tame that they would actually eat from the young boy's hand.

One evening Pedro's father, Machado Luiz, and his mother, Antonia Maria Francisco, were entertaining some guests. As always, Pedro, despite his youthfulness, was allowed the run of the house, but he also knew to be quiet when the adults were deep in conversation.

"Father, said Antonia Maria, "it is time to eat. Will you say the blessing?"

"Aww – I wanted to say the prayer that you taught me, Mama," pleaded young Pedro in a sad voice.

"Alright, son. Are you sure that you won't be embarrassed to say in in front of our guests?"

"No, Mama!" replied Pedro. He then folded his hands, bowed his head and prayed.

"Com Jesus me deito (With Jesus I go to sleep),

Com Jesus me levasto (With Jesus I awake),

27

Com a grac'a de Deus (With the grace of God),

E do Espirito Santo (and of the Holy Spirit), Amen."

After he finished praying, he sat down at the dinner table next to his papa and listened to him talk with a person who was held in high regard throughout the Azores.

"So, Machado, as a man of prominence in Portugal, what was it that brought you to our tropical paradise?" the man asked.

"Oh, I guess the best answer is the politics," Machado replied.

"So, it would seem that you found yourself on the wrong side of the power struggle," the man replied knowingly.

"Actually, it wasn't so much that we were on the wrong side. No, we chose not to take sides. But when King Joseph decided to make the Marquis de Pombal the real ruler, everything began to fall apart. First it was the so-called conspiracy of nobles to murder the king and Pombal himself. Actually, I don't really know if there was a conspiracy or not, but that was all that Pombal needed to begin his purge of anyone the least bit suspicious. Then, all the Jesuits were expelled, or worse, God forbid. Even though we had never aligned ourselves with any of those involved, a good friend with a connection to the power of the throne warned me that my noble family might be targeted. Really, we had no choice but to escape."

That conversation brought some clarity to Pedro. Even though he was very young, he did indeed remember living a royal life in Portugal, residing in a castle with manicured grounds and servants who took care of every need. He then recalled the family loading up several carriages and wagons in the dark of night and boarding a ship that traveled for several days before making landfall there on Terceira. He recalled asking his father where they were going, but there had been no reply.

What he didn't remember and had no way of knowing was that his father had secured the family's wealth and brought it with him. It was what made possible their passage on the ship that had brought them there. That was how his family could now live, even though Machado never had to work, and it was how his father could build such a magnificent home.

Although it had taken several months to construct, and the family had lived in somewhat less desirable quarters for a time, the home at the top of the hill was indeed breathtaking. The walls, soft brown and with quite a rough texture, were made of crushed shells and sand, which, when mixed with water and dried, were as solid as rock.

Inside, four rooms were dedicated as sleeping quarters, and there were rooms for dining, for food preparation, and a gathering room where Pedro had overheard his father's conversation. Outside, an arbor had been constructed, where hydrangeas of every color were planted with great care. Off to one side was a courtyard where Pedro and his sister liked to play with an oversized ball. Because of the ruggedness of the surrounding terrain, a simple set of iron gates and minimal fencing were all that were needed to secure the property from those who would be jealous of the family's apparent wealth.

This night, as the boy listened to his father conversing with guests, was a crisp evening in May, and the clouds had just cleared, making way for the sun's rays to light up the lush, green mountainside in Porto Judeu. Spring flowers on Terceira Island, with blooms in full color as if to invite bees in for the nectar, drank from the seasonal showers.

29

Pedro came running up the gravel hill and through the iron gates at his parents' home. He had just come back from evening church services on this holy day, although he could not remember the actual importance of this particular occasion. In fact, he was never especially fond of going to church in the first place. The problem was that he always had to get dressed up in clothes not entirely suitable for a young boy bursting at the seams with exuberance. Today he had worn a short jacket over a fancy blouse with ruffled cuffs and collar and a knickers-type pair of pants. The only thing that didn't bother Pedro about this costume was his shoes. He loved his shoes. They had prominent buckles that bore the initials P and F on the right and left shoes respectively. These had been made from silver extracted from mines in the north of Spain.

Pedro was completely out of breath when the rest of the family finally caught up to him holding onto the gate. "Mama, do we really have to go to bed? The sun isn't even down past the mountain, and sister and I didn't get to play ball in the courtyard yet," Pedro whined.

"Tomorrow morning is going to come early, Pedro," said Maria, "and we are going to the market right after breakfast, so I want you to be well rested."

"But, mama, you promised that we could play in the courtyard," Pedro insisted.

Maria turned to Machado. "Papa, what do you think?" she pressed on behalf of the children.

"All right, you have thirty minutes, but then you two are going straight to bed," replied Machado. He leaned down and kissed them both on the head and said, "I love you!" Giggling and skipping, Pedro and his sister ran off through the garden and into the south side of the courtyard where they liked to kick their ball back and forth. As the sky turned shades of azure and violet, Maria and Machado headed inside to settle in for the evening. Machado customarily took his shoes off and sat down in his favorite chair, one that he had brought from Portugal.

Playing in the corner of the courtyard at a makeshift net that his father had purchased from a fishing boat in the harbor, Pedro tried unsuccessfully to block the ball his sister had kicked past him. They had been playing for only a few minutes when they heard a noise across the courtyard outside the gate. The noise piqued the boy's curiosity because it sounded like one of the Azorean buzzards that he so liked to feed. After listening to the sound for a few seconds, Pedro ran off to find the tropical bird that he assumed was chirping.

"Come back here, Pedro!" yelled his sister as she hurried after him. "Mama and Papa will be angry." Either he couldn't hear his sister or he just wasn't paying attention, although the latter probably was the case. In any event, the lad never broke stride as he sought at least a glimpse of one of his favorite island creatures. His was a singular purpose, a purpose that would ultimately change his life forever.

As he rounded the corner to the gate, he stopped dead in his tracks. His feet were frozen in the brown dirt and his eyes grew wide. He thought for a fleeting moment that he should be afraid, but he wasn't, at least not yet. There before him were two men, sailors by the looks of them. Each wore pants that were ragged at the bottoms, and well-worn shirts with a variety of colored patches to cover where they had been torn, and bandanas on their heads. Both of them wore a wide, brown, leather belt into which they had tucked a flintlock pistol and a fearsome dagger. Despite the ominous appearance, however, Pedro was drawn by

31

a small sack of some sort carried by one of the men. He had stopped about ten feet in front of them, with his sister nearly catching up to him.

Before he could utter a sound, one of the men looked the young boy in the eyes and smiled. "We just sailed in from Portugal, and your dad asked our captain to bring these sweets back as a gift. Now be a good boy and take these inside to your father," he said.

For a fleeting moment, Pedro thought that maybe these were bad men like Mama and Papa had warned about so many times. Then again, he had always had a sweet tooth and the very thought of some candy, a rarity on the island, was far too tempting for him to resist. As he started walking towards the men, his sister rounded the corner and saw the dingy-looking thugs enticing her brother.

"Pedro, stop!" she screamed.

When he turned to look at his sister running towards him, one of the men lunged forward throwing a burlap sack over his head. In a single motion, he flipped the sack onto his shoulder with Pedro in it. Pedro's sister let out a scream as shrill and as loud as she could muster. The other sailor ran toward her and tried to grab her, but he only caught the hem of her sweater, and that pulled off. The man stood there clutching the sweater and looking at his comrade as if to say, "Now what do we do?" But they turned and hastily made their way down the hill toward Porto Judeu.

Meanwhile, Pedro's sister, still screaming in terror, was approaching the house. Hearing the commotion and instinctively recognizing the panic in her voice, Machado came running outside to see his daughter with a look of terror on her face, pointing toward the iron gate. She was mumbling something about Pedro and two mean-looking men. Machado, grasping the seriousness of the situation, bolted past her. Unfortunately, the thugs, having a significant head start, were well on their way down the path to the harbor. In the distance, Machado could see one of the men with a burlap bag slung over his shoulder, and he could faintly hear his son yelling, "Papa, Papa, help. Help me, Papa." Machado immediately knew that he couldn't possibly catch up with the kidnappers if he followed the winding path -- they had gained too much ground. But if he took a straight path through all the bush and bramble, maybe, just maybe, he could catch them.

Despite the fact that he was barefoot, without hesitation the father gave chase. He had run only about twenty paces before the bayonet palms and sawgrass began to take their toll on his upper body, and his arms and chest were cut and bleeding liberally. Still he pressed on. The soles of his feet were gashed by lava rock and pierced with sand spurs, whose little points could inflict an inordinate amount of pain. Still he pressed on. He felt none of the pain, worried none about the slashes and cuts. Adrenalin was driving him now, and he was gaining. Machado could hear someone yelling, "Pedro. Don't worry. I'm coming for you." It was only later that he would come to realize that it was he, himself, who had been shouting.

Just then, Machado saw one of the men look back at him. He got near enough to just barely reach out and touch the man carrying Pedro on his back, but then the criminals began to gain an advance. As Machado also tried to run faster, he stumbled over a rock and began tumbling. Along the way, his wrist caught a tree root and he heard a horrible snap of bone, which shattered his wrist. The pain should have been unbearable, yet he was oblivious. Eventually the momentum of his tumbling enabled him to get upright, and he continued to run as fast as he possibly could.

Fear and rage are powerful motivators, and Machado was completely under their collective spell. His mind began to race with him. "Suppose I do catch up with them. What do I do then? There are two of them and only one of me. I must concentrate on the one with Pedro -- perhaps I can free him and he can escape. I will take any beating they inflict, to save my son!" Just then he saw the men with Pedro reach the dock. Seeing others on the wharf, he shouted for them to stop the sailors, but he was still too far away for them to hear. No one seemed to take notice as the two men ran toward the end of the dock where a small skiff was tied up and waiting, with several other sailors manning the oars. The man carrying Pedro tossed the sack to one of those waiting in the small boat, and even at this distance, Machado could see them stuff it under some planks. The two abductors jumped in, and the others pushed away from the dock and began to row toward a three-mast ship several-hundred yards out in the harbor.

The race to save Pedro was over, and Machado had lost.

Though he walked slowly to the dock, his mind began to race again. "If they seek a ransom, I will pay anything they ask." Stumbling onto the dock's weathered, wooden planks, he walked methodically to the end. Those working there looked in amazement at the man most of them knew – a man of stature and gentility -- with his shirt soaked with blood, his wrist dangling limply at his side, and his feet leaving bloody footprints with every step he took. Torment was written across his sweaty, dirt-caked face. Machado sat down at the very spot where the small boat had been moored and watched that boat arrive at the ship far off shore. As some of the men climbed netting onto the ship, a package was lifted up toward the deck.

That was the very last that the desperate man would ever see of his son, and deep inside he knew it. There would be no demand for ransom. His son was gone...forever. He held his head in his hands and began to cry, his tears making rivulets through the dirt on his cheeks and falling like raindrops into the ocean, to be washed away with the lapping of the waves.

When he looked up once more, the ship had already set sail. The other men on the dock crowded around, asking Machado what was wrong. He couldn't hear them. He couldn't hear anything except his own heartbeat...and heartbreak.

3

KIDNAPPED BY PIRATES

The moment the burlap sack dropped over little Pedro's head, his entire world literally turned dark and upside down, for in that instant the man who had approached him with the candy had turned from friend to menace. As if the world going dark wasn't enough, Pedro felt himself being picked up and flung over the man's shoulder, knocking all the air out of him. Just as suddenly, he felt himself spun around, the man apparently was running, because Pedro could feel his ribs bouncing up and down, rising and falling on the man's shoulder as he bounded down the hill. The force was such that it took Pedro several moments to catch his breath. As loud as he could, he began to call for his papa to come and help him, and a few times he thought he heard his papa yelling that he was coming to rescue him. All the while, the pounding of his rib cage on the man's shoulder never let up, and the pain became excruciating.

After what seemed like an eternity, Pedro sensed something different. It was the sound of the man's boots no longer running in dirt but on wood. The captive wondered where in the world they could be taking him. Maybe they were going to throw him in the water. The thought terrified him, for he was not a strong swimmer.

All of a sudden, the man stopped running, and the boy was airborne. In those fleeting seconds, he thought his life was about to end in a watery grave. He had already seen the bloated bodies of people who had drowned and washed ashore, and the thought of being like them was almost more than he could bear. Then abruptly, he felt himself being clutched out of the air and slammed onto a hard wooden surface. Once again, pain beyond description shot through every fiber of his body. He tried to rise, but there was something above him. That something, which he would later recognize as the cross plank seating in a longboat, also kept Pedro from removing the sack that covered his head and shoulders. He could hear talking, but even though they were talking in Portuguese, he couldn't quite understand what they were saying. Lying there wondering what would happen next, he sensed motion and listened to oarsmen dipping their tools of the trade into the ocean. It became quite clear that he was on a boat, and he soon realized that wherever this boat was going, it was gaining speed to get there.

The next few minutes seemed like an eternity, when the young boy again felt himself being manhandled. Someone grabbed him from the floor of the boat and in the process knocked his head on the seat plank. Pedro let out a scream and he heard someone say, "Easy there, the lad's not worth anything to us if he's dead." Once again he was hoisted over someone's shoulder, but this time, instead of running, he seemed to be climbing. No matter, his ribs had already taken a pounding, and the misery of his pain was almost becoming numbing. Then he felt someone grab him under his armpits, hoisting him the final distance to the deck of a much larger boat than the one that had brought him there. His shoes caught on a railing, causing one to come halfway off his foot.

"Oh, no!" Pedro thought. "I can't lose my shoes. I love my shoes. What will Papa and Mama think if I lose my shoes?" At that moment, the lad put all of his strength into scrunching his toes so as not to lose the shoe adorned with the buckle initialed "F."

With that, the boy was stood upright with enough force to push his shoe back solidly onto his foot. The burlap sack was removed from his head and, as he faced westward into a sinking sun, his eyes, having been in total darkness for several minutes, hurt from the combined glare of sunshine and water. Instinctively he brought his hand up to shield his eyes.

The first thing Pedro saw was a group of at least 25 men, all resembling the sailor who had enticed him and his sister with candy. Almost every one wore tattered clothes with bandanas on their heads and had scruffy beards. One man in particular stood out, for he had no right leg. Instead, from the knee down there protruded a cylindrical piece of wood making a distinct thumping sound on the wood deck with each step he took toward Pedro. Every man was armed with guns and daggers or swords.

"Alright, boy," the man said, "Down you go below deck. We have a real nice place for you to stay." The sneer on the man's face told Pedro that this wouldn't be such a nice place after all. He spun Pedro around by the shoulders and hurried him toward a slightly raised portion of the deck with a doorway of sorts, one only half as tall as a fully-grown man.

Despite the quickness with which the man pushed him forward, Pedro was able to get a look around the schooner upon which he had been deposited. She had two large sails suspended from spars reaching from the top of the huge masts and extending toward the back of the ship. Another mast stood at the bow of the ship. There were also rows of cannon flanking both sides, at least seven on each side, as well as he could count. The wood all around was old and weathered, and there were ropes everywhere, neatly wound in concentric circles or tightly secured on the rails of the ship. The ship, typical of schooners of the day, had a very shallow draft, so she could be pulled as close to shore as possible for a short escape for the longboat.

The man behind Pedro barely had a grip on the boy. But as his eyes wandered toward the stern, past the raised structure that led to a second deck with a large wheel, little Pedro could see Terceira Island fading in the distance. For a brief moment, pushing the fear of drowning to the farthest reaches of his mind, he thought about diving overboard. After all, which would be worse -- drowning or dying at the hands of these pirates? Diving into the water was certain death. At least he might have a chance, if only a small one, to live if he remained aboard this ship.

Taking his mind away from those thoughts, a door beneath the stairs that led to the second deck suddenly flew open, and from it emerged a man different from any of the crew Pedro had seen. This man seemed larger than the others, wearing a big blue coat that made his shoulders look broader than those of the other pirates. He wore pants without patches and boots that rose over his calves almost to his knees.

40

Two flintlock pistols were in his wide black belt, and from a leather sash hung a large sword in a most ornate scabbard.

As he approached Pedro, everything in this man's bearing brimmed with authority. Pedro guessed him to be a soldier, like those he had seen as a youngster in Portugal. But this was no member of the military. He was a pirate, and he was not to be trifled with.

As the man strode across the deck, he never once took his eyes off Pedro. If someone got in his way, he pushed them aside. If something was in his path, he kicked it away. In only a few moments, the fierce-looking man stood directly in front of the lad, staring down at him with coal black eyes and a deathly cold look. Perhaps, Pedro thought, drowning would have been the better fate. Taking his eyes off Pedro for the first time, the man glanced at the one-legged sailor behind him. "So this is the so-called treasure that you say is worth so much to us, the reason we've given up raiding other ships and islands?"

"Yes, Captain," the sailor replied. "He's the one I was told we should kidnap and take to Brazil. My contact in Lisbon was quite clear, and he's already paid us half a king's ransom to do his bidding. We'll get the rest of the gold when we deliver this package to our fellow Portuguese in the New World. Of course, it would have been better if we had grabbed up the girl, too, but the boy was always the real prize."

"So be it, then," the captain grunted. "But mind you this -- even though I appointed you quartermaster, I'll not be sent on a fool's journey. We could have just kept the first payment and been about our business, so if we are to collect the rest, it'll be on your head to make sure we get 'im there alive. If we don't, or if they don't pay the rest of the gold, I'll have your head on the bowsprit for all to see."

41

"Yes, sir. I'll see to it."

As the captain walked past them, the quartermaster spun Pedro around again and bent down so that they were face-to-face, nose-to-nose. Pedro tilted his head slightly away from the foul-smelling breath. "Listen here, boy, for I'll only be sayin' this once," one-leg said. "For the life of me, I don't know why you're worth your weight in gold. In fact, I'll be thinkin' you might even be worth more than your weight. But this'll be no journey of pleasure. You'll do as you're told and make no fuss, or I'll make your life miserable. Do ya hear me, boy?"

Pedro, too scared and confused to respond, shivered in silence.

"Do ya hear me?" The last words were accompanied with spittle that struck Pedro on the cheek and forehead.

Pedro mumbled a weak, "Yes, sir."

"Then you'll be gettin' below, and you'll be good an' quiet."

With that, Pedro Francisco was shoved toward shallow stairs leading below deck. Forced into darkness again, he could barely see, and he began to stumble. He reached out to steady himself but caught his hand on one of the old beams. He yanked his hand away, full of splinters, though that was a small pain for the little boy to endure on a day already punctuated with pain. The quartermaster grabbed Pedro around the waist to steady him. "Wouldn't do to havin' you break your neck before we reach your final destination. Mind your step now."

In the bowel of the ship, Pedro's eyes began to focus again. This was obviously a cargo hold, as there were wooden crates of all sizes stacked along the sides of the hull. Pedro had no trouble standing, but the quartermaster had to stoop as he ushered his prey around a corner where a pen with bars stood before them. The sight of the pen was frightening

42

enough, but the stench was overpowering. It even made the pirate's breath, so odorous only a few moments earlier, seem like the sweetest island flower fragrance. Suddenly the little boy vomited all over his favorite shoes.

"Aw, now look what you've done. Never mind. You'll get used to the smell after a little while. Every one of our other guests has." And with that, the quartermaster burst into sinister laughter, opened the door to the pen, and shoved little Pedro inside. Then he spun on his good leg and made his way back up the stairs. The boy listened with some relief to the cadence of the step-thump going across the upper deck. Then he looked around at his surroundings and realized he was alone, with the exception of a few mice that made their home down there. As the ship pitched and heaved, so did Pedro's stomach, and he threw up again and again, until he couldn't anymore. The darkness was as thick as the stench, but there was a little bit of light coming through the cracks in the planks above his pen. The cage, about four feet by six feet, was perhaps big enough for a fully-grown tiger. The wooden bottom of it was stained with urine and blood of others who had been imprisoned before him. In one corner was a small bucket of water. There was also a small empty bucket. Pedro scooped out some water with his hand, but immediately spit out the stagnant stuff. Exhausted, he curled up in the slimy straw that was left as bedding and cried himself to sleep. That night, the sound of waves lapping against the side of the ship became a monotonous companion.

Soon Pedro was awakened by those oddly different footsteps coming down the stairs again. His eyes, now accustomed to the dark, saw the quartermaster round the corner. Pedro pressed himself into the farthest corner of his cage.

"Now, now, boy," the pirate said. "Not to be afraid. After all, you heard the cap'n. My survival depends on your survival. Here. Look what I brung for ya." The pirate held out his hand and Pedro could make out an orange in it. "You'll be eatin' this or you'll be gettin' scurvy, and that wouldn't do. That wouldn't do a-tall. I s'pose you found your water bucket. The other bucket is for doin' your business. I'll come and fetch it every couple of days. Now, eat the orange. There's a good boy."

As the days wore on, this scene repeated itself over and over. On some days, the quartermaster presented Pedro with a bit of stale bread or some rancid meat that was frequently infested with maggots. Initially, Pedro would eat the meat and immediately throw up, but eventually his seasickness abated and the taste of maggots became tolerable.

Without the benefit of full sun to gage the days, Pedro lost track of time. A night did come, however, when the quartermaster not only offered Pedro some food but the opportunity to spend some time on deck as well. Reaching the top of the stairs, the weak boy took a deep breath. The fresh sea air was welcomed into lungs that had experienced only stench for days…or was it weeks now? A hand in his back pushed him forward. Making his way out onto the deck, he looked up at a full moon playing its light along soft waves of ocean as far as the eye could see, like a never-ending silver ribbon. Even the stars looked brighter than ever before, and each one seemed to twinkle with a benevolence that belied Pedro's true situation. Regardless, he was thankful to finally be outside as he continued to take deep, uncontaminated breaths and feel a cool breeze on his face.

Near the stairs that led to the upper level deck was a small barrel lashed to the side of the ship. The quartermaster motioned Pedro to sit there. The one-legged man, seeming almost kindly toward the captive, sat on the third step from the bottom. "I know you're scared, boy. I know you're scared. I s'pose I'd be scared, too, if I was in your shoes."

With that, Pedro looked down to see his silver buckles glint in the moonlight.

"I don't know why, boy," the quartermaster continued, "but your papa must have made some bad enemies back in Portugal. We're gettin' paid a lot of gold to deliver you to Brazil. But I'm sure you'll be well treated. Just doesn't make sense to pay all that much to do you harm, so..." There was a long pause. "Best be gettin' you back below deck, now. Wouldn't do for the captain to see you out here."

Days turned into weeks, and Pedro and the quartermaster developed a relationship of sorts, each relying on the other for his very life. And Pedro was getting better food than initially, accompanied by more frequent visits above deck.

One day, raindrops started to pour through the cracks above Pedro's pen. The ship began to pitch and yaw, and Pedro's stomach, which had become accustomed to life at sea, started to churn as it had when he was first brought on board. As night approached, he could see flashes of lightning through the planks and could hear the wind howling above. He tried to stand but whenever he did, he was thrown down on the floor of his pen, so he stopped trying. Unknown to all aboard the ship, they were in the middle of one of the most powerful hurricanes the Atlantic Ocean had ever experienced, a storm born as a tropical wave just off the coast of Africa but turning into a monster storm as she made her way across warm ocean waters. There were times when the storm seemed to have ended, only to return a little while later in all its fury. Pedro longed for a visit from the quartermaster, but he never came. Finally, all was calm again. Yet the quartermaster, the boy's only human contact since being brought down to the bowel of the ship, never arrived with any food or company.

That night Pedro could hear loud voices above him on deck. It sounded like a lot of arguing, and then a shot rang out. He tried to sleep but couldn't stop wondering what had happened and why his friend had not come to visit and bring him food. In fact, two whole days went by with nobody coming down the stairs to check on the little boy.

On the third day since the storm began, dawn sent tiny shafts of light into Pedro's pen. Suddenly he heard the door from the deck open. At last the quartermaster was coming to check on him, he thought. But as he listened to the steps, he could tell they were not those of the one-legged man. These footfalls were even. Pedro focused his eyes on the corner just as another pirate came into view.

"Get up, you brat," the man said. "Get up, get up, get up, now!"

Pedro had never known the name of the quartermaster, so he asked, "Where is the one-leg man?"

"You'll not be worryin' about him," the pirate shot back. "You'd be best worryin' about yourself, you little curse." With that, the pirate opened the door, reached in, and snatched little Pedro by the front of his shirt. He then pulled the boy from his pen and marched him up the stairs, pushing him in the back each step of the way. As they reached the doorway leading out to the deck, Pedro clamped his hands over his eyes. He hadn't seen real sunlight – albeit foggy – in weeks. Another sharp shove in the back caused him to stumble and fall face down on the deck, bloodying his nose. As he rolled over and looked up, the lad saw the body of the quartermaster hanging limply from a cross beam of one of the masts. On the front of his shirt was a large red stain, and sea gulls were pecking away at the body.

Without warning, Pedro could feel himself being lifted up and held out over the rail where another pirate grabbed him and took him into the longboat below. Hoping that he was going back home, the little captive looked out across the water to see if he recognized his surroundings, but he couldn't really make out the shore because of the dense fog.

Fear began to set in and he yelled, "Papa! Papa!"

The closest pirate to Pedro grabbed him and covered his mouth with his filthy hands. "Say another word and I'll slit your throat where you sit. God above must surely hate you or us to have brought that storm on us, but we'll be takin' no more chances. You already cost a good man his life. You'll not be takin' any others. If it was up to me, we'd feed you to the fish, but to his last breath, the quartermaster begged for your life, so do as you will with it and good riddance."

The little boat soon came more clearly into sight of land, but Pedro could recognize nothing. This was most certainly not Porto Judeu or any other part of Terceira Island that Pedro could remember. His little heart sank.

It wasn't long before the longboat docked at a wharf in the breaking dawn. There was almost no activity, especially at this far end. Quietly one of the pirates directed Pedro to a small, makeshift ladder, and as he clambered up onto the pier, the longboat turned around and disappeared into the early morning fog and mist.

4

ALONE AND ABANDONED

The rippled wake of the longboat faded away as Pedro Francisco began to fully comprehend what had happened to him. Only a few weeks ago, he had been a happy youngster with a warm and wonderful family. He had been whisked away from that idyllic life only to be tossed into a seagoing dungeon of sorts. At least the one-legged man had befriended him, but now that man was dead, and here he sat on a dock somewhere he did not know. And he was alone, completely alone. It was June 23, 1765.

The wharf itself was undistinguishable from dozens just like it. It was large and, like so many others, the old wood was weathered to various shades of gray. Pedro looked down at the water and noticed a school of fish swimming carefree in their never-ending hunt for food. At first, the little boy was too stunned at the most recent turn of events to do anything but stare at the water, but as he contemplated his idyllic past and his uncertain future, tears began to well up in his eyes, and he cried softly. Just as his father's tears had mixed with the rolling waves at the end of the dock in Porto Judeu, so, too, did Pedro's here at the end of the wharf at City Point, Virginia. It was all just too much for a five-year-old little boy to deal with, and soon the tears turned to sobs followed by racking wails so strong they shook the boy to his very core.

Further up the wooden walk, dockworkers were just arriving for their early morning workday. The noise they heard at the end of the dock sounded like a wounded animal in its death throes, and they each looked curiously at the small brown shape sitting there where the wharf ended and the James River began. Almost in unison, they set off toward Pedro, running the length of the wharf, their heavy boots raising a hollow racket as they pounded along the wooden planks. Even old Caleb, the dock's night watchman, who had just settled down in his cot to sleep, joined the procession. The first men to arrive just stood there staring in amazement at the boy still crying uncontrollably. Where had he come from, and how long had he been there? Why was his skin so dark? Certainly, he was no African. He was too lightly colored for that, and he wore such fine, though disheveled, clothes. They also took note of his eyes and hair, each as pitch black as the night itself.

Meanwhile, Pedro looked up at the sea of faces surrounding him. Who are these people, he thought. Why are they staring at me? They don't look like pirates, but what will they do to me? Why is their skin so white? The little boy's mind was racing. These men looked a little like the pirates, but they were dressed far better.

Caleb, who thought of himself more as a dock master than a watchman, elbowed his way through the crowd of men to assume what he thought of as his rightful authority.

"Well, well, well, what have we here?" Caleb intoned. "A lost little boy? What's your name, son?

Pedro knew the man was speaking to him, but it only sounded like gibberish. These were words he had never heard before, and that frightened him even more. The man's dress was different from the others, too. He had on dirty white pants that buckled below his knee, a white blouse and red waistcoat over which was a dark blue, long coat with gold trim around its edges. Most prominently, he wore a tri-cornered hat. Pedro had seen one of these before, atop the pirate captain's head.

Still not entirely sure of the intent of this crowd of unfamiliar men, Pedro pushed himself closer to the edge of the wharf, to the point that he could have fallen into the water had not one of the men grabbed him by the arm.

"Now, now," Caleb said in a gravelly voice. "There's nothing to be afraid of here."

Sensing that these men meant him no harm, his trembling began to subside a little. Still, he couldn't help but be wary. Just then, another man arrived at the scene, but instead of wearing clothes of laborers, this man was dressed in the finest clothing of the day, and people stood aside to allow him access to all their attention. Even Caleb snapped around upon the man's arrival.

"Mr. Durrell. What would you be doin' here so early in the day?" Caleb asked.

51

James Durrell, a noted merchant from Petersburg, surveyed the situation and looked down at Pedro. "I'm just here to check on a shipment of goods, and I couldn't help but take notice of all the commotion down here. What's going on?"

"Seems that we've come across a lost lad," Caleb replied. "Don't know who he is...don't know where he came from. He was just sittin' here cryin' when the sun came up. I've been tryin' to talk to him, but so far he hasn't said a word. Maybe he's deef and dumb."

"Well," said Durrell. "Let me try to make some sense of it." Durrell squatted low so that he could get a closer look at the youngster who looked so totally confused and afraid. "Now, then, lad, tell me your name," Durrell inquired. In an instant, Pedro opened up with a stream of Portuguese such as the men on the dock had never heard before. Durrell looked all around at the men who had gathered.

"Well, he's not deef. Does anybody understand what he's saying?"

"Sounds a bit like Spanish," a voice from the back of the crowd said. "But I can't rightly say fer sure."

Durrell turned his attention back to Pedro, reaching his hand out to the little boy and pulling him to his feet as he did. "Let's have a good look at you," Durrell said. "You look to be about seven or eight-years old. Your clothes are filthy, but I can easily tell they were made of some of the finest cloth...European, if my merchant's eye is correct." Just then, Durrell took note of the buckles on Pedro's shoes. Once again, they gleamed in the sun. On the right shoe was the letter "P" and on the left shoe the letter "F." A thought came to Durrell. Pointing to the shoes, he asked the boy, "Is that part of your name?" Are your initials P.F.?"

52

"Pedro...Pedro Francisco," the little boy shouted. He puffed his chest out as if proud that he was finally communicating with these men. "Pedro Francisco," he repeated.

"Ah. Now we're getting somewhere," said Durrell. "Though I daresay that may be the most we get from him for awhile." Durrell signaled Caleb to follow him off to one side, and a couple of the other men joined the conversation, while the rest remained crowded around Pedro. "Does anybody know where he comes from, how he got here?" asked Durrell.

"No," Caleb piped up. "We just all heard this awful crying – wailin', it was – comin' from here. Don't nobody know how he got here."

"Well, the question now is what do we do with him?"

"I s'pose he kin stay with me in my wharf shack for the time bein', though I can't say as I have an idea of what to do with him," Caleb offered.

"I guess that'll do for now, but there are strict laws about runaways and waifs," Durrell responded. "If someone doesn't come to claim him in a couple of days, we'll have to inform the folks over at the poor house to come and get him."

The men turned their attention back to Pedro, and Caleb reached out to grab him by the arm. Immediately, Pedro drew away. Durrell knelt down again so as to look the little boy square in the eye. "It's all right. Old Caleb here won't hurt you. Nobody here wants to hurt you, Pedro. By the way, Pedro isn't a proper name here in the New World. From now on, we'll call you Peter. Peter Francisco." Durrell looked to see if the boy understood. Then he jabbed himself in the chest with his thumb. "James

53

Durrell. James Durrell," he repeated. Then he pointed his index finger at Pedro. "Peter Francisco. You are Peter Francisco."

Understanding crept into the little boy's eyes. He poked his thumb to his own chest and mimicked, "Peter Francisco!"

Rather than grabbing Peter's arm, Caleb reached out his hand. It was rough, scarred, and calloused, and his fingers were gnarled from years of hard work on all sorts of wharfs. Nevertheless, it offered an act of kindness that Peter gratefully accepted. He slid his much smaller hand into that of the night watchman, while the dockworkers parted, creating a path through which Caleb and the boy could walk back to the old man's shack.

Durrell knew what he had to do next for the boy called Peter, who looked as if he hadn't had a decent meal in weeks, an accurate assumption. He strode from the dock, turned left down the adjoining street and walked directly to the home of Edna Watkins.

Edna Watkins was well known in this area. Her husband was a tanner who made some of the finest leather goods in the territory. In fact, Durrell had bought some of his offerings from his own store. But leather was not the order of the day, food was, and Edna Watkins was recognized as one of the best cooks anywhere. Durrell walked up the three steps and onto a small, well kept porch. He approached the whitewashed front door and knocked four times.

"Why, Mister Durrell. What a fine surprise," said Edna as she opened the door. "But my husband's not here. You'll find him at the tannery."

"I've not come to see Albert," said Durrell. "It's you I'll be having business with today."

54

Edna came onto the porch, for inviting a married man into her home when her husband wasn't there would have been frowned upon by the neighbors.

Durrell began to relate what had taken place at the wharf earlier in the day.

"The youngster looks to be famished, and I can't really trust old Caleb to take care of his needs. Would you mind getting together some real home cooked food for the lad and taking it down to the dock?"

"Why, of course, I will. Of course. I'll see to it right away."

Durrell reached into his purse and produced eight shillings, coins of the realm, and offered them to Edna.

"Oh, no, Mister Durrell," Edna said. "There's no need for that."

"Edna," said Durrell, "I know how tough times are. Between all these new taxes and crop failures in the colony, things are tough for everybody. But I feel responsible for the boy, and I'll be thanking you to do this fine thing."

As Durrell turned to leave, Edna Watkins touched his arm. "God will be blessing you, sir."

A couple of hours later, Edna Watkins, laden with all sorts of food for the youngster now known as Peter Francisco, was headed toward the dock. She had roasted chicken, green beans, and some of the best tasting, most delicious smelling fresh baked biscuits known to man. For dessert, there was a fresh baked apple pie. She arrived at Caleb's little shack and knocked on the doorframe, since the door was nothing more than an old blanket tacked across the top. Caleb pushed aside the makeshift door. Durrell had told him of the arrangement, and he was expecting Edna's arrival.

"Oooooh, that smells good," he said, lifting the cloth Edna had used to cover the food and to keep it warm. Edna slapped his hand.

"That's for the boy, not for you, although from the looks of ya, you could use a decent meal, too. Whatever the boy doesn't eat, you can have the rest." She looked past Caleb and her eyes rested upon the most pitiful looking youngster she had ever seen.

"Oh, you poor thing," she said as she crossed the few steps to the cot where Peter was sitting. "Everything is going to be alright by and by, you just wait and see." She offered Peter the food, and he tore into it ravenously. Caleb was left to wonder if there would be anything left for him, but Peter's stomach could hold only so much, and before long he stopped eating.

Edna reached over and ran her fingers through Peter's dirty, uncombed hair, then looked at his filthy face and hands. "My, my, my, you are a sight," she said. "Come along with me, and let's get you cleaned up." She reached out a hand, and this time Peter gladly placed his in hers. Hers were a bit softer than Caleb's, though they were considerably harder than his own mother's. Along the way, Edna chatted up a storm even though Durrell had told her that the boy didn't speak a word of English. It didn't really matter. She figured the boy wouldn't be so frightened if he heard some kind words, even if he didn't understand them.

The kind woman took Peter directly into the kitchen and brought in a wooden tub from the back porch. In it she put some water and then set about to boiling some more water in a big kettle over the fireplace. After she poured the hot water in with the cold, she gently removed Peter's clothes, helped him into the tub, and began to scrub away weeks' worth of grime from his body. Peter, like most boys his age, wasn't especially fond of bathing, but this was more than that. This was someone showing him true kindness, and he was grateful for that. As she rubbed the washcloth over his arms, Edna took note at how well defined his muscles were for a boy his age. "Goodness, aren't you going to be the strong one when you grow up. Yes sir, you will." After toweling Peter off, she went to a chest and found some clothes for him to wear. "These belonged to my precious departed son," she said. "He was only ten when the pox took him away, but I think they'll fit you just fine."

Peter didn't mind the new clothes. In fact, he was happy to get out of the ones he had been wearing. As soon as the dressing was complete, he jumped to put his shoes on. He wasn't about to give up his good shoes. Not now. Not ever. From that same chest, Edna dug out an old stuffed animal, although what it was supposed to be Peter could not imagine. Regardless, when she offered it to him, he plucked it out of her hands and hugged it close to his chest.

"My son always called this Pookie," Edna said.

Peter looked at the stuffed toy. "Boneca de trapo," he declared. "Boneca de trapo." In Portuguese, that meant rag doll.

Late that afternoon, Edna Watkins delivered Peter back to the dock and to Caleb's shack. The tired, clean, satisfied boy walked in, crossed the few steps to the cot, and laid down, still clutching his new best friend. Before Edna had the chance to say anything, he was asleep. She touched his cheek with the back of her hand. "Sleep well, young Peter Francisco, sleep well," she said.

For several days, the same scene was repeated. Edna showed up with some of the best food Peter had ever eaten, provoking and gaining his appetite. Poor Caleb had barely enough leftovers to feed a bird. Each day, she and the boy would go back to the Watkins' house. Some days, Edna would give Peter another bath, though for the life of him he could not imagine why one needed to be so clean. On other days, Edna just sat in the kitchen and talked to him. He still didn't understand all that she had to say, but he was beginning to pick up some words here and there, words like food and water and sleep.

One day, very early, there came a rapping on Caleb's doorframe. It was too early for Edna – Peter knew her name now – it was too early for Edna to arrive. Caleb, who had just settled down to sleep, rose and pulled the blanket door aside. There stood James Durrell.

"Caleb," he said. "your duties are over. I'll be taking young Peter with me."

"But why?" Caleb asked. In the back of his mind, the watchman knew there would be no more home cooked meals once Peter left. "Ain't I been doin' a good job lookin' after the boy?"

"It's not that," said Durrell. "I've been talking with the authorities, and we all think it would be best for Peter to go to the Prince George County Poor House. They have an orphanage there, and Peter can play with kids and learn our ways and customs. Besides, this is no place for a boy his age to be brought up. You know that as well as I do."

"Well, of course. You know best, sir," said Caleb. "I was gettin' used to havin' the lad around, but you know best." He spent a few moments gathering up Peter's belongings, including the fine clothes he was wearing when he was kidnapped, along with a number of pants and shirts Edna Watkins had donated. And, of course, he couldn't forget boneca de trapo, even though Caleb couldn't figure out what it was supposed to be either.

Durrell took charge of Peter and led him off the wharf and straight up a hill toward one of the largest buildings Peter had ever seen, other than the family castle in Portugal. Every once in a while, he looked up at James Durrell with a questioning look on his face.

"I know it's not been easy, son," said Durrell, "but you're gonna like it here. They'll take real good care of you, and you'll have other kids to play with and everything. They'll even teach you to read and write. There's nothing to worry about. One day, who knows? Someone might just come along and claim you or something."

The building loomed even larger than it had appeared from Peter's vantage point on the wharf. It was two stories tall, all white, with a clapboard-like siding. From behind the house, Pedro could hear the sounds of children playing and having fun. As they reached the steps leading up to the porch, a much larger porch than that at the Watkins' house, a woman opened the door to greet Durrell and young Peter.

"Peter, this is Miss Smyth, Miss Mary Smyth," Durrell said. "Miss Mary, this is Peter Francisco."

Peter looked up at the lady with wide eyes. She was younger than Edna Watkins, but he wondered if she was as kind as Edna.

"How do you do?" Miss Mary said.

"He doesn't speak much English," Durrell broke in. "In fact, we still haven't figured out what it is that he does speak."

"That's all right," Miss Mary responded. "We'll take real good care of him, and we'll have him speaking the King's English in no time."

Durrell then patted Peter on the head, thanked Miss Mary for taking over his care, turned and walked back down the hill toward the wharf.

Miss Mary Smyth took Peter by the hand, a hand almost as soft as his own mother's but not quite. She led him to a large room occupied with beds of a sort that Peter had never seen. They were stacked one on top of another and obviously made of scrap lumber. Peter counted four of these contraptions, making sleep space for eight. Other than that, and throughout the rest of the house for that matter, the furnishings were a mix and match mess, all donations from the community. Mary showed the lad to a bed and told him to put his belongings in a small trunk at its foot. Peter pushed at the mattress. It was full of feathers and was so soft. This was much better than the cot at the wharf. Plus, there was a feather-filled pillow. It was so nice that Peter could hardly wait to go to bed, although there was still plenty of daylight left. Miss Mary signaled for him to follow her as she led him out the back door to the back yard, where about 15 children of all ages and sizes played. Seven of them were boys and the rest girls. Peter had obviously gotten one of the last beds to be had.

"Boys and girls," Miss Mary spoke loudly to be heard. "I want you all to come here." As the children gathered around, she introduced Peter. "Peter doesn't speak much English yet, so you'll all have to be patient with him and help him for a while. Now everybody go back to playing, and take Peter with you." As the children ran back to playing their games, Miss Mary gently shoved Peter in the same direction, then went back into the house. Once the door had closed, three of the boys came over to Peter.

"So. Peter Francisco, eh?" one of the boys said. "Well, let me tell you something. I run things around here. I've been here the longest, and I run things."

Peter looked at the boy quizzically. The boy was a good three or four inches taller than he was.

"Do you understand me!" the boy shouted. "I'm the boss around here."

"Didn't you hear Miss Mary?" one of the other boys interrupted. "He doesn't understand English."

"Well, maybe he'll understand this," the first boy said as he took a glance at Peter's shoe buckles. Then he began to kick dirt all over Peter's shoes. Even though the boy was bigger than Peter and probably a few years older, Peter didn't hesitate. He launched himself at the taunter and knocked him flat on his back. Peter, not really knowing how to fight, jumped on top of him and pinned the boy to the ground. Although the boy from the Azores had arrived on these shores malnourished, even emaciated from his ocean voyage, the sustenance that had been provided of late had restored his natural vitality and strength.

Just then the back door to the house was flung open and out came Miss Mary. She rushed over to where Peter was holding the other boy down. "What in the world is going on here?" she yelled. "Who started this?"

"He did," came the reply from the boy underneath Peter.

"No, he didn't," said a small voice. It was one of the girls. "I saw the whole thing, and Johnny was kicking dirt on the new boy's shoes."

"Peter, get off Johnny," Miss Mary said.

Peter looked around at Miss Mary. He had understood his name, his new name, but he hadn't comprehended the rest. Realizing this, Miss Mary reached down and touched Peter on the shoulder and motioned him to get up. He did.

"Johnny O'Neal, didn't you hear what I said? Didn't I tell you to be nice to Peter? Now shake hands and make friends," she demanded. Reluctantly, Johnny extended his hand. Peter didn't quite know what to make of the gesture, but he also held out his hand. Peace, at least for the time being, had been restored.

"Come now, children," Miss Mary said. "It's time for supper."

As the kids began to file into the house, one of the other boys came up from behind Peter and draped his arm around his shoulder. "Way to go. Way to put O'Neal in his rightful place."

That evening's meal was good, not as good as Edna Watkins', but good nonetheless.

Weeks passed, and although Johnny O'Neal and Peter never became what one would call friends, the other children seemed to take the newcomer under their wing. They included him in their games and tried their best to help him with his lessons, although reading and writing were all too much for Peter to really grasp. However, he was picking up the language, and he could communicate in a rudimentary fashion.

A couple of months had gone by when a distinguished looking man came to visit. He told Miss Mary that he was looking for a young boy to come and work on his plantation, Hunting Towers. "I don't want an older boy," the man said. "I want a boy who can be trained in our ways. I don't want a boy who already thinks he knows it all. I have a certain way I want things done. A lad about eight or nine would do well."

Miss Mary lined the boys up in the back yard for the man to inspect. One by one, he grabbed the boys by the shoulders and gave them a shake to check their sturdiness. When he came to Peter, he guessed that the boy was seven or eight, but when he shook him, he could feel how solidly built he was.

"This one here," he said. "This one will do fine. I notice that his skin is really dark. Do you have any idea where he came from?"

"No, sir. They just said that they found him at the main dock in town. That's about all I know about young Peter," she said. "But he's one of the hardest working boys we've ever had at the orphanage. No chore seems to be too big for him."

"Well, that's what I'm looking for, and with his dark skin, he'll fit right in with my Negroes. My slave master will probably put him to work cleaning the horse stables or something like that. But, there are 3600 acres' worth of chores, so we'll make sure that he stays busy. Will you take 50 pounds for him?"

"Well, first I think you should know that his name is Peter Francisco," Miss Mary said. "But he doesn't speak much English, and he can't read or write a lick."

"That's not a problem. He's got the makings of a fine farm hand, and that's exactly what I'm looking for. Again, I ask you, how much? Will you take 50 pounds for him?"

"With all due respect, that is how much I'm paid for the white kids, but this boy has dark skin like a Negro, so I'm asking for 200 pounds. That's the going rate for a slave his age," argued Miss Mary.

"Fine, fine, 200 pounds it is. Get his things together. We've a bit of a journey before us, and I'd like to get home before dark."

As Miss Mary went in the house to put Peter's few belongings in a sack, the man bent down to look at him more closely. "My name is Judge Anthony Winston," the man said. Even though Miss Mary had told him the boy's name, he looked directly into Peter's black eyes and inquired, "What's yours?"

"Peter, Peter Francisco," the little boy said, and he stuck his chest out as proud as a peacock, as if he instinctively knew a whole new chapter of life was about to begin.

5

SLAVERY NOT SCHOOL

When Miss Mary handed Peter his sack of belongings, she looked at him and said, " I know this is all a bit unsettling, and I'm not even sure that you understand me all the time, but this is your lucky day. The judge here is a wise man, and he's a nice man, and he's well thought of hereabouts. Oh, my, I'm just going on and on. Just remember, life is going to be a lot better for you now. Now run along -- best not to keep the good Judge Winston waiting."

As the two of them exited the front door, they saw Judge Winston standing next to a carriage. Peter's eyes grew wide. It was magnificent. With a luxurious deep brown color, it was so highly polished that sunlight danced off each delicate curve in the hand-hewn woodwork. Truly it was a piece of art. There was a folded top that could be raised in rainy weather, but today was far too glorious for that, so it was neatly compacted behind the passenger area, which had room for two or three people. Forward of the carriage body was a raised seat, and there sat the blackest man Peter had ever seen. The sight of him startled Peter for just a moment, but that's when he saw the horses.

There were two of them -- American Cream draft horses. Their coats looked as rich as the best buttermilk Peter had ever tasted, and beneath their beautiful coats was the pinkest skin, almost the shade of Miss Mary's skin. Lush, pure white manes and tails adorned the horses, and one had distinctively beautiful, deep amber eyes. Both horses were females, stood a good sixteen hands tall, and weighed about 1500 pounds. Peter couldn't take his eyes off these magnificent creatures; he was in love.

"Over here, lad." said Judge Winston as he motioned Peter into the carriage. "We've a ways to go before dark sets in."

Peter, trailing his sack behind him, climbed in and settled into the farthest portion of the seat. When Judge Winston sat down next to him, the leaf springs, crafted by Winston's own blacksmith who was driving the rig, sagged slightly and pushed back under his weight.

The black man in front tapped each of the horses on their rumps with a long stick and said, "Gidup." The horses, only recently acquired by the judge, made a perfect U-turn and began a slow trot down the path, the path to Hunting Tower Plantation, the path to a life that Peter Francisco could never have imagined.

Judge Winston began with some small talk, little of which Peter understood. Then mindful of Peter's limited English, he grew silent. Perhaps he had made a mistake. Perhaps it would be too hard to train this boy in the ways of the plantation. Then again, many of his slaves had come to Hunting Tower with even less understanding of spoken English, and they had all worked out.

Along the way, Peter marveled at the landscape. At home on the island, he had been accustomed to palm trees and tropical vegetation. But this was different. Their journey was taking them through forests of oak and maple, and with fall in the air, these trees were varying shades of red and gold. Scrub brush was plentiful, as though God had laid a green carpet on each side of the path on which they were riding.

Even in the midst of this beauty, however, Peter couldn't keep from glancing toward the front of the carriage where the two beautiful horses effortlessly pulled the three passengers to their final destination. As the sun began to fade away, Peter noticed that they had turned off the path and were heading toward one of the most magnificent houses he had ever seen. Nearing the main house, he could also see several out structures. Some looked like small houses, but the most noticeable was a huge, white building with an angular roof and large, open doors at the top of one end.

Judge Winston, stepping down first, offered to help Peter, but the youngster literally leaped from the carriage with a single bound, still gazing at the house. Winston smiled at him. "Independent little guy, aren't you...Then again, aren't we all?

Suddenly the front door opened and the first to rush out was the littlest Winston, daughter Martha, followed by Alice, Anthony, Jr., and the eldest, Sarah.

"Father, Father," Martha squealed. "What did you bring me for my birthday?"

"Now just hold up there, little lady," Judge Winston responded. "Your birthday isn't until tomorrow and if I ruin the surprise, your momma will have my hide." He did, however, motion toward the carriage boot just to let young Martha know that he hadn't forgotten.

Alice, the shyest of the three Winston girls, gave her father a hug and then simply stood to one side. Anthony, Jr., however, the most outgoing, gave his father a bear hug and a clap on the arm. "Father, we're so glad you're home."

Sarah, although not the least bit shy like Alice, was always the most reserved and never showed much emotion. "I trust you had a good trip, Father," she said as she kissed his cheek.

"Yes, yes." the judge said. "It was a good trip, and I was able to negotiate a fine price for our hemp crop."

Even though Judge Winston had only been gone for a little more than four days, this was the typical greeting from his family.

Although most of the surrounding plantations produced tobacco as their main crop, Judge Winston had wisely decided to diversify his 3600-acre plantation, planting hemp on a goodly part of the acreage a few years ago. Now, while other plantation owners were weighed down by several years of tobacco crop failures, his hemp crop, commonly used to make rope, paper, and canvas, was helping to fill in the gaps. However, it wasn't enough to entirely offset the poor tobacco yield, but the judge was never one to discuss the family finances, even with his wife, Alice, who had just appeared at the doorway.

"Anthony," she said. "It's good to have you home. I daresay the children missed you terribly. And what do we have here?" Her gaze had settled on Peter standing by the carriage, taking in the whole scene.

"This," said Judge Winston, "This is Peter Francisco. I just purchased him from the Prince George County Poor House so that we'll have plenty of help come harvest time."

"But, what is he?" she said. "He's not white like us, but he isn't colored like our Negroes either. Is he a half-blood?"

"I don't think so, but nobody is really sure. They think he may come from Spain or Portugal or Italy or someplace like that." Judge Winston related Peter's story as well as he knew it from Mary Smyth. "I suppose the biggest problem is that he doesn't understand English real well yet, but we can get Petunia to help out with that."

Pulling Peter in front of him, the judge proceeded to point at his children and tell him their names. Then, he pointed to his wife and said, "Mrs. Winston...Mrs. Winston."

Immediately, Peter jabbed his thumb to his chest and said as proudly as he could, "Peter Francisco...Peter Francisco." As usual, he stuck out his chest.

"Anthony," Mrs. Winston said in a quiet but perturbed voice, "For the life of me, I don't know why you didn't get a white boy like we talked about. It would have been so much easier, and at least he would have spoken English. Sometimes I just don't..."

Judge Winston cut her off. "He was by far the best of the lot, and the decision has been made." Mrs. Winston was not too pleased to be admonished like that in front of the children, but family life in the New World was a true patriarchy, and the judge's word was always the last word.

"Get Petunia out here," Judge Winston said. "I want her to meet Peter." Coincidently, Petunia, who served as a house slave and had her quarters as part of an attached dwelling off the back of the main house, was just coming around the corner.

"Oh, there you are," said the judge. "Come here, Petunia, there's someone I want you to meet." Peter's eyes almost popped out of his head. This little girl was even darker than the man who had driven the carriage.

"Petunia, this is Peter Francisco," said the judge. "You'll be in charge of him, except for his chores...the slave master will see to that. I want you to show him around and introduce him to the others; but most of all, I want you to help him to learn English so that he will speak it as well as you do and can understand what he is told. For the time being, he'll be staying in your quarters with you. I'll get a mattress brought in there in a little while."

Petunia eyed Peter up and down with some suspicion. She really didn't want to have to take this boy under her wing, and she surely didn't want to have to share her quarters with him. But Petunia had been a slave all her life. In fact, she had been born on this very plantation, and she knew that a slave didn't sass the white master.

"Yes, suh, Mister Judge," Petunia said. "I'll takes real good care of 'im." She immediately took Peter by the hand and guided him around to the back of the house. As they crossed the threshold into Petunia's small room, Peter glanced around. The furnishings were quite simple, although Petunia had the luxury of a small bed that occupied one windowless wall. Alongside the bed was a little three-drawer dresser with a metal washbasin on top.

As Peter surveyed his new home, yet another black man came in carrying a straw mattress. He looked at Petunia, who motioned him to put it on the opposite wall under a window. The man was her father and lived with Petunia's mother and two brothers in one of the outbuildings.

"Daddy," she said. "Mister Judge say I gotta have this boy live with me, an' I don't like it...don't like it one bit."

"You knows the rules, Petunia," her father said. "What Mister Judge say is what it will be...ain't no use to gettin' all upset about it. Tha's just the way it is."

"I know, I know, but it ruins everything. I always used to move my bed by the window on hot nights and then move it over here on the cold ones so's not to take a chill. Now what am I gonna do?"

"I spect we'll be havin' lots more cold nights than hot this time of year, so don't you go worryin' on it so much," her father commented.

Sam, the old slave's name, took a look at Peter. "My, oh my, my, my. You don't look like no Negro, but you don't look zactly white neither. What in the world is you, boy?"

Understanding that he had been asked a question, Peter puffed himself up and jabbed his thumb to his chest. "Peter...Peter Francisco."

"He don't speak hardly no English, yet," Petunia said. "That's what Mister Judge says I gotta do...I gots to teach him some English."

"Then you do as you been tol', girl...you do as you been tol'. You be only 14 years, and here you are sleepin' in the main house, so you gots it pretty good if you be askin' me. Anyway, I gots to git back to your momma now. She's got supper waitin' on me."

71

Peter was trying his best to take in all this conversation, but it had been a long day, and he was tired and hungry. He wondered when he might get something to eat.

Petunia looked at the boy and motioned him to put his sack of stuff at the foot of his bed. She may have to share her room with Peter, but she wasn't about to give up any of her dresser space.

As he did as instructed, Petunia became resigned to this whole disruption of her life, and her demeanor began to soften. "You don't understand much of what we been sayin', do ya? Well, tha's alright. I'll be learnin' ya to speak proper in no time...anyway, are you hungry?"

Hungry was a word that Peter had come to know early on at the orphanage. "Hungry...yes hungry," he said.

"Well, I kin fix that. I'll jus' go into the kitchen and get us a couple of plates. Livin' in the main house means we gets to eat what the Winstons eat. You wait right here. I'll be back. Wait here."

Petunia then opened a door opposite her bedroom door. It led directly into the kitchen, where she spent each morning peeling potatoes, gathering eggs, measuring out the biscuit flour, and setting out whatever meat they would be having that day, preparing the food for Mrs. Winston to cook. The slave girl never did any of the actual cooking; Mrs. Winston insisted that she and her daughters tend to that. When Petunia returned to her room with the food, Peter was already sound asleep. His straw mattress didn't match the feathered one at the orphanage, but it was comfortable enough for the tired little boy. Petunia sat his plate next to his bed, took her own plate to her bed, and ate in silence. The sun was long gone now, and tomorrow was a big day.

The eastern sky was just coming to life when Petunia shook Peter awake. He hadn't even heard the insistent crowing of the plantation rooster, but sometime during the night he had awakened and had eaten all his dinner. Today was a new day, and it promised to be a big day on the plantation. Today was Sunday, usually a day off for everybody, even the slaves. But it was also Martha Winston's birthday, and there would be a great celebration.

As the house servant, Petunia had plenty to do to prepare for the afternoon party, so she took Peter down a short path past the big white building he had noticed on the way into Hunting Tower. He could hear horses whinnying from inside, and he wanted to go see them, but Petunia held tightly to his arm and guided him to a building that measured about 15-foot square. Opening the door, Peter could see four straw beds on one side and four more on the other side. Some of these were stacked like the beds at the orphanage, although they were a bit better constructed. Petunia's family lived in one half of the building and four more male slaves occupied the other side with the bunks. The floor was packed dirt, but these were some of the best accommodations on the plantation. There was a fireplace on the back wall and some pots and cooking utensils.

Peter immediately recognized Sam, Petunia's father, and nodded at the man. Then Petunia introduced him to her mother, Lizzy, and her brothers, Joseph and George. They were 16 and 18 years old, and they took to Peter immediately.

"I'm s'posed to show Peter around, but I gots to be fixin' the stuff for Miss Martha's party. Will you do the showin' for me?" Petunia asked her brothers.

"Don't you worry 'bout nothin'," said George, the oldest. "We'll see that Peter sees the place." And they did, spending the rest of the morning taking the boy around to the other slave quarters, showing him the crop fields and even the vegetable garden, where tomatoes, cucumbers, potatoes, green beans and corn were all grown. This particular plot was well over an acre, and Peter had never seen so many vegetables in one place at one time. He also got a look at a fairly large fenced in area where about thirty head of cattle were grazing. He had not seen cattle like this before, and he thought they were odd looking creatures. As he and the others approached the place that Peter wanted to see most, Alfred, the slave master, came out from a side door.

"I was just coming to look for you," Alfred said, nodding toward Peter. "Mister Winston told me he had made a purchase at the orphanage."

Peter looked up at the man. He was not as tall as Judge Winston, but he had a stocky build and a no-nonsense look about him.

"Come here to the barn tomorrow morning. I want you to report to Arthur. You met him yesterday. He drove the carriage, and he's in charge of the horses and everything else in the barn." Amazingly, Peter seemed to understand. This was the place that Peter most wanted to see, so if he was to work here, then all the better. He nodded yes to the man. "Now you three run along," Alfred said. "Miss Martha's party will begin shortly. Joseph and George, I assume you'll be entertainin'."

"Oh, yes, suh," said George. "We'll be dancin' and fiddlin' till the cows come home."

"Fine, fine. Just be sure you save some of that energy for the harvest. We gots a lot of work to do tomorrow. Now run along."

The brothers took off in a trot, and Peter, with no place else to go, went into the barn to take a look around. Arthur was there cleaning some of his tools, and he looked up as Peter entered.

"Well, if it ain't my new helper. I'll be glad to have a second set of hands 'round here. Yes, indeed. These old bones are gettin' a bit too tired for muckin' out all these stalls." Even though they had spent several hours together on the previous day's journey, neither man nor boy had exchanged a single word.

Arthur had been the first slave Judge Winston had bought and was the longest serving and oldest slave at Hunting Tower. As well as he could recollect, he was about 70-years old. Over the years, Arthur had served the judge as a stable boy, carpenter, driver and blacksmith. Though not very tall, he was quite broad across the shoulders, with biceps befitting the work he had done all his life. Because of his strength, he was also the judge's trusted bodyguard, although at his advanced age, it was debatable as to who was guarding whom.

At that moment, a loud bell rang, and Peter looked at the soft-spoken slave questioningly.

"That there's the bell to start Miss Martha's party," said Arthur. "We best be gettin' up to the main house, now." As they left the barn and walked toward the main house, all the other plantation slaves were running in the same direction. Even though Peter had met most of them earlier in the day, seeing them all together was something to behold. There must have been at least twenty of them, and Peter was amazed that their skin tones were very dark yet different from each other's, nonetheless. Some were as dark as night, while others were more like chocolate. Peter wondered where they had all come from.

As they reached the massive front porch of the main house, the Winston family members were all taking their seats to watch the show that the slaves were to present in honor of Miss Martha. One of the slaves played a banjo, another played a fiddle, and another played a homemade drum. The rhythm was almost intoxicating, and many of the slaves started dancing or doing back flips and the like. Such a spectacle Peter had never seen. After a while, some of the slave women set up a long table consisting of wooden planks and barrels that had been brought out by the men. Before Peter knew it, tablecloths had been laid over the planks, and the ladies started a procession of food from behind the house. When they had finished, a veritable feast had been laid out on the makeshift table. Peter could not ever recall seeing so much food. There were three turkeys, two hams, fried fish, all types of vegetables and potatoes, and cakes and pies. He could hardly contain himself at the sight of such a bounty.

As Peter was about to arise from the bench, where he and Arthur had been sitting, the old Negro touched his arm. "We waits until the Winstons have their food. Then we gets to eat. But this here birthday party sets me to wonderin' just how old are you, Peter. Do you know?" Peter didn't understand the question, so Arthur tried again, using as many gestures as he could think of. "How many parties like this have you had?"

Finally it struck Peter what was being asked of him. He didn't know the word, so he held up his hand displaying four fingers and his thumb.

"You is jus' five years old?" said Arthur astonished. "Good lord, you is gonna to be a big one, you sho is."

As was the proper custom, after each of the Winston family members had filled their plates and retaken their seats, the slaves lined up to do the same. For them, this was quite the treat. Normally, the slaves would have a breakfast of hominy, fried potatoes and onions, and some scrambled eggs. Lunch was usually a bit of beef or pork with biscuits, and dinner generally consisted of a small amount of chicken plus biscuits and thin gravy. It was enough, but just barely. Nevertheless, the slaves at Hunting Tower considered themselves lucky, as they had heard the stories of slaves at other plantations having far less and being treated much more poorly. Peter ate and ate and ate, then ate some more. He wanted to taste absolutely everything.

Well into the evening, Judge Winston produced a large box that had been hidden in the carriage boot just the day before. He handed it to Martha, who tore at its ribbon and opened it to find inside a dress she had seen while on a shopping trip in town a few weeks ago. She had pointed it out to the judge, and he had remembered how much she loved it.

"Mother, Father," she exclaimed. "How did you know this was the exact dress that I wanted? How did you know?"

"How, indeed," responded Judge Winston, smiling at his daughter with a twinkle in his eye "You haven't stopped talking about that dress since you saw it." As the birthday girl ran into the house to try it on, Judge Winston signaled that the party was over.

"Alright, everybody," said Alfred. "Back to your quarters with all of you. There's a lot to do tomorrow, and I don't want any laggards. Off with you now." Quickly and efficiently, the dishes were removed and the table taken down, after which the field slaves slowly made their way back to their respective shacks. Peter remained seated with Arthur, who hadn't made a move. Alfred may have held sway with the others, but Arthur, having been on the plantation the longest, held a special part in the judge's heart -- at least as special as a slave could.

"Best you be gettin' along now, boy," Arthur said as he finally began to stir. "I've got lots to show you tomorrow, so you best be awake; don't intend to show you more than jest'one time."

Peter understood and made his way to the back of the house. Since Petunia wasn't there yet, he crawled onto his mattress, pulled his stuffed animal to his chest and fell fast asleep.

The next morning, Petunia didn't have to wake the lad up. The rooster had positioned itself right under his window as the sun scaled the eastern sky. At the first crowing, Peter threw on his clothes and made his way to the barn. Along the way, he saw almost all of the slaves, carrying hoes and rakes and spades, making their way to the fields.

Breakfast would have to wait this day, because Peter's real interest was in seeing the horses, and he wanted to see Arthur, as well. He liked Arthur and he sensed that Arthur also liked him. As he walked into the barn, he saw the old man was already stoking the fire in the forge. A few feet away sat a heavy anvil, all black and shiny, sitting on the stub of a massive tree trunk. Next to the anvil was a bench with several large hammers and a mandrel that Peter would later learn was used for shaping the softened iron being taken from the forge. In his hand, Arthur held grabbers, a set of pincer-like tools. With these, the blacksmith held a long, slender piece of iron from which he would make nails that day. He was just beginning to set the iron in the forge when he looked up and noticed Peter watching him.

"Ah, there you is, and right on time," said Arthur. "We've got lots to do this fine day, so let's be gettin' you to work." He crossed the barn and returned with a pitchfork. "Ever worked with one of these?" he asked, holding out the implement. "This be a pitchfork."

Peter took a step back. He had understood the word fork. He had learned it at the orphanage. But this thing -- this thing must have been made for giants.

A smile came across old Arthur's face. "Come 'ere. Let me show you." He led Peter over to a large pile of straw and drove the pitchfork deep into it. Then he lifted it and a large quantity of hay came out with it. Arthur whirled about and took the straw over to one of the stables. At that moment, Peter finally noticed what he had come here for, at least in his own mind. The horses. He looked at them in wonderment.

There to one side were the two Cream Drafts that had pulled the carriage the day before. They each had their own stall, and next to them were three larger stalls housing three Canadian horses. Originating in France, they made their way as a breed to Quebec, then were slowly integrated onto the farms in the colonies. They stood almost as tall as the Cream Drafts, but Peter could easily tell they were not as broad-chested and didn't weigh nearly as much.

Just then Joseph and George came through the big doors. "Mister Alfred sent us to fetch the Canadians," said George. "We also gots to get their hitchin' gear. I guess Mister Alfred wants to bring in a mess of crops today, so we is s'posed to hitch these horses to the carts."

Arthur pointed his thumb to a far wall. "There be the hitchin' gear, and here's the horses. Don't be waitin' fer me to do your jobs."

Joseph grabbed the horse collars and bridles while George dropped rope nooses over the necks of the animals. Then the two of them led the horses out of the barn and on to a hard day's work. After the boys had left, Arthur began again to show Peter what he was to do with the pitchfork in cleaning out the stalls and replenishing the hay. A short time later, as Peter was getting the hang of his new duties, Alfred came into the barn.

"How's the young lad doin'?" he asked Arthur.

"He be doin' just fine, but he 'aint as old as I think you think, Mister Alfred."

"What do you mean?" queried the slave master.

"Well, when we was sittin' at the party yesterday, I asks him how old he is. It took a while to get my point to him, but he finally tells me with his fingers that he be jes' five years old."

"Imagine that," said Alfred. "I figured him for at least eight or nine. Imagine that. Wait till I tell Judge Winston. Young Peter here is gonna be a big one."

"That's what I said." But the slave master hadn't waited to hear the old Negro's last words. He was already headed for the main house to report what he had found out. As he went up the steps of the front porch, Judge Winston and his wife were just coming out the front door. "Wait till you hear what I just found out about Peter," Alfred said.

"Oh, I just knew it," said Mrs. Winston, her voice revealing her stress over this new information. "He's probably got some terrible disease, and he'll infect all our crop of slaves. I just knew it."

"Hush, woman," rebuked the judge. "What is this about Peter?"

"You know how you said you thought he was seven or eight?

80

"Yes."

"Well, he's not even close. That boy is only five years old."

"How on earth do you know that?"

"Arthur got it out of him."

"Well, I'll be."

"That's just great," Mrs. Winston interrupted. "He'll eat us out of house and home."

"Will you please hush," the judge snapped. "What he'll do is give us a whole lot more work than the average slave, that's what he'll do. Now go back inside and tend to...tend to...tend to something." Given the level of exasperation the judge was beginning to show, Mrs. Winston knew when not to provoke her husband any further. She promptly retreated back inside the house.

Weeks passed and the fall was quickly headed toward winter. Even though, or perhaps because, the days were getting shorter, the pace of work picked up to beat the arrival of the first real cold weather. Except for Sundays, each day was pretty much the same for Peter. He'd arise at the crack of dawn, chomp down a quick breakfast, and head off to the barn to do his chores. He'd work until dark, taking a few minutes for a midday meal, then trudge off to his room where Petunia would help him learn English as they ate dinner together. He was a quick student. After dinner and learning, Peter would curl up with boneca de trapo, which nobody else on the plantation could identify either. In moments, he was sound asleep....until the rooster came calling to start another day.

FROM BOYHOOD TO MANHOOD

Months turned to years at Hunting Tower Plantation – time seemed to fly by. Peter, under the tutelage of Petunia, became fairly well versed in the slave-style-English spoken word and could understand just about anything that was said to him. He was also growing in other ways for by his thirteenth year, he was well over six feet tall and weighed better than 200 pounds of steeled muscle. This was largely due to the fact that Arthur had been teaching him the blacksmith trade.

By now, Peter had his own living quarters, as Judge Winston had deemed it inappropriate for him to continue sharing a room with Petunia. As a result, Peter and Arthur had constructed a room right next to hers on the back of the house. Although it did not have a direct door into the main house, it was attached and reasonably well furnished with an actual bed that stood off the floor, and not one but two dressers to hold the clothing that he seemed to grow out of every few months. Most of these had been made by some of the female slaves working on the plantation, but every once in a while, when Judge Winston went to town, he had Peter drive the carriage. While on these trips, the judge frequently took Peter into the general store for better clothing than the slaves were able to provide. In fact, one of his store-bought pair of pants had been adorned with his salvaged silver, initialed buckles, since his feet had long ago outgrown his favorite boyhood shoes. It was on one of those occasions when Peter first became personally acquainted with Susannah Anderson, whose family lived on a plantation near Hunting Tower.

It was a summer Saturday in 1773, and the judge wanted to go to town to make arrangements for shipping that year's hemp crop for processing in Richmond. He had asked Peter to drive the carriage, as Arthur was not feeling very well - something which was happening more and more frequently of late. As Peter took his place on the driver's seat in front of the Judge Winston, the judge asked him to stop at the main house. At the last minute, he had decided to take his daughter, Sarah, on the trip as well. All of the Winston children relished a trip such as this, and it had been a long time since Sarah had been off the plantation. As he approached the carriage with his pretty daughter, Peter jumped down from his seat, doffed his tri-cornered hat, a gift from the judge a few years earlier, and bent slowly at the waist.

"Good day, Miss Sarah. I trust that all is well with you today," the young man said.

Sarah Winston was astonished and even Judge Winston was taken aback. "Why, Peter," she said. "Where in the world did you learn such lovely manners?"

"Oh, I've been watchin' when we get guests here at the main house. I seen and heard people do it all the time, so I thought it was the right thing to do. I didn't do nothin' wrong, did I?

"Of course not, Peter," the judge cut in. "Of course not. You are learning our ways well."

Peter extended his hand to Sarah and assisted her into the carriage. Repositioning himself just behind the Creams, he gave them a soft-spoken "Gidup", and the horses quickly responded, taking the happy party of three off to town.

Upon their arrival, the judge told Sarah to go across the street and pick out something nice for herself. He always did that when he took one of the children along, which was one of the reasons they always wanted to go with him. Then he told Peter to wait with the carriage and entered an office that sat right on the main street. Peter sat back on the hard rail that provided a backrest for the driver and was soon lost in his thoughts.

Suddenly there was a commotion from up the street as a single-horse wagon careened down the street in Peter's direction and he immediately saw that there was no driver aboard. People were running behind it yelling, "Stop that wagon! Stop that wagon!" Peter leaped from his seat with every intention of running out and grabbing the horse's collar.

At that very moment, Susannah Anderson had just exited the store in which Sarah was doing her shopping. Peter had seen Susannah several times when the Andersons had come to visit the Winstons, but he had never actually met her or even exchanged a word of conversation, especially since she was a few years older than he.

Susannah was carrying a heavy load of packages that blocked her view of the oncoming runaway wagon. Though she subconsciously heard the commotion, she was so lost in her own thoughts that she stepped into the street directly into the path of the driverless wagon. Seeing this, Peter dashed into the street and crossed its breadth in only a few steps. Just as the horse and wagon were ready to plow Susannah down, in a single motion, Peter swept the young woman off her feet, tucked her behind himself like a human shield, and turned to face the onrushing horse and wagon. Fortunately, the horse recognized Peter as a rather formidable object in its path and swerved at the last second. Nevertheless, it nicked Peter with quite a force, and it was all he could do to maintain his balance and that of Susannah, whom he had successfully shielded. Turning sharply to the left, the wagon overturned, spilling flour and other items into the street. Thankfully, it had also stopped the horse.

As Peter loosened his grip on Susannah and turned around to check on her welfare, their eyes met for the first, but most certainly not the last time. Susannah's packages were strewn at her feet, but she couldn't take her eyes off the tall, dark Portuguese who had just saved her life. It took several moments before she could gather her composure.

"You're Peter -- Peter Francisco, aren't you? You live at Hunting Tower, don't you?" Susannah said as she began to regain her senses. She, too, had noticed Peter on her visits to the Winston Plantation, but the propriety of the day would never have allowed her to initiate a conversation with him. This occasion, however, was quite different. "Do you know what you just did?"

"Yes, Miss...ah, no Miss...ah, I don't know, Miss," Peter stammered. He too was flustered, but not because of a close brush with death. "Are you alright, Miss? I didn't hurt you, did I?"

"Am I alright? Am I alright?" she mindlessly repeated. "I am, but only because of you. You just saved my life. You do know that, don't you?"

"I...I guess so," replied Peter, still looking so deeply into Susannah's eyes that forming sentences had become difficult. Peter and Susannah just stood there looking at each other for a moment, and in the next moment, Sarah came out of the store, and Judge Winston exited the office. Both of them had been drawn by all the activity and racket, and they were quick to notice Susannah and Peter in the middle of the street.

"Well, well, what do we have here?" said Sarah, noticing the longing gazes of the couple standing in the street, surrounded by packages.

"Oh, my," said Susannah, finally breaking eye contact. "Why, your Peter, here, just saved my life from a runaway horse."

"What do you mean?" asked the judge as he approached the two girls. "And what in the world happened?" he asked, looking around not only at Susannah's packages but also at the overturned wagon with its contents scattered all about.

"That wagon," said Susannah, still a bit shaken and pointing to the wreckage, "would have run me down if it weren't for Peter here."

"Do tell," the judge replied. Other townspeople began to gather around as well.

"Did you see what he did?" questioned one man

"Sure did," said another. "Never seen anything like it. That horse plowed right into this fella, and he never even flinched...never seen anything like it...never"

"Just exactly what did happen?" Judge Winston asked.

Everyone who had gathered around had his own version of the story, and, of course, each version was slightly different from the other. In the end, however, Judge Winston had a pretty good idea of what had taken place.

"Seems like you are a bit of a hero," commended the judge, slapping Peter on the back approvingly. "I'm right proud of you...right proud. Now, let's help Miss Susannah gather up her things."

Peter was quick to that task, too, being a bit embarrassed by all the attention. Soon enough, he was carrying all of Susannah's purchases to her carriage, which had just arrived on the opposite side of the street. He placed them in the carriage boot and offered his hand to Susannah to climb into the carriage. As their hands touched, she looked warmly into Peter's eyes and he into hers. They lingered for a moment before Susannah broke the silence.

"Thank you, Peter Francisco," she said sincerely. "Your bravery will not go unrewarded. I'm sure my father will want to have words with you when I tell him what happened today." Susannah sat down and told her driver to take her home, but as the carriage drove off, she turned in her seat to take one last look at her hero. Peter, not moving a single muscle, watched the carriage drive out of sight.

Judge Winston walked up behind Peter and slapped him on the back. "Well done, Peter, well done. But we must be getting back to Hunting Tower now, before the sun goes down much further."

"Yes, sir," Peter complied. They stowed Sarah's purchase in their own carriage boot, and Peter began the trip home, prodding the Creams on with just his voice.

In the passenger area, Sarah looked at her father. "Did you see how they were looking at each other?" she commented quietly so that Peter could not hear her.

"No, I didn't," replied the judge. "What do you mean?"

With all the wisdom of a teenaged girl, she answered, "I think Peter is in love, and I think Miss Anderson is, too."

"You don't say. I'm not sure if that's a good thing or not, them coming from two different classes and all. Besides, Mr. Anderson and I don't exactly share the same views on a lot of things. Still, I like having the Andersons over for a lively debate now and again. I guess we'll just have to wait and see what happens next."

Ever so softly, so that only her father could hear, Sarah began to murmur, "Peter's got a girlfriend, Peter's got a girlfriend." The judge just smiled.

The next morning, the rooster, which had now taken up crowing outside Peter's new window, alerted him that a new day had indeed begun. He was quick to put on his work clothes and head off to the barn, anxious to see if old Arthur was feeling any better. As he was leaving his private dwelling to check on the old man, a thought struck him. His hearing was a lot better than the judge and Sarah had supposed, and once he had overheard the judge comment about Susannah and him being of different classes. But just what class did he belong to, he wondered. His new accommodations had signified a certain standing among the rest of the plantation's residents. He was not truly a slave, yet he still answered to the slave master, he worked from sunup to sundown every day except Sunday, and he had been purchased from the orphanage. Nor was he an indentured servant. Indentured servants had a contract with their master and at some point would be set free. He had no such arrangement with the judge. On the other hand, he had certain luxuries and privileges that the black slaves did not. He had his private place to sleep. He ate better food, and the judge just treated him differently than the others. This was all too perplexing, and Peter tried his best to push the thoughts out of his mind. He really did want to see how Arthur was doing. But there was something he couldn't stop thinking about -- the look in Susannah's eyes yesterday and the way her hand felt in his. For the first time in his life, he had felt hands that were even softer than his mother's.

As he pushed open the huge double doors to the barn, there stood Arthur putting some hard maple wood into the forge to get it fired up. The old Negro turned to see who was entering his domain.

"Ah, there you are, the hero of the day," greeted Arthur.

"What do you mean?" responded Peter naively.

"You knows what I mean. The way I hears it, you jes' 'bout flattened that runaway horse in town yesterday."

"Oh, that. That was nothin'. I just did what was needed. 'Sides, you'd a done the same. But how'd you hear about it?"

"I mighta tried to do the same thing, but these old bones probly woulda stopped me...and you know how news like that travels fast on the plantation. Jes' you remember this, Peter, you is big...bigger than any other boy your age I ever seen. You is strong. You is already stronger than anybody else at Hunting Tower and you is gettin' stronger every day. And you is smart. Lordy, lordy, lordy -- you is smarter than jest' 'bout anybody I ever met, 'cept the judge and some of the folks that come to visitin' the main house."

"Well, let's just get to work and forget all this foolish talk," said Peter. He crossed over to the back wall of the barn, grabbed his smithy's apron from off a wooden peg and tied it on. Over the past year, Peter had been doing more and more of the blacksmith duties as Arthur's advancing age was truly slowing him down. It wasn't long before the sound of hammer on molten iron began to ring out for all to hear, and Peter could really make that hammer sing once he got going. Every time he slammed that ten-pounder down on the anvil, his biceps seemed to gain more muscle. Arthur was right. For a man of any age, Peter was one of the strongest on the plantation, in the county, maybe in all the colonies, for that matter. And he was going to grow even bigger and stronger.

Peter's relationship with Arthur had also grown -- the two of them were almost inseparable. They spent nerly every day together, working from sunrise to sunset, and they often spent evenings in deep conversation. Peter had come to love the old man, and Arthur, initially happy with just the help in the barn, had begun to look at Peter as the son he had never had.

During one of their after-dinner talks in Arthur's cabin, Tom and Richard, two of the several other male slaves he shared the cabin with, came in arguing. They hadn't noticed Peter and Arthur in the dark corner. "So what reason we got to stay here on the plantation? Give me one reason," Tom's voice was agitated and adamant. "All we ever do is pick tobacco and hemp and plant and works all day." His voice was excited.

91

"Yeah, I knows," said Richard. "Believe me, I knows, but where ya gonna go tha's any better? And s'pose you get catched? You know what they do to runaways. If'n they don't shoot ya, they hang ya, and if'n they bringed you back here, you know Mister Alfred would nearly whip the hide offen ya."

It was true that Judge Winston treated his slaves better than those owners on a lot of other plantations, but he gave Alfred his lead to maintain discipline in whatever he was thought necessary. Peter could only remember one time, his first year on the plantation, when one of the slaves had back sassed the master. Alfred had promptly had that man strapped to a tree. Twenty lashes with a bullwhip later, the slave's back had been laid open raw. It was a sight that had turned Peter's stomach and one he would never forget. The next day, that slave was gone, never to be seen or heard of again.

"It don' matter. I jes' gots to get away from here. I gots to be free," Tom insisted.

"You listen to me," said Richard. "No matter where you goes, you ain't never gonna be free. Free is for white folk, and you ain't no white folk."

Arthur had heard enough and cleared his throat to make his presence known. From his dark corner where he and Peter had been talking, he crossed the room. The fireplace light played on his features.

"You best be listenin' to Richard, Tom. He be dead right. You two was born slaves, you is slaves today, you be slaves tomorrow, an' on the day you dies, you still be slaves," Arthur told them. "Besides that, you got one o' the best mas'ers around. Best you remember that, "

Arthur turned to Peter, "And best you be gettin' some sleep. We gots a long day tomorrow."

Peter rose, walked across the room and strode out into the cool night air. What he had just heard was making his mind run in all sorts of directions. Freedom. What a curious idea. Other than his first five years of life with his family, a time that was quickly becoming a fading memory, Peter had not known real freedom. First he was a prisoner of pirates, and then he was a ward at the orphanage, followed by his life here at Hunting Tower Plantation. Now that he was approaching manhood, he wondered -- what exactly did it mean to be free? Peter didn't know. Didn't even know who to ask. But he was determined to find out. That night, alone in his bed, he couldn't get the idea of freedom out of his mind, and he slept restlessly.

The next day was one that Peter would never forget. He and Arthur were working in the barn when Alfred came in. Motioning toward Peter he said, "Judge Winston would like to see you up at the main house."

Peter wondered what he might have done wrong. As he approached the house, he saw the same carriage that had whisked Susannah Anderson homeward on the day he had rescued her from certain death. He also noticed that an older gentleman accompanied Susannah, and the thought made his hands grow clammy, his breathing grow shallow. Before he could reach the carriage, Susannah and the man were already standing and being greeted by Judge Winston.

The judge turned toward Peter. "Ah, here he is. Peter, come over here. I have someone who would like to meet you."

Peter's mind raced. After all, he had already met Susannah, so the judge must mean he wanted him to meet the man…but whatever for?

"Peter," said the judge, "this is Mr. Anderson, Susannah's father, and he would have words with you."

"Peter," the man broke in, "I wanted to come here today to thank your for your gallantry and bravery in saving my little girl's life a few weeks ago. I would have liked to do this sooner, but things at our plantation have been so busy. I hope you'll forgive me for not coming directly."

Peter stood there a bit dumbfounded by all this attention. He had basically understood what Mr. Anderson had said, although the word gallantry was not yet a part of his vocabulary. "I'm just glad I was there," said Peter.

"Well, we're glad you were there, too," repeated Mr. Anderson, "and as a small token of our appreciation, I've brought you something I hope you can use." Mr. Anderson reached into the carriage and produced a package wrapped in brown paper. "Peter, this is for you. Wear it well."

Peter accepted the gift and looked at Susannah. "Open it, Peter, please do," she said.

He looked at the judge as if seeking permission. "By all means, Peter. Open it," he insisted.

Peter tore at the paper and produced a magnificent, dark blue tri-cornered hat with silver trim. For a moment, he just looked at it. His own hat was well worn and dirty, covered in sawdust. This -- this was a real gentleman's hat. Peter was tongue-tied.

The judge piped in to rescue him for the awkward moment. "I think Peter would do well to say 'thank you,' but I see that your fine gift renders him speechless."

"Thank you, sir, thank you," Peter said. "I...I...," his voice trailed off. Peter had turned his attention back to the most beautiful creature in the world, Susannah Anderson.

"Do try it on, Peter," she said.

The reluctant hero removed his own work hat and placed the new one on his head. It fit like a glove on a hand, much to everyone's approval. For the second time, Peter was actually embarrassed by all the attention.

The silence became a bit uncomfortable before the judge spoke again. "Where are my manners? Please, come into the house, you and Miss Susannah. I'm sure we have some refreshments at hand." Turning to Peter he said, "That will be all. You can return to your chores now." As the three of them went into the house, Susannah turned again to look at Peter. She silently mouthed a thank you, and Peter could feel his blood rushing to his cheeks.

When the door closed, he set out for the barn as instructed, but not until he had taken his new hat to his room, where he placed it on top of the dresser so he could see it as soon as he entered the room later that day and every day.

****

The radiant hues of that fall's leaves soon gave way to bare branches with sparse leaves, yet the work on the plantation was not sparse. Each day, Peter and Arthur worked side-by-side in the barn as they crafted farm implements out of iron and wood. By this time, he was also becoming well schooled in carpentry, and he could wield an auger and a gimlet with the best of them. He especially liked using the wide variety of chisels and gauges, drawknives and spokeshaves, which he used to transform wood into all types of useful shapes. The pride he took in his work always showed in the finished product.

Peter also attempted to grasp the whole idea of freedom. He watched the slave children as they played in the evenings, rolling hoops, walking on stilts that Peter himself had made, or engaging in a game of ninepins. He thought of Arthur and the rest of the slaves. Even the food they ate was of far lesser quality than that of the Winston family. Corn meal was one of the main staples, while the Winstons, Petunia and even Peter feasted, as it were, on Fish Muddle, Welsh Rabbit and, Peter's favorite, Shepherd's Pie. Indeed, there was a difference between free and not free, but the line of separation was becoming more and more obvious in Peter's mind, and it was a line that he didn't much care for.

As the long winter finally gave way to the spring of 1774, there seemed to be more and more activity in the main house with frequent visitors. Always wanting to put on a show for his guests, Judge Winston asked Peter to act as a doorman for those who frequented Hunting Tower, and as they arrived, Peter greeted them, led them to the front door, and announced their names as they entered the main house. It kept him busy, as these gatherings were getting larger, and more guests meant more need for Peter to be doorman.

On one particular occassion , a gentleman of obvious stature arrived in one of the most magnificent carriages Peter had ever seen. He had noticed this man several times from afar, but this time when the servant held open the door to the carriage, the man stepped down and extended his hand to Peter. "You must be Peter Francisco. My uncle, the judge, has told me a lot about you. My name is Patrick Henry."

Peter shook his hand and replied courteously, "How do you do, sir." He always wore his new hat for this assignment, sweeping it from his head while giving a slight bow, evidencing his refined manners. Peter was quite impressed by Patrick Henry's bearing and by his height. This man, although a few inches shorter than Peter, was a good six feet tall, a full half-head taller than most men of the day. When Peter announced Patrick Henry's name upon opening the main house front door, he did so with a flourish reserved only for guests he knew to be extra important.

On this same night, the Anderson family -- with Susannah and her brothers Thomas and James, Jr. included -- was in attendance, and as usual Peter found himself somewhat weak-kneed when their carriage arrived. Whenever the Andersons visited, Peter felt as though his heart was about ready to jump right out of his chest; yet he was always anxious for their visits, for it gave him an excuse to touch Susannah's hand as he helped her from the carriage – and yet another chance to gaze into her eyes. Tonight was one of those times.

When all the guests had arrived, and the judge told Peter that his services would no longer be needed, he retired to his room. Since it adjoined the main house parlor, Peter was easily able to hear what was being said.

"What you speak of is tyranny," said one of the voices. "Tyranny, I say." The voice sounded like Mr. Anderson's.

"Tyranny! Tyranny! I'll tell you what tyranny is." This voice was unmistakably that of Judge Winston. "Tyranny is all these taxes...taxes that we're having to pay because the King had to fight the French. He should have kept that war in Europe where it belonged. Tyranny was the Stamp Act!"

"But that was repealed," rebutted the first voice. Peter knew it was Anderson speaking now.

"Then how about the Townshend Act? The king wanted to tax everything of value coming to the Americas," said the judge.

"That, too, was repealed," retorted Anderson.

"Yes, it was repealed, but not until the king's men shot down several peaceful people at that square in Boston. Shooting your own people, now that's tyranny." This voice belonged to the man who had introduced himself earlier in the day. This was Patrick Henry. "And what of the Proclamation of 1763? The colonies can't even expand to the west because of this cowardly act to protect the very Indians who would have had our scalps only a few years earlier. And the Sugar Act, and, and, and...oh, I could go on and on. Gentlemen, I say that those of us in the colonies know best how to govern our interests. We are taxed and we are told what to do and when to do it, yet we have no voice, no say in the matter. Such talk of rebellion is not tyranny. No, it is the reason that so many sacrificed so much to settle in this new land...it is the talk of freedom, and it is freedom we must have."

There was that word again. Freedom. Slowly, Peter was beginning to understand. Freedom was a good thing, and people were willing to fight and die and sacrifice for it. Still, Peter was confused. Mr. Anderson had been so nice to him, and he had the deepest feelings for

Susannah. Yet he was arguing against what Peter knew deep in his heart was a good thing...Freedom. This made no sense.

The arguing back and forth went well into the night, but Peter, exhausted from another long day's work, could fight sleep no longer. The voices faded, and Peter found himself dreaming...dreaming of Susannah Anderson...dreaming of freedom...dreaming of the freedom to make Susannah his wife. Would that, could that possibly ever happen?

In the spring of 1775, Judge Winston came to a decision, one that had been in the making over the past few years. One Friday morning, he felt the time had come to put his decision into action.

Peter and Arthur were hard at work in the barn when an early morning shadow cast itself upon the wide double-door opening. They looked up to see Judge Winston standing there -- truly unusual, since the judge most often sent Alfred to relay any messages or information he might have for them.

"Peter," said the judge, "I would like to speak with you."

Arthur, sensing that this was to be a private conversation, was the first to respond. "Yes, sir, Judge Winston, I'll jes' go out here and check on some other things."

"No, Arthur, I want you to stay as this concerns you, too," replied the judge.

"Peter," the judge repeated. "You've been with me for about ten years now. You've certainly grown as a man. Just look at the size of you. You're as strong as -- no, stronger than -- any I've ever seen. You're also smarter than most, even though you don't read or write. Now, Arthur, here, he has been as loyal to me as anyone. I've depended on him for a lot of things over the years. He's been my driver, my bodyguard; and he's been my faithful companion all these years." There was a long pause, as the judge seemed to be looking for just the right words to say. "Arthur, I think you'd be the first to admit that time has caught up with you, with both of us, for that matter. I know that riding around the countryside has become a painful experience, though you never complained, not even once. I also know that if the situation arose, you would gladly lay down your own life for my safety."

Arthur interrupted, something he seldom did when the judge was speaking, "Yes, sir, Judge Winston, I sho'ly would."

"Yes, Arthur, I know you would. But the times are different now. These are perilous times for us all. I feel that the time is rapidly approaching when the views of those of us in the colonies and those of the King of England shall be in total opposition. Certain people will be considered enemies of the crown, and danger, perhaps even bloodshed, is coming to the land. Arthur, if ever a white man could love a Negro and vice versa, we share that kind of love. But from this day forward, I will be having young Peter here as my driver and bodyguard. Peter," continued the judge as he looked at the massive teenager, "you have earned this privilege. If you can assume these duties and perform them even half as well as old Arthur here, I will be forever grateful."

Peter, who hadn't spoken a word, cleared his throat. "Of course, I will. Yes, sir, and I'll be honored to."

"Good then," said the judge. "It's all settled. In a couple of weeks we have a journey to make to Richmond. My nephew, Patrick Henry, will also be there along with some other very important people. Good day then." The judge's very tone spoke volumes as to his feelings about the old Negro and the young Portuguese.

100

As Judge Winston left the barn, Arthur looked at Peter with the eyes of a father to a son. "I hates admittin' that I is gettin' old, but I is real proud of you, Peter Francisco. I is powerful proud.

7

A CALL TO ARMS, MARCH 1775

Peter's mind began to settle on his new assignment as Judge Winston's carriage driver and bodyguard. But he couldn't help pondering the words he had just heard both inside and outside the St. John's Church. Inside, Patrick Henry had created a frenzy of shouts with his stirring speech. Even now, the bedlam that ensued continued as delegates shouted at one another. Outside, Susannah Anderson's father had rebuked Peter for siding with those calling for freedom from England's tyranny, and the young lady herself. The woman who had so easily won Peter's heart had called him a fool.

Regardless, he was trying to understand the concept of freedom, knowing full well that it was something good, something he wished very much to attain. How could the Andersons not see this as clearly as he?

How could they possibly be so wrong? Peter, struggling with his thoughts and emotions, felt a tap on his shoulder. It was Judge Winston.

"Peter, my boy," the judge said, "Did you hear what my nephew had to say? Did you understand what he meant?

"Yes, sir." replied Peter, standing up to show proper respect for the judge. "I heard Mr. Henry speak. I didn't understand everything. Some of his words I never heard before, but I think I understood enough -- enough to know that everyone wants to be free, but some really don't know what real freedom is or how to get it. It just seems that some folks don't want things to change."

"Very good, Peter. I think you probably understood more than you think."

"But what about those who don't think like you and Mr. Henry? What about those people? When they left, Mr. Anderson wouldn't even speak to me, and Susannah called me a fool and you, too!"

"You have to understand, Peter, that not everyone wants to possibly risk all that they have, perhaps their very lives, for something they don't fully understand. They are pretty happy with the way things are. What they fail to see is that, if we were to allow things to go on as they are, the King of England will strip us of all that we have tried to acquire for the sake of families and ourselves. Many of our ancestors came to this new world to escape the very tyranny with which we re now faced."

"Does that mean that the Andersons are wrong? Or that someday they may agree with us?"

"That's hard to say, Peter. I know that young Susannah has won your heart," the judge said knowingly. "I've seen the way you look at her

104

when they visit. But Mr. Anderson is pretty set in his ways. We call him a loyalist, and I'm not too sure that he will ever see things our way. Peter, I say this to you as though you were my son. I would think that any further thoughts of Susannah should be put to rest. There will be plenty of other young ladies to capture your fancy. Besides, there's still considerable work for you to do at Hunting Tower. I'm going to be relying on you even more in the future. I'd better be getting back inside now. The day's business still is not done." The judge turned and disappeared inside the church as other delegates filed in with him.

Peter took a moment to look down the road -- the road down which Susannah and her father had disappeared in a cloud of dust. Now the judge's words rang in his head. Was he never to see her again? Would the future he had imagined for himself and her only a couple of hours before never come to be? Was the judge right that he should just forget about her? It was all just too confusing. Peter strolled over to the horses he loved so much. At the very least, he could always depend on them.

With the approach of evening, the delegates -- including the judge, Patrick Henry, George Washington and Thomas Jefferson -- began to leave the church. While some walked in near silence, others spoke excitedly. As the judge and Patrick Henry neared, Peter held the door open when he saw the judge and Patrick Henry nearing the carriage.

"Peter," the judge spoke, "my nephew and I will be dining together this evening, so he will be riding back to the inn with us."

"Very well, sir," Peter said. Nodding toward Patrick Henry, he added, "I liked your speech today, sir."

"You don't sound all that enthusiastic," replied Henry.

"Oh, no, sir, those were some of the best words I ever heard in my life."

"Patrick, " the judge interrupted, "you have to understand that the boy is having some mixed feelings right now. I suspect young Peter liked what you said just fine, but the young lady he had his cap set for seems to disagree. You know her -- Susannah Anderson, James Anderson's daughter."

"Ah, yes," Henry recalled. "Her father and I have had many a lively debate. But I'm sure you'll find some other winsome lass to take your breath away again."

"That's exactly what I told him," the judge chimed in. "Now let's be off, before the dining room at the inn gets too crowded."

Peter closed the carriage door behind the judge and Patrick Henry, took his place in the driver's position, and guided the Creams out onto the street. Most of the other delegates had the same idea, and dozens of carriages were trying to exit the church grounds at the same time. But the mere size of the Creams and their driver caused other horses and drivers to make way for the Winston carriage.

Peter dropped Judge Winston and Patrick Henry off in front of the inn and then drove down the street to the livery stable, where he unhitched and stalled the magnificent animals, pulled the carriage behind the building, and returned to rub down and feed his horses. He took his time with each of them, while letting his mind wander back over the day's events. He knew full well that he would always embrace the idea of freedom and that he was in total support of what Patrick Henry had said that day. On the other hand, he wasn't about to give up so easily on

Susannah Anderson, no matter what the judge and his nephew had said. There just had to be a way.

Reaching into his pocket, Peter discovered the biscuits the innkeeper's wife had made for him the previous night. The day's events had been so unsettling that he had forgotten to eat them. For that matter, since he still had no appetite, he offered the biscuits to the horses, which readily gobbled down the treat.

The next day played out much as the last three had. Peter arose early, prepared the wagon and drove Judge Winston to the St. John's Church for more meetings of the Second Virginia Convention. Ultimately, Patrick Henry introduced a resolution calling for the establishment of militias throughout the Virginia Colony. Although the delegation was quite divided on the proposed action, everyone knew there would be ramifications, and they dispersed on the final day with full knowledge that war with England, like it or not, was just around the corner.

On the journey back to Hunting Tower, Peter contemplated the role he might play in the upcoming conflict. After about an hour of driving in silence, the judge addressed his driver from inside the enclosed carriage. "Peter? Peter, can you hear me?

"Yes, sir, Judge Winston," was the reply.

"Peter, I think you understand there's going to be a war."

"Yes, sir, I think I do."

"Do you know what that means, Peter?"

"Men are going to fight, and men are going to die, and in the end, we will all be free."

"Well, not exactly. Not everyone is going to be free. The slaves back at the plantation will still be slaves. But our country will be free. Free from the oppression of England. Free from the king. Free to determine our own destiny as a country. Do you understand what I'm saying?

"Yes, sir. I think so, and I've been thinking that I should join the army, too."

"Well, Peter, while I admire your noble thoughts, I think there are a few things we must consider. First, you are simply too young to go off fighting in a war. After all, you're just barely fifteen years old, even though you're bigger than most fully-grown men I know. The other problem is that there's no real army to join. Right now, it looks like we're just going to have some local militias to protect our interests here in Virginia. But what's most important is that we can do so much important work right at Hunting Tower, and that includes you, Peter. I'm planning to convert most of our cropland to growing more hemp. That way, when the time comes, we'll be able to produce more and more rope, and rope is going to be a vital commodity for our troops and especially our sailors. We will all have a roll to play as the conflict draws near, and that includes all of us at Hunting Tower. With Arthur's health such a concern, I'll need you there now more than ever before."

"Yes, sir," Peter replied with resignation.

Not another word was spoken as each man contemplated his own thoughts during the rest of the trip.

Upon returning to Hunting Tower, Peter discovered that Arthur's health was indeed rapidly declining. More often than not, the old Negro arrived at the barn no earlier than midday, if at all. Thus Peter found

108

himself especially busy doing the work of two men in caring for all the horses and doing all the blacksmith and carpentry work that the busy plantation required on a day-to-day basis.

In early May, a rider galloped up to the main house, dismounted before his horse barely had time to come to a complete stop, bounded up the steps to the porch and pounded on the front door. When the judge opened the door, he and the excited rider spoke for a few minutes, the man then leaving just as quickly as he had arrived. Peter, responding to all of the racket, stood in the double door opening to the barn. The judge walked over to where he was standing.

"Peter," said the judge soberly, "it would appear that the fight has just begun."

"What? Where? How?" asked Peter.

"In Massachusetts. Some places called Lexington and Concord. The local militias there exchanged gunfire with the English."

"But isn't that far away?"

"Indeed, it is, but there has also been some trouble right here in Virginia in Williamsburg, and it involves my nephew."

"Mr. Henry?"

"Yes, Peter, my nephew Patrick. It seems that when Governor Dunmore heard about the conflict up north, he decided to move fifteen half barrels of gunpowder out of Williamsburg to make sure nobody could get their hands on it. Well, Patrick and a bunch of others heard about it, and they rode to Williamsburg to stop the transfer. The governor sent his family away and then threatened to set fire to the whole city. From what the messenger just told me, they spent several days in a standoff before the matter was settled."

"Is Mr. Henry alright?" questioned Peter.

"Yes, yes, he's fine, though your concern is deeply appreciated. However, Dunmore issued a proclamation against Patrick and others accusing them of treason, so I fear that this will all begin to press forward to all-out war very soon. In fact, the Second Continental Congress is set to convene in just a couple of days, and Virginia's representative, a fellow named Richard Henry Lee, has been instructed to propose that the colonies declare themselves as free and independent."

"What does all that mean, sir?" asked Peter.

"It means that we are pressing ever closer to the war we all know is coming."

"So, what should I do?'

"I know what you're thinking, Peter, but forget not what I told you on the way back from Richmond. You are still too young to fight, and there's plenty for us to do here to help the war. Now go back to what you were doing, and let's not talk any further about you going off to fight."

"Yes, sir." Peter knew when not to contradict the judge's wishes, even though, deep inside, he was sure that it was his destiny to fight – fight for the freedom of his country, and fight for his own freedom."

That evening when Peter went to his quarters, he rummaged through one of the dresser drawers until he found his best pair of britches. At the area where they were buckled, just below the knee, were the silver buckles with P and F that had once adorned his shoes.

Peter sat down on his bed and looked at the buckles. They were the only remnants of his childhood in the Azores Islands, a place where he had once been free. Surely one day, though he didn't know how, he would be free once again. Even though the judge had been kind to him, he had always known his place at Hunting Tower. If the judge told him to do something, he did it. If the judge told him he couldn't go off to war, then so be it. But Peter knew -- he just knew -- that the day would come when he would fight in this war and that, through that struggle, he would one day be free.

He also thought of Susannah. What was she doing right now? Were she and her father finally seeing the truth of the matter? Did they finally understand that fighting the English was the right thing to do? Was there any possible chance that he would see her again? As Peter lay back on his bed, clutching the silver buckles, he pictured Susannah in his mind and drifted slowly off to sleep.

The next morning, Peter slept a bit later than usual. Even the faithful rooster had no effect on his slumber. When he entered the barn for his day's work, he was pleasantly surprised to see Arthur already hard at work. It had been nearly a week since the elderly man had felt up to working, although Peter had made it a point to visit with him each evening.

"My, my, my," Arthur said looking up from the forge. "Look who couldn't get up out of bed today."

Peter just stood there looking sheepish.

"Well, snap to it, boy. We gots lots o' work to do 'round here, and it ain't gettin' done with you jes' standin' there."

"Do you remember the night when we heard Tom and Richard talking about running away? Do you remember what you told them?" asked Peter.

"Of course, I does. I may be gettin' feeble in the body, but I remembers everything. Why is you askin?"

"It's just that whole thing about freedom and being free."

"Peter, why you just keep goin' on about all this, I jes' don' know. It's 'bout all you talk since you be comin' back from Richmond. Peter, you needs to get your mind right. You may not be nearly as black as me and the other slaves, but the judge paid good money for you, and you'll be doin' as he pleases, no matter what. 'Sides, the judge, he treats you better than jes' 'bout anybody else 'round here, 'cept his own family. He even treats you better 'n that old slave master Alfred."

"I know, Arthur, I know." Peter said as he began to gather up his blacksmith's tools. "But don't it bother you wondering what it would be like to be free?"

"Peter, maybe I'm jes' too old to remember a time when I be free, but I do know this -- I've lived a pretty good life here at Hunting Tower, and I 'spect this is where I'll end my days. An' I understand what a young buck like you might be thinkin'. But you need to be puttin' them kind o' thoughts outta your mind. Now let's not be talkin' no more 'bout it. We gots lots o' work to do, and it don't get done talkin'."

Peter was a bit confused at Arthur's way of ending the conversation. Arthur had always been his sounding board, but today it seemed as though the old darky didn't want to discuss the matter anymore. Peter tried his best to forget about the whole thing, and soon he had anvil, hammer and hot iron singing in perfect, three-part harmony. Still, the idea of freedom haunted every waking hour of his day and most of his dreams, too. Nevertheless, he stopped talking about it with anyone.

As the days pressed into June, at Hunting Tower riders were an almost daily occurrence bringing Judge Winston the latest news. Of course, one way or another, Peter heard what was happening either directly from the judge or sometimes from the riders themselves, when he tended to their horses.

Early in June, fearing for his life, Governor Dunmore had left Williamsburg, certain that the rebels would do him harm if he stayed. Initially he fled to Porto Bello, his hunting lodge in York County. Later he and his family took refuge on the British warship Fowey, which was anchored in the York River at the time.

But to Peter, more important than that announcement was the announcement that on June 14 the Continental Army had been established. At least now one of the judge's objections to Peter's going to war had been eliminated. Now there was an actual army to join. The very next day, the tall gentleman that Peter had seen in Richmond was appointed as that army's chief commander. Peter tried his best to remember his name. It was George...George something...George...George...George Washington...that was it. Peter couldn't have been happier. Even though he had not spoken with the man, he could just tell that he was a leader of men.

Unfortunately, the news that came only a couple of days later was not nearly as uplifting. The American forces had suffered a dramatic defeat at the hands of the British at somewhere called Bunker Hill. From what Peter could gather, the Americans had fought gallantly and inflicted heavy losses on the English but in the end were forced to retreat.

That very evening, Judge Winston knocked on the door of Peter's quarters and entered without waiting for an answer. Peter could not recall the last time the judge had actually paid him a visit. The sole kerosene lamp barely lit the room, even with the wick fully up, and the judge's shadow played across the wall of wooden planks.

"Peter, I would like to speak with you," the judge said soberly. "I know you've been hearing all the news about the war, and I know you would love to join the army. But before you get that notion back in your head, I want to put an end to it right here and right now. The truth is that you are just too valuable to me here at Hunting Tower. Alfred has just informed me that he is planning on leaving to join the Continental Army in New Jersey. I have to admit that I never thought a great deal about him as a slave master, but he kept things running around here for a good many years. I'm going to ask Anthony, Jr. to assume that role, but he's not had much experience, so I'm going to rely on you to help him as much as you can. You seem to get along with all the slaves, and Lord knows you and Arthur seem to have a special bond. I think everyone will listen to you. The reason I'm telling you all this is that, while you might be thinking the time is right for you to go off and fight, now is just not the time, and I'll hear no talk of it. I need you here. And my decision has been made." Without waiting for any response from Peter, Judge Winston opened the door and left.

Peter just sat there in silence. Indeed he had thought of going to the judge with another request to join the army, but now that seemed out of the question, at least for the foreseeable future.

Days went by, then weeks and months. That season's crop of hemp was by far the largest ever grown on the plantation, and the judge was especially pleased, although rather than take it all to market, though he decided to store a good deal of it in the barn until the time was right to send it for processing for the war.

Anthony, Jr., with a good deal of help from Peter, successfully took over as slave master, and the little farming community known as Hunting Tower seemed as productive as ever. Peter's influence was especially prominent, as the slaves looked at him as one of their own, even though he had always been treated better than they had. Of course, in no small measure, Peter's relationships with Petunia and Arthur had also helped.

Meanwhile, news from the war itself was not good. Although the Americans were inflicting great casualties on the British troops, the redcoats always seemed to have the advantage. They had more and better trained soldiers, more equipment, especially artillery, and what seemed like an almost endless ability to supply their troops with the basics.

As winter settled over Virginia and Hunting Tower, Judge Winston was particularly anxious about how the war was being waged. He had gambled a great deal in supporting the drive toward independence. If that gamble failed, surely the king would take retribution, and the judge and his family would probably be forced into poverty or worse. He had also gambled with his switch to an even more highly concentrated crop of hemp, and that gamble was doubled by not having sent a goodly part of the previous harvest to market. However, the burning of Falmouth in the northern campaign was instrumental in the decision of the Continental Congress in establishing a navy, which would increase the demand for hemp, and that did set the judge's mind at ease a little.

The judge was also concerned with the well being of his nephew, Patrick Henry. Patrick had been one of the most outspoken of patriots, and the royal crown would stop at almost nothing to secure his capture, trial and, presumably, quick hanging. The mere fact that they were related caused the judge to fear for his own life and that of his family. But there was little he could do about it, for these were also difficult times financially, and the Winston family had had to refrain from frivolous spending. In fact, at one point, the judge had offered a portion of Hunting Tower for sale, though no deal was ever consummated.

For this reason, Patrick Henry almost never visited his uncle anymore, as he had in the past, for fear that their association might cause even more problems.

In December, there did come some good news that the colonialists won a decisive victory in the Battle of Great Bridge, an important shipping point to the port city of Norfolk. As a result, on New Year's Day, 1776, Lord Dunmore began a bombardment of Norfolk that would eventually leave a majority of the city in ashes. Nevertheless, it was less an action to win territory than it was revenge on the part of Dunmore, as British rule in Virginia had essentially come to an end.

The balance of the spring and early summer passed without significant news, and life at Hunting Tower settled into a familiar routine. Crops were planted and tended, and Peter and Arthur worked hard to keep the farm supplied with tools and other necessities in addition to seeing to the well being of the horses.

Although the Continental Army had been established more than a year earlier, the time-consuming task of recruiting and training troops continued. On August 27, 1776, though, those troops were finally ready to do battle with their British counterparts at the Battle of Long Island. According to reports that filtered back to Hunting Tower, this was truly the first major battle of the war, and it didn't go well. Under the command of General Washington himself, the Americans were forced to withdraw. A few weeks later, Patrick Henry ignored his own self-imposed banishment and rode to Hunting Tower to confer with his uncle, Judge Winston. Peter, who had been working in the barn, had seen Patrick arrive and came out to see what was so important that he would ignore the danger and visit the plantation. As Patrick dismounted, he saw the big teenager approaching. "Peter," he said, "would you look after my horse and then join me and my uncle in the main house? I have news of the war, and I think you may be interested in what I have to tell him."

"Yes, sir, Mr. Henry." Peter replied. "I'll see to it right away." Peter took the horse to the trough outside the barn and allowed the horse to quench its thirst. Walking to the open doors, he caught Arthur's attention and asked him to take care of the horse once he had finished drinking. It was unlike Peter to let anyone complete a task to which he had been assigned, but he was anxious to hear what Patrick Henry had to say. He quickly proceeded to the main house and knocked on the door. After waiting a few seconds with no response, Peter was about to rap on the door again when it opened and Judge Winston looked at him with some surprise.

"Peter, what do you need?" the judge inquired.

"Mr. Henry told me to come to the house for news on the war."

"Well, for the life of me, I don't know what it is that would concern you, but come in, my boy, come in." Peter followed the judge to the parlor where Patrick Henry, seated in an overstuffed chair, was drinking tea. Standing near the fireplace was Anthony, Jr.

Patrick looked up and said, "Good, good. I'm glad you could join us, Peter, because what I've got to say concerns you, too." Addressing the men in the room, he continued, "As you probably know, the war has truly begun. General Washington has done the best he can, although he is quite constrained with limitations in troops and materials. Unfortunately, after the Battle of Long Island, he was forced to withdraw from the field. He led his troops, some 9,000 strong, to Kip's Bay, and although the retreat was orderly, some of the troops took to looting and deserting, and morale was disintegrating rather rapidly.

"I was told that the remaining troops did manage to dig in, but the English sent their navy and bombarded with such a barrage as even the most seasoned soldiers have never seen. Then the British conducted an amphibious landing, and some say that our boys were buried with so much dirt from the cannon fire that they couldn't even return fire. From what I hear, General Washington was absolutely furious as our troops began a somewhat disorderly retreat. I've even heard tales that the Hessians were bayoneting Americans who were trying to surrender.

"Most of the remaining troops were able to make it to Harlem Heights, but the next day -- I think it was September 16 -- the British came after us intent on crushing our army on the Island of Manhattan. We were down to about 2000 troops, and the good general was determined to keep what remained of our forces intact, so they were again in retreat.

"That's when the English made a rather formidable mistake. They sounded the foxhunt bugle call and, rather than intimidating our

118

lads, insulted them and they turned back to fight. According to reports, our boys faced 5000 British troops, and, even though they were outnumbered by more than two to one, they pushed the English back until it was the British who were in retreat. We were able to win our first major battle.

"However, unless we can recruit some reinforcements, I fear we shall not prevail in our worthy cause. That's what I've been doing for the past several days, and it's why I'm here now."

"What do you mean?" asked Judge Winston.

"In this room, uncle, we have two strong lads who would most certainly do us both proud if you would let them join the conflict. I know this is a difficult thing for you to consider, but consider it you must, for we are desperate for able-bodied men. I truly believe that Anthony, Jr., with the proper training and with his breeding, could well be promoted to an officer's position within a short period of time. As for Peter, he will make a fine soldier and will be an imposing figure on any battlefield."

The judge's face went pale as he contemplated what he had just been asked. Allowing Peter to go off to war was one thing. After all, Peter had been pestering him to go to fight ever since the convention in Richmond. But the thought of sending his only son off to battle was not something that the judge was willing to entertain. "I'm afraid you ask too much, Patrick," responded the judge, speaking as though neither of the subjects of conversation was in the room. "Sending Peter off to war is one thing, though I fear that our productivity at Hunting Tower shall suffer the consequences. But to send both Peter and Anthony would cause great harm to our abilities to function and fulfill our obligation to provide hemp to the war effort. I will agree to let Peter go, but as for Anthony, I must decline your request."

There was a long, awkward silence in the room. Secretly, Anthony, Jr. was breathing a sigh of relief. Peter, meanwhile, was so elated he could barely contain himself. This was what he had wanted all along -- a chance to be free, a chance to fight for freedom for his adopted country.

Finally, Patrick Henry broke the silence. "I understand," he said to his uncle. "Of course, you need young Anthony to run things here at the plantation, and your efforts have not gone unnoticed."

"I appreciate your understanding," replied the judge in a formal acknowledgment. Then he looked directly at Peter. "If I didn't know any better, I'd say you conspired with my nephew. But I know how you feel, and I release you from any further obligation to me and to Hunting Tower so that you may join the army. I would only ask that you take a couple of weeks to help train someone else to assist Arthur."

"Yes, sir," replied Peter. "I wouldn't think of leaving until all was in order. Thank you, sir." Immediately, he said goodbye to Patrick Henry and left the room. He didn't want to show too much emotion, especially in light of how the judge had treated him over the past ten years, but deep inside he felt elated that this was one of the best days of his life. Though he vaguely recalled happy days with his family in the Azores Islands, those memories now lived in the furthest recesses of his mind.

As Peter stood on the porch surveying the place he had called home for almost a decade, his thoughts turned to Susannah Anderson. He must see her before he left Virginia for New Jersey, where his training would take place. But how? And when? Contemplatively he descended the steps of the porch and crossed the short distance to the barn where Arthur was still at work.

"Arthur, I have the most wonderful news," Peter said. "I'm to be allowed to join the army."

Arthur looked up from where he was working on a carpentry project. It seemed like forever before the old slave could summon the words. "I knows how much this means to you, Peter. I really does, but I'm goin' to miss you a powerful lot. You've been more like family to me than anyone else I can remember. You've been like a son, and I fears that the day you leave, I'll never see you again. But I is happy for you, Peter. I is happy for you."

Peter walked the few paces that separated the two men. Arthur didn't look at him, not wanting Peter see the tears welling up in his eyes. The young man took Arthur's face in his hands, lifted his head and looked directly at him.

"Know this, and know it well," Peter said. "I love you, and I always will. You have been the father I needed desperately after losing my family so long ago. I will always remember the time you spent teaching me everything about being a blacksmith, being a carpenter and..." Peter's voice cracked..."and being a man. Besides, nothing's going to happen to me, and I'll see you sooner than you can blink an eye."

The two men embraced. Arthur could say nothing. However, it was not Peter's safety that he feared for. Arthur had been feeling poorly, his body was failing him in more ways than he had let on, and he was certain that his days were soon to come to an end.

121

8

PREPARING TO LEAVE

The next few days were a flurry of activity for Peter as he prepared for what he was certain was his destiny, to gain and fight for freedom. At Hunting Tower, he set about teaching Richard, his replacement, how best to help Arthur in the barn. They covered the care and feeding of the plantation's horses. He also showed Richard all the various carpentry tools and the use of each. The most difficult part was attempting to teach Richard the tricks of the blacksmithing trade.

Understanding what the tools were for and how to use them wasn't the problem. Richard was quite intelligent, so it wasn't long before he knew what his responsibilities were. It was the actual doing that presented the problem. Richard had always been assigned to fieldwork. There he had developed sinewy muscles best suited to flexibility and endurance. But work as a blacksmith required pure power and the kind of massive muscles that Peter came by naturally. By far, Peter was one of the largest men in all the colonies. In fact, he may have been the largest, had an accurate accounting of size been taken. Richard was no match for that brute power, but he was slowly adapting, and Arthur, despite his failing health, would continue the training long after Peter had left.

Peter also had to decide what he was going to take with him. He knew that his precious silver, initialed buckles would definitely go with him wherever his travels might lead. He would also be taking the tri-corner hat that Judge Winston had purchased for him many years before, but the hat that had been a gift from Susannah's father, James Anderson, would be staying here at Hunting Tower, as the judge had assured Peter that the plantation would always be his home. Clothing was another matter altogether. It had been some time since Peter had gotten any new clothes, and most of his shirts and trousers were well worn with the hard labor he had performed. In addition, Peter had filled out to a massive 260 pounds, and many of his clothes simply didn't fit.

Sitting on the bed of his room, sorting through his meager clothing selection, he heard a knock on his door. Judge Winston walked right in, again such a rarity that Peter was a bit startled.

"I see you're packing, Peter," intoned the judge. "You know, you'll be sorely missed here at Hunting Tower. You've become as much family as anyone could possibly be, save my very own flesh and blood."

"Yes, sir," replied Peter, "except for Mrs. Winston. I don't think she really likes me."

"Well, Peter, Mrs. Winston is quite set in her ways. She's not much for a change in routine, and when I showed up with you some ten

124

years ago, she was not too pleased, I'll admit. She's become used to you, though, and I hasten to say that she'll probably miss you, though I doubt that she'll ever admit to it. How is the packing coming along? Do you have everything you need?"

"Yes, sir, I think so."

"Let me see."

Peter held up a couple of shirts, the best he could find in his small collection.

"No, no, no." said the judge. "Those won't do at all. You're going to be representing Hunting Tower and Buckingham County, I dare say, and you need to look better than that. What about your trousers?" Again, Peter showed the judge what he was planning to take. After a few moments of studying Peter's selections, Judge Winston was not too pleased. "Peter," he said. "I believe a shopping trip is in order. We need to procure some better clothes for you."

"Yes, sir." Peter agreed. The very thought of new clothes that fit was exciting all by itself. "I'll go hitch a team to the carriage. Which one would you like to take?"

"No need for that. You'll be going by yourself. After all, in a couple of days, you'll be on your own to join the army. You don't need me to go with you to town. Just go to the mercantile, select a couple pair of britches and a couple of shirts...oh, and a jacket to keep the chill off during the northern evenings at this time of year. Just have them put your selections on my bill at the store.

"By the way, when you decide which horse to ride into town, choose wisely. That horse is my gift to you...any horse except one of the Creams, that is"

125

Peter hardly knew what to say. He stammered a couple of unintelligible syllables before the judge walked over to where he was standing at his dresser. Judge Winston opened his arms and, considering Peter's size, gave him as big a hug as he could muster. At first, the giant young man just stood there with his arms at his side, trying to decide what to do. After what seemed like minutes that were actually only seconds, he raised his arms and returned the judge's embrace. When they broke away, Peter could see tears welling in Judge Winston's eyes. This was the second time in recent days that a man more senior than himself had shown such emotion. Although Peter wasn't quite sure how to react, there was a feeling in his heart that was new to him. This affection wasn't the same as it was with Susannah Anderson, but it was quite genuine in its warmth and sincerity.

The judge held up his index finger. "No words, Peter, no words. Just know that I love you almost like a son, that I shall miss you, and I shall pray for your well-being and safety every day." As in his previous visit, the judge did not want nor did he wait for a reply. Rather, he turned around, exited the room, and left Peter musing deeply in his own thoughts.

That very afternoon, Peter did as instructed. He chose a horse, one of the Canadians, named Isabel. After saddling her up, he hoisted himself on her broad back, grabbed the reins and trotted her out of the barn. He had usually driven a team of horses sitting behind a carriage or wagon, so sitting on top of one was a fairly new experience. His innate relationship with horses served him well, though, and he was soon comfortable astride the filly.

On the trip to town, his thoughts turned back to the day when Judge Winston had purchased him from the orphanage. As then, the fall of the year was now turning the leaves on the trees hues of red and gold, and there was a crispness and freshness in the air. But the part that most occupied Peter's thoughts was the feeling of being a free man. The result of that glorious thought made the trees' colors seem more glorious -- the red leaves were redder, the gold leaves were more gold. And the smell of the air -- that was unmistakable. That was the scent of freedom filling his nostrils.

Feeling as happy as he could ever remember, when Peter arrived in town, he hitched Isabel to the post in front of the store and strode in with a confident step. He glanced around and saw a variety of bolts of material for bedding, curtains and the various types of things that went into fine furnishings. There were also leather goods, perhaps made by Edna Watkins' husband, and that brought to his mind how kind Edna had been to him while he had lived in old Caleb's shack on the wharf at City Point. Then, remembering what his purpose was in the store, he surveyed the layout and recalled that the shirts were kept in the back left-hand corner. Women's clothing was displayed on the right side of the store, and Peter took a glance in that direction, also. What he saw made him lose track of his purpose altogether.

About halfway to the back of the store, thumbing through some of the finer dresses that were displayed there, was Susannah Anderson. Peter felt his heart skip a beat, accompanied by a discernable weakness in his knees. He wanted to speak to her. He wanted to sweep her into his arms. He wanted to hold her tight to his chest and never let her go. He felt his voice rising from his throat as he was about to call out to her, the

127

lovelicst young girl in the county. Wondering if anyone else had caught him staring at Susannah, his eyes darted about the store. But recalling her sharp words in Richmond, when right after Patrick Henry's speech she had called Peter and those who thought like him fools, Peter quelled the instinct to call out to her. In fact, he thought it best to avoid any contact whatsoever, so he turned a hard left toward the men's side of the store and cautiously ducked down to conceal his frame, as much as any man that tall could. His detour took him to the trousers rather than the shirts. He selected two pairs of tan britches and determined that the waist would fit him well, though he cared not about the length, since his habit was to simply roll them up just below the knee and buckle them. Besides, not a single pair would have been long enough for anyone as tall as he, and he knew it.

Furtively, Peter took a look over his shoulder. Susannah had still not noticed him as she made her selections and decided on her purchases. So far, so good. Peter then made his way to the back where shirts were displayed and chose two, a brown and a tan, like the britches he had already chosen. Once again, he glanced in the direction where Susannah had been standing, but she was gone. Immediately, he felt the conflict in his heart and mind. His mind told him that it was just as well that she had left the store without confrontation. His heart told him that perhaps, just perhaps, he would never see her again, and that made him sad. Since his heart seemed to be winning the battle, Peter was more than a bit disappointed.

Remembering what Judge Winston had told him about getting a winter coat, Peter made his way to the center of the store where all winter outerwear were kept in anticipation of winter's onset. Just as he rounded the corner, however, Susannah Anderson, once again carrying so many parcels that she could not see over the top, crashed right into Peter's chest.

"Oh my, pardon me," she said, packages tumbling to the floor. Never looking up, she bent over to gather up her purchases. Peter, ever the increasingly refined gentleman, of course bent down to help her, and her eyes locked on his. An awkward silence seemed to linger before Peter finally spoke.

"It was entirely my fault," he apologized. "I should have seen you coming and gotten out of your way -- although I must say, you need to have someone help you with your things so you don't have to pile them up so high. Thank goodness there are no wild horses in here," he chided.

Susannah just looked at him for a moment and then threw her head back in laughter. "Why, Peter Francisco, you've just made a joke. I didn't think you had it in you."

"Yes, I guess I did, but please don't think it was at your expense."

"Well, of course, it's at my expense...and I deserve it. Oh, Peter, how have you been, and what are you doing here?"

"I've been well, Susannah. But I don't think you want to know why I'm here."

"Why in the world not?"

"I'm buying things to take with me to sign up for the Continental Army."

"Oh, I see." Susannah seemed to be gathering her thoughts for a moment. "Peter, can you ever forgive my rudeness when last we spoke?

My words were quite harsh, and the times have found Father thinking differently than when I chastised you in Richmond."

"How is that?"

"We've been following the events very closely. England's rule has become almost unbearable. We have family in Boston, and they have convinced us that our path is undeniable. We must claim the colonies for ourselves or suffer the consequences. In fact, Father has accepted a commission to establish a militia here in the south. He is to be a captain"

"Susannah," Peter said. "What unexpected good news. Does this mean we can be friends again?"

"Of course...yes, of course. I just hope you can forgive my words. I am so sorry."

Peter took her hand and they both stood up, oblivious to the fact that Susannah's packages were still strewn on the floor.

"Forgive you? How could I not forgive you?" Peter said. "How could I not forgive the woman I love?"

"You...you love me? Oh my dear Peter, I love you, too," Susannah confessed quietly, so that no one in the shop would hear. "I have ever since the day you saved me from the horses on this very street," she whispered, moving toward the storefront.

Peter's heart nearly leaped from his chest. Then a disheartening thought occurred to him. "Do you realize that we've spent this last year-and-a-half in silence? Do you realize how much time we have wasted?"

"Yes, Peter, I do...but we have our whole lives ahead of us."

"But first I must go to fight in the north. I must! It's the reason that Judge Winston has granted my freedom, and it's that very freedom that gives me the courage to ask if you'll wait for my return."

There was a moment of hesitation. Then looking up at him, she spoke with all honesty, "I don't want you to go, but I do understand why you feel you must. Of course, I will wait for you. I will wait the rest of my life if that is what it takes."

Peter reached out and drew Susannah close. They didn't notice that the store's other patrons had gathered around. Peter could feel her tremble in his arms, or was it he who was trembling? It mattered not. He buried his face in her hair and drew a deep breath so as to always remember its scent.

Suddenly, one of the men in the store, a man who had witnessed Susannah's rescue at the hands of the giant, raised his fist in the air. "To Peter and Susannah, huzzah, huzzah, huzzah! May Peter return home safely and may they have many offspring." Everyone gathered began to clap. Though a formal marriage proposal had not been proffered -- that would have to wait until Peter could ask Susannah's father -- the nature of their relationship was becoming clear, and every witness knew it.

Looking around, a bit embarrassed by all the attention they had drawn, the two set to the task of gathering up all their packages. Peter stopped at the counter, requested that his items be placed on the judge's account and carried both his and Susannah's items to place them in her carriage.

As Peter assisted Susannah into the enclosed carriage, she turned and looked at him. "Promise me that you'll stop by our farm before you go off to the army. Please promise."

"I will be there tomorrow afternoon," Peter replied. "I promise."

Susannah's hand lingered in Peter's until the carriage driver began to pull away. As the carriage made its way out of town, Peter saw her lean her head out of the window, looking back at him. Even the dust flying from the wheels of the carriage, this had been a far better ending than the one at Richmond.

Peter barely needed Isabel to transport him back to Hunting Tower, the only real home he had known for the past ten years. The way he felt, he could have floated back to the plantation. Every once in a while, he could hear someone yelling "Huzzah, huzzah!" After a time, he realized that it was he who was doing the hollering.

The fall dusk was just settling when he arrived home, and Judge Winston was coming out onto the front porch. "Peter, my boy. I was wondering what had happened to you. You were gone a long time. How much of a bill did you ring up?"

Peter looked at the judge thinking he might be in trouble, but then the judge started to laugh.

"Come and show me what you bought for yourself. I hope you made your selections as wisely as you did in choosing Isabel for your horse."

Peter walked up the steps to the porch, and the two men sat on chairs while he showed the judge his trousers and shirts.

"But what of the winter jacket I told you to get?" the judge inquired.

"I was on my way to get it, but I got distracted," said Peter a bit sheepishly, and he related the story of his encounter with Susannah.

When he had finished telling his story, the judge looked at him and said, "Well, that's fine, Peter. But remember what I told you. You always have a home here, and I hope you'll come back to us someday."

"Thank you, sir," Peter said. "I'll never forget that." He rose and shook the judge's hand, then went to find Arthur. There was no one he wanted to spend time with more than the old slave who had taken him under his wing and taught him so much. Their final hours together passed much too quickly before they bade their last goodbye and shared their last father-son embrace.

With his mind continuing to think about everything that lay ahead of him, Peter slept but a single fitful hour. He had said all his farewells the night before, and he wanted to get an early start. So well before the faithful rooster could announce the dawn of another day, he finished packing his few possessions in a satchel, slung it over his shoulder, saddled Isabel, and rode away from Hunting Tower for what could be the last time.

There was one more stop he wanted to make before setting out on the long ride that would destine him to the army. He directed Isabel toward the Anderson farm. He would arrive well before the afternoon hour he had promised Susannah, but he was certain she wouldn't mind.

9

OFF TO WAR

The ride to the Anderson plantation normally took about an hour, but Peter was so excited at the thought of seeing Susannah again that he had Isabel at a near full gallop, and he covered the distance in about half the time. He rode up to the main house, dismounted and knocked on the door. James Anderson answered.

"Peter," he said, extending his hand, "how good to see you."

"Thank you, sir. It's good to see you, too, sir."

"Susannah told me about your meeting yesterday as well as your plans. I know this might sound a bit strange coming from me, especially in light of our last encounter, but I think what you are doing is quite commendable. I'd like to apologize for my conduct in Richmond, Peter. It was I who acted the fool, and I am sorry."

"No need to apologize, sir. We each have our different views."

"Of course, Susannah told you that we have changed our thinking, and I am to be commissioned as an officer in the militia."

"Yes, sir, she did say that, so I guess we'll be fighting in the war together, even though we may be hundreds of miles apart."

"Yes, I suppose we shall. But enough of this talk. I know you've come to bid goodbye to Susannah, not to talk to me. Besides, she'd have my head if she lost any of the precious little time you two have remaining. Let me go and find her while you make yourself comfortable here on the porch."

Peter sat down on a two-person swing suspended by chains from the veranda roof, and it wasn't long before Susannah came around the corner wearing a working dress, as she had been tending to the small vegetable garden behind the house.

"Peter," she said with surprise, "I didn't expect you until later in the day."

"Yes, I know, but I couldn't wait to see you again."

"Well, I must look a sight. I was picking the last of the tomatoes, but since you have arrived early, I don't look my best for you."

"I suppose I could get back on my horse and circle the plantation for a while," Peter said dryly.

"There you go again, making another joke," she smiled. "Anyway, you wait here for just a bit while I go make myself more presentable."

"You look just fine to me," replied Peter approvingly.

"Well, wait here anyway." Susannah disappeared into the house, returning shortly in one of her finest dresses and bearing a pitcher of cold tea. After pouring a glass for each of them, she took a seat next to Peter on the swing. This was exactly what he had hoped for -- the chance to sit close to the young lady who had captured his heart and soul. They spoke of what was to come, but their conversation wasn't nearly as important as was the opportunity to just sit together and enjoy each other's company. Though it didn't seem like it, three hours disappeared as quickly as the morning mist on a warm summer's day.

Soon Susannah's father approached. "I realize you two have a lot of catching up to do, and I know how difficult it is to know that you'll be apart for some time, but if young Peter is going to make any headway on his trip, he should be getting on his way."

"Of course, sir. You're absolutely right," Peter agreed. Turning toward Susannah, he continued, "Your father is right. I do have a long journey ahead of me, and I have no certainty as to where it leads. But know this deep inside you," he said, looking into her eyes, "I will return. No matter how far away I go, no matter how long it takes, I will return to you, my dearest. I will return to you."

"Peter," responded Susannah, "that's all I need to know. And when you return, I will be here waiting for you, my love." She then pulled a dainty handkerchief from the sleeve of her dress. "I want you to have this. I want you to keep it with you at all times. Take it out and think of me whenever you get lonely, knowing I will be with you always."

Peter took the handkerchief and held it to his nose, smelling the sweet scent of Susannah. "Thank you," he said, smiling at her. "I will forever carry it near my heart."

They both looked around and were surprised to find that Susannah's father had withdrawn to give them a last few moments of privacy. Glancing back at each other, their faces were drawn closer and closer, and soon they felt the warmth of each other's lips. They lingered in that kiss for several moments before Peter pulled away.

"Forgive my boldness, Susannah," Peter said. "Perhaps I shouldn't have done that."

"If you hadn't," Susannah interrupted, "I would have. My lips and my heart are yours to keep, Peter Francisco, and don't you ever forget that. Will you write to me to tell me how you are?"

"I don't know how to read or write," he said regretfully, "but I will enlist the aid of someone more educated than I am. So, yes, my dear, I will write to you."

Peter blushed and rose from the swing, offering his hand to assist Susannah to her feet as well.

"Where are you headed when you leave here?" she inquired.

"To western Virginia to join up with the 10th Virginia Regiment. Those were the arrangements that Patrick Henry made for me."

"Then your journey is indeed a long one, so I'll not keep you from your destiny any longer. Just remember that I love you. I'll always love you."

Almost unintentionally, as naturally as breathing, they walked hand-in-hand, descending the porch steps. When Peter stepped down the first couple of steps, he turned back one last time. Susannah's hand was still in his, and they were once again almost face-to-face. He let go of her hand, reached for her and pulled her closer. He kissed her again and they embraced one last time.

Peter walked down the last few steps, then reached into his satchel for something. When he removed his hand, he was holding

Boneca de Trapo. He walked back to the steps and held out the cherished rag doll to Susannah. "This is one of my only childhood possessions, and I want you to keep it for me until I return." After mounting his horse, he looked at Susannah from atop Isabel and said, "I love you with all my heart. Wait for my return."

"I love you, too, Peter Francisco. Keep safe, my love."

The young soldier-to-be wheeled his horse around and headed off the Anderson plantation, yet as he reached the main road, he couldn't help but turn around to wave the sweet-smelling handkerchief. She waved back as he tugged at the reins and headed down the road. It was a road that would lead to celebrations and misery, to victories and defeats, but Peter could know none of this. What he did know was that someday, somehow, he would return on this road to claim Susannah Anderson as his wife.

Heading northwest toward the mountains of western Virginia and the Shenandoah Valley, Peter maintained a steady pace throughout the rest of the day. Sometimes there were traveled paths on which to journey, but as Peter continued to make progress toward the setting sun, he found himself riding deeper and deeper into pristine forests and places where no man had preceded him. Pine trees and other conifers dominated the landscape, and their scent filled his nostrils and lighted his senses. Abundant deer and squirrels curiously watched the lone traveler as they went about foraging for food. Peter had never been in such a land, a land almost devoid of human presence, a land unpolluted by human endeavors. The topography, with gently rolling hills and majestic forests, was unlike any he had seen. Truly, this was a land worth fighting for, he thought, and he felt as one with the earth. The only sounds to be heard

139

were those of Isabel's hoofs rising and falling in the lush forest blanket and those of the birds chirping from the highest boughs of the trees.

A mix of magnificent colors painted the far horizon as the sun gradually dropped out of sight, and Peter began looking for a clearing where he could camp for the night. Eventually he found a spot thick with pine straw, which he thought might make a comfortable mattress. Though he had ridden for many hours, the fatigue was not great, as the time had passed quickly with his thoughts constantly drawn back to the image of Susannah waving goodbye from her family's porch. Dismounting Isabel, he unsaddled the horse, removed her bridle, and hobbled her. Then he searched for some kindling with which to build a small fire to take the chill off the night. After clearing a large circle so as not to set the forest itself on fire, he opened a second satchel containing dried beef and pork and biscuits, a going-away present of sorts from Petunia. As he ate, his mind contemplated what the future might hold, but he could never have imagined what was in store. Soon the day's events left him too weary to fight off slumber any longer, and using the saddle as a pillow, Peter Francisco fell into a sound and dreamless sleep.

The next morning, there was no rooster to rouse Peter from his bed, only the light of the new day streaming through the trees, but ass he opened his eyes to the morning sun, he sensed that he was being watched. Rolling over, he came face-to-face with an inquisitive raccoon. Startled as he was by the creature's black-as-coal eyes, Peter lashed out with his hand, but the raccoon was too fast and bounded off into the underbrush. He then grabbed his water jug, slaked his morning thirst, and used the remainder to fully extinguish the dying embers of his fire. Then he saddled Isabel, ate a couple more of the biscuits, refilled his water jug from a nearby brook, and continued his journey. When Peter reached the edge of the Shenandoah Valley, he noticed that the terrain began to change and that to the west were mountains like none he had seen before. They rose majestically skyward, jutting into the middle of the azure skies. Patrick Henry had told Peter that the sight of these would indicate he was to head in a more northerly direction, up the heart of the valley that bordered the mountains.

He spent a second night much like the first, and on the third day, about mid-afternoon, Peter cleared a small ridge and came upon an encampment near what would one day be Waynesboro, named for General Anthony Wayne. The center of the clearing was populated by all sorts, shapes and sizes of canvas tents clustered around campfires with steaming kettles suspended over them. Around the edge of the clearing were lean-tos, somewhat less accommodating structures. These had been built by the mountain men of western Virginia, men whose prowess with their long rifles would have a great impact on the war.

Peter was surprised to notice the number of women also inhabiting the camp. There were some children to be found as well. Surely, he thought, they were only there to bid their men folk farewell when they left for the Northern campaign. Something else also stood out -- the wide variety of clothing worn by the camp's occupants. Some of the men wore clothing much like Peter's, while others appeared to be going off to a formal tea rather than a war. Most startling were the clothes of the mountain men. These were obviously the skins of animals that they had killed. Some were fairly plain. Others were adorned with colorful beading, and many had fringe strips on the sleeves of the shirts. Even their footwear was of animal skins. As Peter rode Isabel slowly into camp, people tended to stop whatever they were doing and stare at the huge man joining their legion. There was only one word to describe someone of his stature…giant.

One tent situated toward the center stood out from the others. It was considerably larger and was whiter than the rest. It also stood out because the men standing in front of it wore conforming uniforms. Although Peter couldn't be entirely sure, this was probably the tent belonging to Captain Hughes Woodson, the man to whom Patrick Henry indicated he should report. Peter dismounted as one of the two men standing on either side of the tent flap approached.

"Good day," said the soldier. "What business have you here?"

"My name is Peter Francisco from Buckingham County. I was told to find Captain Woodson when I arrived, and I've just arrived," he said with a sly grin.

"Well, well," mused the soldier looking up at Peter. "Aren't you the big one? Well, you've come to the right place. I'll tell the captain you're here." Retreating into the tent, the man soon reappeared followed by a young man who carried an air of importance as he strode to meet Peter.

"Oh, my goodness," Captain Woodson said, with eyebrows raised while, extending his hand. "Aren't you the big one?"

"So I've heard," replied Peter. "I was told to report to you so that I can join the army."

"I must say, it's nice to be getting two men for the price of one." Although Peter had developed a dry sense of humor over the years, he wasn't quite sure what the captain meant. "Alright then," the captain continued. "Come with me to sign your papers."

142

As they entered the tent, Captain Woodson indicated a small folding stool on which Peter was to sit. However, because of his size, the newcomer chose a solid wooden stool to the right of a makeshift table, which was just some planks spanning a couple of barrels, much like had been used during plantation feasts back at Hunting Tower.

The captain handed some papers to Peter, who looked at the two sheets for just a moment and then looked at Woodson. "I don't know what these say," he told the captain.

"I'm sorry. Rest assured, you're not the first one unable to read or write, and I daresay you'll not be the last. Let me explain. By signing these papers, you are agreeing to serve in the Continental Army for a period of three years. In return, you'll receive 100 acres of land, the sum of $6.67 each month and a fine uniform. The uniforms have not been delivered as yet, although it might not be so easy to find one for your size. Do you understand?"

"Yes, sir, I think I do."

"Very well, then," Woodson said as he turned to the second sheet of paper. "Just make your mark there," he said, pointing to an area at the bottom of the page."

"Mark?" inquired Peter.

"Yes, your mark. Most men just make an X."

Peter did his best to make a perfect X and handed the paper back to Woodson.

"Congratulations, Peter Francisco, and welcome to the army. You are now officially a member of the 10th Virginia Regiment, Company 9. By the way, we are also called the Prince Edward Musketeers, since muskets will be our primary weapon." The captain then summoned the soldier who had greeted Peter outside the tent. Addressing him, Woodson ordered, "Show our newest recruit around, assign him to a tent and issue him a musket."

The soldier stepped out of the tent just behind Peter, who took another look around. What had appeared to be a crazy quilt of scattered tents was actually a group of fairly neat rows. Every group centered around a common fire. The soldier motioned Peter to follow, so the new musketeer took the reins of Isabel and fell in behind the young man. At the outer edge of the clearing, just a few paces in front of the lean-tos, the man came to a stop and pointed to a tent. "You'll be staying here for the time being, and you have three other tent mates, although I don't know where they are at the moment."

"Thank you," said Peter. "I'll meet them later. Where should I take my horse?"

"Up there," said the soldier, indicating the edge of the forest. "We have a makeshift corral set up, but I suggest you keep your saddle and bridle here with you."

Indeed, he did meet his tent mates that evening, though none was especially distinguishable. Of course, each commented on the newcomer's size, and Peter was beginning to become a bit self-conscious about it all.

After a welcomed hot evening meal prepared by some of the camp women, Peter made his way to where the mountain men had staked their claim to temporary land. They were gathered around a campfire where they prepared and ate their own meals without the help of any females, and one of them was playing a harmonica. Since these men generally stayed to themselves and weren't attuned much to social skills, they looked up at Peter as he entered their area, none of them saying a word. Those who knew each other spoke among themselves. In a few minutes, Peter began to recognize the repetitiveness of the harmonica's tune, and he started to hum along with it in a marvelous tenor voice. All conversation stopped as he began to harmonize with the music, and when it was over, several of the mountain men voiced their appreciation and introduced themselves to him. That night he slept comfortably in the thought that, for the first time, he had made friends with his peers. His dreams, however, were not of new friends but of the young lady he had left behind.

Since the regiment was not yet at full strength, the next several mornings Peter spent becoming familiar with army life, including taking and delivering orders, understanding lines of authority, and learning the basics of marching as a unit. This was not especially to his liking. After all, he was here to fight. That's what he wanted to learn most, and that's why he liked the afternoons the best, because that's when the enlistees were taught how to use their weapons.

Each man had been issued a musket, a bayonet and a fighting sword. The men were taught how to load their nine-pound, five-foot long muskets using a cartridge of powder and ball. First, they were to tear the cartridge open with their teeth, prime the pan or frizzen, load the barrel with the balance of powder and the ball, and ram it all home with a rod. They were also shown that they could substitute the ball with pellets or even use a combination of pellets and ball. Once the weapon was loaded, rammed, and primed, the soldiers were to cock the musket, aim and fire. According to the Continental Army manual, this was actually a thirteen-step process, and it was expected that the soldier could complete the steps in about twenty seconds.

Peter had a fairly good aim, although he couldn't quite get the hang of reloading his musket as quickly as most of the others. On the other hand, his height, and especially the length of his arms, made him quite proficient in the use of his bayonet, which, when attached to the end of the musket, made quite a formidable weapon for close quarters' fighting. But that same size also made Peter uncomfortable in wielding his sword, and he oftentimes found himself swinging the blade too high and completely missing his intended target. This led to some lively discussions around the campfire with the mountain men, but Peter, being naturally of good humor, usually took the kidding in stride.

It all began when John Allen, one of the men in the group, commented that he had heard that Benjamin Franklin thought the troops might be better equipped with bows and arrows, since that weapon could be fired six times compared to just once for a musket.

"Heck," said Allen, "if we was countin' the Virginia Giant, the bow and arrow could be fired a *dozen* times for every shot Peter got off." Laughter rang out from the others. "Now I'll be the first to admit that it takes a bit longer to get off a shot with our long guns, but I kin hit a squirrel at better 'n a hunerd yards, and them muskets can barely hit a cow at fifty yards."

"I'm not looking to shoot a cow," Peter shot back. "That is unless the cow's wearing a red coat." The other men at the campfire guffawed, but John Allen began to think that their laughter was at his expense. As with most of the men in the group, Allen carried a tomahawk in his belt, and he withdrew it just as the laughter reached a crescendo.

"I kin hit any target you kin with your musket, and alls I need is my tomahawk. Go ahead. Pick a target, any target, and I'll jes' betcha I kin hit it."

Peter pointed to a tall pine tree and indicated a target area about ten feet up. "There you go, John Allen, see if you can hit that split in the branches."

Allen stood up, drew back with his weapon and let her fly. And he stuck his tomahawk right where Peter had pointed. "There, you see," Allen boasted. "I put 'er right where you pointed."

"Well," said Peter, trying to hide a smirk. "I guess I'll not be starting a tomahawk war with the likes of you, John Allen. Just tell me one thing...how are you going to get that tomahawk down from that tree?"

This time the laughter of the others was uncontrollable, and this time John knew it was indeed at his expense. "I ain't much used to bein' laughed at," he growled, and at the same time, his hand reached behind him where he kept his skinning knife.

Peter's eyes narrowed, and for a moment he thought he might have a fight on his hands. Then he thought the better of it. "John, I'm sorry if I offended you. Come here and I'll help you get your tomahawk." The two men walked over to the pine tree, and Peter held his hand out palm up. "Sit on my hand," Peter said.

"What, are you daft, man?" retorted Allen.

"Just sit down," ordered Peter impatiently.

147

Allen did as instructed, and Peter calmly lifted the mountain man's entire weight up and over his head until Allen could easily reach the embedded tomahawk. Then he gently set him back on the ground. Allen looked at Peter and said, "I'll be startin' no kinda war with you, Peter Francisco." The two men shook hands and everyone had one final laugh before calling it a night.

Days became weeks while the men continued to drill and become proficient with all of their weapons, and new men continued to filter into the camp. Almost a month after Peter's arrival, Colonel Edward Stevens was commissioned to be in charge of the regiment. More and more men came to sign up, and on December 15, 1776, the 10th Virginia Regiment finally met her quota of just over 700 men and was officially accepted into the Continental Army.

In the early months of 1777, the regiment received orders to join the main army, under the overall command of General George Washington, telling them to report to New Jersey to help defend Pennsylvania's capital, Philadelphia. Uniforms had finally arrived, but none was of suitable size for Peter, which was just fine with him. He had struck a kinship of sorts with the mountain men who were not issued any uniforms, and Peter found himself among them during their march north. Interestingly, at least to Peter, the women and children continued to tag along.

10

A BATTLE AND A FRIEND FOR LIFE

In May, Peter and the rest of the regiment arrived at Middle Brook, New Jersey, where the main body of the Continental Army was assembling for battle. This army and its militia were a rag tag group, but Washington was pleased to count as many as 10,000 men under his command, especially since he'd had only about 1000 just a few months earlier. The problem was that many of the men, especially the militia, were volunteers who felt no obligation of a long-term commitment. Frequently, men stayed only for several weeks or months before leaving to attend to their farms and businesses. This group seemed a bit more stable, though, and was swelling by the day, so Washington felt that the time was ripe to make a stand against the Redcoats as they threatened Philadelphia.

In July, British General Sir William Howe set sail from Sandy Hook, New Jersey with the intent of sailing up the Delaware River to make his assault against the colonial capital, Philadelphia. Wanting to reassure the residents of the city that their welfare was not in peril, Washington decided to parade his troops through the city. Thus on August 24, a Sunday morning, almost the entire Continental Army marched for two hours through the city streets.

Because so many of the troops, for a variety of reasons, had not been uniformed, they were all ordered to wear green sprigs in their hats. They were also commanded to polish their weapons to the highest sheen possible. To both of these orders, the men responded quite favorably. There was one other order to which many of the men were not nearly so inclined. It was rumored that some 40,000 people would line the streets to watch the parade, and many of the viewers were said to be extremely pretty girls. Some of the troops saw this as an opportunity, but Washington, in an attempt to show dignity and respect, notified his officers that any man who left the ranks during parade would be subject to 39 lashes as punishment.

Each regiment and division was led by its respective cavalry, followed by foot soldiers and artillery marching twelve abreast. Fife and drum corps interspersed throughout the parade route. Standing head and shoulders above his comrades, Peter Francisco was not happy about becoming a spectacle, for he had left Hunting Tower and the love of his life not to be gawked at in a parade but to fight the British. It had been well over half-a-year and he had yet to see battle, but that long wait was about to come to an end.

150

At four o'clock in the morning, on September 11, 1777, the British began their march toward Philadelphia, bent on destroying the colonials and ending this rebellion quickly and savagely. Relying on what would turn out to be faulty intelligence, General Washington had stationed the majority of his troops near Brandywine Creek at Chad's Ford. This was where he expected the primary thrust of General Howe's troops to attempt to break through the American lines. Peter and the 10th Virginia were among those in this battle group.

Standing among his fellow soldiers, Peter could see Washington riding up and down the lines encouraging the troops through the early morning fog. Peter reached inside his satchel and pulled out his silver buckles carefully wrapped in Susannah Anderson's handkerchief. As he held them in his hand, he remembered a Portuguese prayer he had recited as a child. Com Jesus me deito (With Jesus I go to Sleep), Com Jesus me levasto (With Jesus I awake), Com a grac'a de Deus (With the grace of God), e do Espirto Santo (and of the Holy Spirit), Eu vou para a batalha (I go into battle). The last phrase was only now added to his childhood litany.

Soon the sound of English cannon fire broke out, although most of their volleys fell harmlessly. American artillery answered the call, but their aim at an unseen target was just as ineffective. As the sun began to climb the eastern sky, some musket fire could be heard from time to time, but this, too, caused few casualties. Looking across the Brandywine Creek, Peter could see Redcoats taking cover but not attempting to advance any further. They were not truly attacking there at Chad's Ford. Instead, unknown to even Washington himself, this was simply a diversion, while the main body of Howe's forces planned to attack a few miles north. By early afternoon, cannon and gunfire could be heard from just north of their location, so Washington ordered a number of his troops to quickly head in that direction to reinforce the troops there. Peter Francisco's unit was among those so ordered.

As they approached the now full-blown battle, the reinforcing troops, Peter among them, could barely believe their eyes. The colonials were in complete disarray. Many of them were running away. Peter saw one man who was bleeding profusely from his nose, mouth, ears and eyes. This as the first time he had seen someone so badly injured. Some men might have have been tempted to join a good many of the others who had simply thrown down their weapons and run away, but not Peter. Onward the 10th Virginia pressed into an open field where the battle was at full rage. Meanwhile, Peter could see General Washington riding throughout the troops, unconcerned for his own well being and trying to rally the troops to stand and fight. With him was another officer who was frantically waving his saber to encourage the colonials onward into the fray.

"Spread out and stand your ground," screamed Captain Woodson. "Hold them off, boys."

About 200 miles away and facing Woodson's men was a contingent of British troops, marching in formation with fixed bayonets gleaming in the afternoon sun. They were still too far away for the colonials' muskets to be of any use, but there was no cover in this barren field, and Peter thought it foolhardy to just stand and fire once the order had been given. Spotting a medium sized fallen oak near the edge of the field, he ran over to it, wrapped his massive arms around it, and with sheer brute force dragged it to the center of the field so his fellow soldiers could take cover. Woodson saw what Peter had done and ordered the mountain men with their long rifles to take up positions there. Even George Washington took note of Peter's feat and spoke of it with his junior officer. "I've seen that man before. He was at Richmond if I recall correctly."

"Ah, but of course, you would remember him," said the other officer. "Who could forget such a large man?"

The order came to fix bayonets, but the mountain men's weapons could not be fitted with them, so they just waited behind the tree for the British to come into range. As the English advanced to about 100 yards, John Allen looked to Captain Woodson for the order to fire. Woodson didn't have to say a word. Allen could read his eyes.

Snuggling his long rifle tight against his shoulder, Allen took careful aim and fired. A British officer near the front of the line dropped where he stood. Other mountain men began to fire, too, and with each distinctive crack of a long rifle, another Redcoat was laid to rest. Still, the English refused to break ranks but rather just kept advancing.

Soon the British were within range of the regular infantry muskets, and the order to fire when ready came down the lines. Peter had loaded his weapon with both ball and pellets, and when he fired his weapon, another English trooper went down. The air all around Peter filled with musket balls, and he heard several as they whizzed by his head. Kneeling now, Peter did his best to reload in the 20 seconds allowed by the manual, but when he fired again, he could not be sure that his aim had been true, for the air was so filled with smoke that it became difficult to even see what or whom he was aiming at. There was also something else in the air. It was the smell of rotten eggs, the sulfur scent of so many weapons being fired all at once.

Enemies and friends were falling all around Peter. Directly to his left, he heard the sound of a musket ball as it met human flesh. He spun around to see one of his tent mates from the Shenandoah Valley with a dazed look on his face, clutching his chest. When he withdrew his hand, a red stain on his chest spread out all over the man's blouse. The soldier then fell to his knees and dropped face first on the field.

Just then, Peter felt a sensation like no other he had ever known. Every muscle in his large body tightened as if turning to the molten lead he had forged so well as a blacksmith at Hunting Tower. He could hear a roar in his head, but it was not that of gun or cannon fire. His very skin tingled. Enraged, Peter stood and fired his musket, bayonet affixed to the muzzle. "Kill them, boys," he shouted. "Kill them. Kill them all."

He pressed forward toward the tree he had dragged onto the field of battle. There he found John Allen flailing with his tomahawk taking down British troops with almost every swing. Soon Peter and Allen were back to back. Redcoats surrounded them, but each man was dealing out death and destruction with his weapon. In the midst of it all, Peter felt a sharp pain in his left leg, but he ignored it to take down the remaining British around them. Then, without warning, there was an eerie silence. Cannon had not fired for some time since the confrontation had become hand-to-hand. But now, even the muskets fell silent, and the British had resumed positions at the far edges of the field. John Allen and Peter looked at each other in amazement, perhaps stunned to see that they were alive.

"Remind me next time, big fella," said John Allen, "whenever we go into battle, I want you close by."

"I'll remember," said Peter grinning ear to ear.

Allen looked down and noticed blood staining Peter's britches from his thigh down to his knee high socks. "Peter, sit down," he said. "You've been wounded."

Peter did as John told him, but his adrenalin had been strong enough to dull any pain. He straightened his left leg as John cut through his trousers to more carefully inspect the wound.

"Yes, sir," said John. "It looks like you took a musket ball to your leg. You're lucky on this day, though, because it seems that the ball went right through your leg and out the other side."

"Is that good?" Peter asked.

"You bet your life that's good. At least this way, you don't have to have anyone fishin' around in your leg lookin' for the ball. But I think it may be a few days 'fore you kin walk on it."

Although Peter and the 10th Virginia had stood their ground, and the British had vacated the field, the Battle of Brandywine would go down as an British victory, for while the majority of Washington's troops had defended the right flank, General Howe had re-concentrated his forces back to Chad's Ford and pushed the Americans into an orderly retreat, but a retreat nonetheless. Howe's troops, however, were exhausted from the early morning march and battle, and declined to pursue the Americans. The colonials would live to fight another day.

As for Peter, he was evacuated to the home of a Moravian farmer to receive medical attention. There he met a man who would become a lifelong friend. It was evening when he arrived and was helped into a back bedroom dimly lit by two oil lamps. There was a figure lying on a wooden framed bed, and he could see considerable blood on the lower half of the sheet that covered the man. As Peter was assisted to the bed on the opposite wall, the man lifted himself up and looked over at his new roommate.

"Well, look who has arrived to keep me company," the man said. "If it isn't the giant who fights like…like…like a giant." This was the same man whom Peter had seen riding with General Washington as one of his junior officers. "Allow me to introduce myself, *mon ami,*" the man continued. "I am the Marquis de Lafayette, but please just call me Lafayette. And what is your name, or should I just call you Giant?"

"My name is Peter, Peter Francisco, but you can call me Peter rather than Giant."

"Peter it is, then. It's much more dignified than Giant anyway." They both laughed at the thought.

"But what did you mean, monami? I thought I had learned pretty good English back at the plantation," said Peter.

"Please forgive me. I come from France. *Mon ami* is a term of affection. It means 'my friend' in my country. But what brings you here to this farm?"

Peter lifted his left leg as well as he could, and for the first time Lafayette could see the blood stain on his britches.

"*Magnifigue,*" said Lafayette. "We suffer wounds in the same place."

"Well, you might think it's *magnifique,*" Peter bumbled, "but I'm not so sure." Their voices brought a doctor into the room to check on Lafayette.

156

"What's going on in here?" the doctor queried. "I thought I told you to stay calm, General, to lessen the loss of blood."

"But of course, doctor, and I would be doing as you told me except for this big fellow here who keeps me from my slumber."

Peter looked at the Marquis, who gave him a wink.

"This is a good friend of mine and a brave warrior. I know that General Washington personally sent you to take care of my needs, but what I need most of all is for you to take care of my friend."

"Of course, General Lafayette." And the doctor set about tending to Peter's wound. As he cleaned and dressed Peter's leg, Lafayette fell back on his bed in pain and fell into exhausted sleep. Neither did Peter have the energy to stay awake while the doctor fixed his leg. He, too, drifted into exhausted but fitful sleep. For several days thereafter, the two recuperating young soldiers exchanged stories from their past. Peter learned that Lafayette had come from a wealthy family, that he was just 19 years old, and that he had come to America to learn all he could about war and tactics, because he had never actually seen combat.

As for Peter, he remembered being kidnapped about twelve years earlier, so that made him 17. He remembered being abandoned and then purchased by Judge Winston, but he couldn't recall anything about where his own family came from.

"Perhaps I can help," said Lafayette. "Do you remember any words from when you were little?"

Peter recited the prayer he had said just before going into battle.

"But, of course," said Lafayette when Peter had finished. "If I'm not mistaken, that language is Portuguese. You are from Portugal, *mon ami*."

157

"I think you could be right. I remember a conversation my father had in our house on the island in Azores, and he said something about Portugal. I'm Pedro Francisco, and I'm from Portugal." Peter seemed delighted to have finally solved the mystery.

After a few days of bed rest, Lafayette asked the doctor if they could stretch their legs and go into town. Although the doctor wasn't entirely happy with the idea, he also knew better than to keep young men such as these lying down for too long, lest they become so restless that they do something foolish. So it was that Peter and Lafayette headed to a tavern, sharing a couple of local grogs at an old wooden table, carrying on a quiet conversation. One of the patrons of the tavern noticed that Peter still had the green sprig in his hat and, having had more than his share of the local brew, and despite Peter's obvious stature, approached the two men.

"I'll be supposin' that you two are revolutionaries, aren't you? I saw you fellas with your green sprigs in Philadelphia a few weeks back. Now why don't you just turn in your guns and such and just go home where you belong?"

Lafayette looked at the man for a moment. "Perhaps it is just me, but I think you show poor manners. My friend and I are here to relax and enjoy ourselves. You, on the other hand, appear to be what the English call a sot, so why don't *you* just go home and sleep it off…in a barn, if I guess correctly."

Actually, the man was well beyond just drunk, because the first punch he threw was aimed directly at Peter, who was much larger than Lafayette. His first swing missed. His first would also be his last as Peter rose from his chair and landed a blacksmith's right fist squarely on the man's jaw. The man teetered across the room before collapsing at a table where his friends were also drinking too much. The ensuing brawl wasn't really a fair fight, even though Peter and Lafayette were outnumbered by more than three to one. But when it was over, seven Tories lay flat out on the floor, and Peter and Lafayette stood in the middle of the room with satisfied looks on their faces.

Lafayette looked at Peter and said, "I don't think General Washington fully understands what kind of a fighting man he has in his army, but I promise you he soon will."

When they arrived back at the Moravian farm, new orders had come for Lafayette. He was to report to another area farm that could better provide for his comfort. He immediately asked if Peter could be transferred there, too, but it was obvious to everyone that Peter's wound had been less serious, and he was ready to report back to the 10th Virginians.

There was something else waiting for Peter besides his orders to report. It was a letter from Susannah Anderson. It had taken several months, but it had finally caught up with Peter. He opened it and looked at the page.

"What does it say? What does it say? Is it not from your sweetheart?" Lafayette inquired.

"Yes, it is from Susannah, but I don't know what it says," replied Peter.

"Why in the world not?"

"Because I don't know how to read. I never learned."

"But why did you not tell me?"

Peter didn't answer.

"My friend, this is nothing to be ashamed of. Many fine men never learned how to read or write. Please, may I read it for you?"

"Would you? Would you, please?"

"Of course. But, of course, I will." Lafayette took the letter from Peter and began to read.

My dearest Peter,

I am distressed to begin my first letter to you with bad news, but I knew you would want to know. Your friend Arthur has passed away at Hunting Tower. Judge Winston visited us a couple of weeks ago and said that Arthur had passed comfortably in his sleep. I hope you find some small comfort that your friend didn't suffer.

Since you left, I have thought of you every day. I long for you to return. When you left that day, I stood and watched you ride off until you were out of sight, then I went straight to my room and cried my heart out for three days. My father finally insisted that I come out. I miss you so much and shall cherish our last moments together.

It would seem that the British are gathering troops for war here in the south, and my father is preparing to take command of his militia. Word is that they may be sent to South Carolina, but we can't be certain of that as yet.

Please know that my heart aches for you. You are my hero and my love, and I miss you so much.

I must go now, my love, as I want to get this letter posted today. Please take care of yourself and know that my heart is yours to keep forever.

Love, Susannah

"She must be a lovely lady," said Lafayette as he finished reading.

"She truly is," replied Peter. "She truly is. Can I ask you a favor? If I tell you the words, will you write a letter to her for me?"

"I would be honored." Lafayette secured some paper, and Peter began to recite his reply.

Dear Susannah,

It pains me to hear about my dear friend Arthur. Truly, he was the closest thing I ever had for a father, and I shall miss him deeply.

Your letter has found me recovering from a slight leg wound, but I have made a new friend, and it is he who is writing this letter to you. He is the Marquis de Lafayetteand he comes from France. He was also wounded in battle, but he is also recuperating well. As for me, I am healed enough to rejoin my friends in the army, and I shall do so in just a few days.

In the midst of the chaos of battle, I didn't realize that I had been wounded. Afterwards, I couldn't help but think of you and what we would have lost had that musket had a deadly aim.

I, too, think often of our afternoon on your porch, and that memory is one that I shall carry for the rest of my days. I wish we had had more time together, but what I do now is for the great cause. Along with the memory of your beauty, I still carry your handkerchief in my satchel wrapped around my silver shoe buckles. Even though you can't be here with me, I think of you often.

Please know that it is my love for you that keeps me fighting for freedom.

Peter

"Is there anything else I can do for you?" asked Lafayette.

"Actually, there is," said Peter smiling. "When you tell General Washington about what a great warrior I am, ask him to send me a bigger sword, a sword about five feet long, that I could make sing as it cuts down those lobster-backs."

"Indeed, *mon ami*. Indeed. A giant man needs a giant sword, and you shall have it. I promise, you shall have it."

11

NEW BATTLES AND A WINTER OF DISTRESS

After Brandywine and the Battle of Paoli, British General Lord Cornwallis had successfully seized the colonial capital of Philadelphia. Then General Howe, for some reason, decided to split his forces, leaving about one-third of his men to defend the captial and marching the balance north to Germantown to seek out and destroy the colonials.

Just a few weeks after being wounded at Brandywine, Peter rejoined his fellow troops just north of Germantown where, despite their recent defeats, General Washington and his officers were emboldened by the ability of their men to hold their owen against the British professional soldiers. It was with that confidence that Washington conceived a plan that he felt could rout the British.

Thus it was that just after sunset on October 3, the American army, including Peter's 10th Virginia, set out marching toward the hamlet of Germantown. The plan was to arrive barely before dawn and attack from four different directions. Each of the four columns would converge in a pincer-like movement, eventually crushing the British defenders. The plan was bold and called for silently taking out British sentries before launching the full attack. It might have worked, but God Almighty had a different plan in mind.

Throughout the night, a heavy fog settled on and around Germantown. As a result, communications between the four columns became almost impossible, and coordinating the attack -- a crucial part of the plan's success -- was no longer possible. Under the command of General George Weedon, Peter and the rest of the Virginians, having marched an extra four miles, were a bit late in arriving at their position. As he and his comrades took their positions, many of the men stood shivering, with the fog adding to their misery. Peter again reached inside his satchel, removed the buckles that were wrapped inside Susannah's handkerchief and recited his Portuguese prayer.

Almost as soon as he had returned them to his satchel, the Virginia regiment could hear gunfire break out to their right, and Peter could feel that same sensation that had overtaken him during Brandywine. His skin tingled and the roar in his head returned. John Allen stood next to him, sensing that his friend may be losing control in his deep-rooted desire to kill more Redcoats. He reached over and rested his hand on Peter's arm. Just then to their left, a signal flair illuminated the early dawn – one of the British sentries had been able to fire the sparkler just before being bayoneted to death by one of the scouting colonials. The element of surprise had been lost.

"Easy, big fella, easy," John said. "You'll get your chance to kill the lobster backs soon enough."

Peter restrained himself and stood his ground, waiting for the signal to advance. Suddenly, violently, the very air shook with the sound of cannonfire. Although the aim was not accurate because of the early hour and the increasingly dense fog, it made a deafening roar. Almost immediately, musketfire could be heard. Again, there was little significant effect, for no one firing could possibly see what he was aiming at. However, because the smoke added to the nearly impossible visibility, there was a definite effect.

All hell broke loose. The order finally came for the Virginians to advance, and they came within sight of the British. This time, rather than standing in defensive positions as they had at Brandywine, the Americans took the fight to the enemy. At 100 yards, the mountain men again used their long rifles precisely, dropping several British soldiers.

As before, the balance of the troops had been ordered not to fire until they were within fifty yards of their targets, and Peter, whose urge was to charge full speed into the mass of red standing in front of him, did his best to control himself. He customarily loaded his musket with a combination of ball and pellets and, arriving at the correct distance, brought his musket to his shoulder, took careful aim and fired. A British soldier went down. Since the Redcoats were just holding their ground, Peter found the time to reload and fire four more times; each time another enemy fell to the ground.

Meanwhile the fog and smoke mingled, further deepening the obscurity, until the soldiers could see no more than thirty yards in front of them. That's when it happened. Off to one side, some of the

Americans became totally befuddled. Thinking that the British had launched a counterattack, they fired in the presumed direction of the enemy. But they were firing on their own troops.

Cries of "We're trapped! Retreat!" could be heard, and many men threw down their weapons in retreat and ran from the field. Washington's plan was deteriorating rapidly. Peter's Virginians stood their ground, fighting valiantly while at the same time having to let the retreating troops through the lines. Just as at Brandywine, General Washington had tried in vain to rally his soldiers, but the moment had been lost. The British troops surged back at the Americans, and Washington's men were compelled to give up the battlefield. Once again, the battle itself had been lost.

However, Washington and his general staff came to a very important conclusion. It was now obvious to them that they could hold their own against the British military. They could hold their own, and they could drive them back. This was a good omen.

Soon thereafter, the Americans were further encouraged by the outcome of the Battle of Red Bank. The colonials had built two forts on opposite sides of the Delaware River, which were to cut off the British supply line into the city of Philadelphia. If Washington could not physically defeat the British there, he would starve them out.

The Redcoats' next move was to send a large contingent of Hessians – their German allies – to root out the considerably smaller American force defending fort Mercer, positioned on the left bank of the Delaware. In fact, Colonel Karl von Donop was so sure of victory that he declared the fort would either soon be named after him or he would be dead. Three days after the attack on October 22, von Donop died of injuries sustained when the Americans inflicted heavy casualties on the German forces.

Prior to that victory, the colonials had withstood a bombardment of the sister Fort Mifflin, also known as Mud Island. The second and far more intense attack would serve notice that the Americans still had a long way to go before they could have any real hope of defeating their enemy.

November 10, 1777 was a cold, dreary day. Fort Mifflin, to which Francisco had been assigned, had been under occasional bombardment for almost a month now. The cannonfire had taken its toll on the partially completed fortifications, but the impact of war inside the fort was far greater. The men were cold. They were wet. They were hungry. And nearly thirty days of cannonfire had left them sleepless. For Peter, this was not the war he anticipated. There was no musketfire, and there was no hand-to-hand combat, at which the Portuguese soldier excelled. There was only the constant pounding of the British cannon and a headache pounding inside Peter's head. He crouched down behind a bunker on the north side of the fort alongside his friend, John Allen.

"Do you think this will ever stop?" asked Peter of the mountain man.

"Of course, I do," replied John. "After all, they've got to run out of cannonballs sooner or later," he remarked dryly.

The two friends shared a hearty but brief laugh that came to an abrupt halt when the British forcefully opened up with cannonfire. Even the fort's stone walls on the south and east sides were soon reduced to not much more than rubble.

The withering fire continued throughout the day. At one point, one of Peter's friends stood to run for a more protected spot, but a three-pound cannon ball caught him squarely in the chest. His arms and legs were literally blown from his body, sending a mist of his blood settling on Peter and John Allen. Others of the Americans were also blown to bits or suffered horrific injuries, but with most of their artillery destroyed, the colonials could do nothing to return fire.

For the first time since Peter had been kidnapped, he was afraid. It wasn't so much that he feared death itself; he was afraid that his end would come without even the ability to put up a fight -- that he would die under a pile of rubble and Susannah would never know his fate; that he would die without having the future with her which he dreamed of every night. More than anything else, these thoughts made him very angry.

In the midst of a bombardment that later was reported to include one thousand cannonballs raining down every twenty minutes, Peter stood up, aimed his musket at a British ship two or three hundred yards away, and fired.

"Peter," said John Allen. "What in the world are you're doing? You can't possibly hit anything but river fish at this distance, and probably not even the fish."

"I don't care," snapped the enraged Peter. "I've got to do something."

"Well, just stop it. Besides, you're too big a target, and if they aim at you, they'll probably kill me, too."

While Peter was reloading his musket, a cannonball ripped into their embankment, spewing mud and dirt on the two friends and causing Peter's rage to morph to amusement. He broke out laughing.

"Just what do you find so funny about this?" asked John incredulously.

"You, John Allen. You look just like one of the black slaves back at Hunting Tower," Peter shot back.

"Well, you don't look much better. Your dark skin is a whole shade darker now."

Up and down the ranks, others heard the laughter and looked at the two friends who couldn't contain themselves. Although not a word was spoken, most of them concluded that Peter Francisco and John Allen had momentarily lost touch with the reality of war.

The brutal pounding upon Fort Miffin continued for five straight days. By day, the walls and embankments were destroyed. By night, the remaining American defenders reconstructed them, discouraging any attempt by the British to land troops on the island and overrun its defenders. But by October 15, more than half the men in the fort had been killed and the order came down to set fire to anything that would burn. After having done so, the survivors, including Peter and John Allen, made their way by the cover of night to the wharf where three boats facilitated their escape to Fort Mercer.

Having been unable to conquer it less than a month before, the British sought to seize the advantage and turned their attentions back to Fort Mercer. After five more days of sustained cannonfire, the Continental forces were compelled to abandon this last barricade to Philadelphia. Peter Francisco found himself retreating with his comrades once again, and he didn't like it. He didn't like it one bit.

****

169

After several small skirmishes with British and Hessian troops, Peter and the rest of the 10th Virginia Regiment were compelled to follow the whole of the Continental Army from Whitemarsh, New Jersey to Valley Forge, Pennsylvania, where they would camp for the winter. As he, John Allen, and the rest of the Virginians marched, they noticed bloody footprints left by those shoeless Americans. Without even much of their clothing left, they wrapped themselves in blankets in the 20 to 30 degree temperatures. Crossing the Schuylkill River near Gulph, they encountered a snowstorm of such fury that they had to make temporary camp for several days. Conditions were absolutely miserable, but the worst was yet to come. Finally, on December 19, 1777, the troops arrived at Valley Forge. They had marched only thirteen miles, but it had taken eight days. Upon arrival, Peter and John Allen looked around at what would be their home for the next several months. – a fort sitting on a high plateau with the river protecting one side and two small creeks providing natural barriers against an enemy attack.

"Looks like we've at least got a place where we can defend ourselves," commented Peter.

"From what I hear tell," said John, "these armies take the winter off, so I don't think we'll have to do much defendin'."

"Good, then. At least we can rest up a bit. I just hope we can make it through the winter snow and ice."

One of the first priorities in the new location was securing food; the first few days the men existed on nothing more than firecakes, a mixture of flour and water that resulted in a tasteless, sooty biscuit of sorts. Peter, eating his daily ration, longed for some of the biscuits that were served in great quantity at Hunting Tower. John Allen sat down next to him on a log fronting one of the many campfires. After biting into the firecake, he spat it out on the ground. "Enough is enough," he declared. "I can't exist on this." With that he grabbed his long rifle. "With all these woods around here, there's got to be some critters we can hunt." Several of the other Virginia mountain men grabbed their weapons too.

"Mind if I go, too?" Peter inquired.

"Come ahead if you want to," was John's response. "Just don't try shootin' anything. These ain't Redcoats, and you're not that good a shot anyway. This here is serious work, I tell you." Peter was a bit taken aback by his friend's rebuke, but he joined the hunting party anyway. It didn't matter. Most of the animals knew instinctively that the winter would be a hard one, and they were safely tucked inside their burrows. After four hours on the hunt, the party returned to camp with just one raccoon and a few squirrels to show for the effort.

Meanwhile, General Washington had issued an order to build huts to ward off the winter elements. Each 16-foot wide by 14-foot deep hut was to house twelve men. The walls would be six-and-one-half feet high, a height that would barely accommodate Peter's stature. A fireplace made of wood and covered with clay was also to be constructed. Although a $12 reward was offered to the first squad in each regiment that got its hut built, Peter and the mountain men were far behind on the task, because they had spent so much time hunting. However, Peter could wield an axe with the best of them, and his group just barely missed out on the reward. No matter. They were all just glad for the shelter. Unfortunately, the huts were quite drafty with nothing more than a straw floor and a blanket for a door, just like old Caleb's, and a fireplace that belched an overwhelming amount of smoke because of the green wood that had to be used.

Food was the major problem. Supplies were available but getting them to the encampment was difficult at best. The roads and trails to the camp were just about impassable, so even when supplies could be secured, it was impossible for them to reach the soldiers. Although the quartermaster, a fellow by the name of Thomas Mifflin, had been a merchant in Philadelphia, he hated his job and ignored it for the most part.

During the first six weeks at Valley Forge, there were thirteen days of icy rain or snow, causing the morale of the men to rapidly decline. One afternoon, Peter was on the outskirts of camp to get fresh water from one of the small streams when he happened on a shirtless soldier, a sentry wrapped in a blanket, standing with no shoes on his hat. This was the only way he could avoid standing barefoot in the four inches of snow.

"You don't look very comfortable," Peter commented.

The soldier looked at Peter. He was shivering so that his teeth were audibly chattering. "I've never been so cold in all my life," he said. "I come from Virginia, and we don't get winter like this."

"I thought I recognized you," said Peter. "I come from Virginia, too, and right now, I wish I was back there. But listen here, I have a proposal for you. I could just pick you up and hold your feet off the snow while you stand guard, or I could take your place, and you can go back to your hut and get warm by the fireplace."

The sentry looked at the huge man, almost speechless. "You would do that for me?" he questioned, hoping it wasn't some sort of twisted joke.

"Well, now if you mean holding you up in the air, I could do it, but I think it would serve no purpose for us both to be cold."

The soldier looked at Peter for a moment, then spontaneously reached up and threw an arm around one shoulder. When he let go, he said to the man, "I don't know where our paths may lead, but I owe you a great debt of gratitude that I will endeavor to repay some day." With that, the man trudged back to the lines of huts. Peter watched him as, just like on the march to Valley Forge, he left bloody footprints in the snow. The Portuguese soldier began to wonder how much more these men could endure.

Later that evening, as Peter sat in his hut trying to warm himself by the ever-smoking fireplace, a man pulled back the blanket door. Peter, with a blanket wrapped around his torso that nearly covered his eyes, squinted to make out who had entered. Much to his surprise, it was Lafayette.

Peter jumped to his feet and rushed to greet his friend. "Lafayette. It's so good to see you again." The two men exchanged a bear hug after which Lafayette gave Peter a kiss on one cheek and then the other, surprising him by this outward show of affection.

"Do not be offended, *mon ami*," said Lafayette. "This is a greeting between friends in my country. I thought I had told you that when last we were together."

"Well, that's fine with me. After all, we wouldn't want to insult the French, now, would we?" Peter said with a glint in his eye and a smirk on his face. Just then, he started to cough but not from all the smoke in the room. The hacking cough was relentless, and was soon doubled over coughing until spittle and phlegm dripped from his mouth.

"*Mon ami*, my friend. You are not well."

"It's just all this cold and wet and snow. I don't know how people live in a place like this. We had snow back at Hunting Tower, but never like this. I haven't felt good for days, and ever since I got back from standing guard duty, I can't stop coughing and wheezing."

"Well, tonight, you shall share my quarters. They are considerably more comfortable than here. And we shall inquire of the services of a doctor. I'm sure General Washington would agree that we can ill afford to lose soldiers like you."

Peter pulled his blanket close around himself and followed the Frenchman back to his officer's quarters in the falling snow. He was thankful for the respite in Lafayette's hut, but the two men talked well into the night until Peter could stay awake no longer and fell into a fitful, cough-broken sleep.

The next morning when he awoke, Lafayette was nowhere in sight. He tried his best to get up, but he was so weak he could barely raise his head. A few minutes later, Lafayette returned, bringing one of the camp doctors. After examining Peter for a short time, the doctor turned to Lafayette.

"He is quite ill but to provide the proper care, he needs to be transferred to our hospital in Yellow Springs. In any event, this man is not to report for any kind of duty."

"Of course," said Lafayette. "I will see to it immediately."

174

Yellow Springs was the first true military hospital, and Lafayette arranged for Peter to be taken there that very day. As Peter was loaded onto the back of a wagon for the ten-mile trip, Lafayette placed his hand on Peter's arm.

"Be not concerned, *mon ami*. They will take very good care of you at the hospital." Lafayette was looking at the doctor who was to accompany Peter and several others on this journey. "They will take very good care of you or they will feel the wrath of a very unhappy Frenchman." With that, Lafayette winked at his friend.

Peter, in a voice weakened by his condition, murmured, "Thank you, my friend. Thank you. I don't know how I can ever repay you."

"You need not worry about repaying me. Rather, take down a few more lobster backs when you return to the battlefield. Get well, my giant friend, for the British wish they had seen the last of you." As the wagon left the encampment, Peter managed to raise his head a little to see Lafayette wave goodbye.

When the wagon pulled up to the hospital, the patient was feeling a bit better and was able to get out of the wagon unassisted. Standing there in the snow, he savored the sight of the three-story building that could accommodate as many as 300 men at a time. As he made his way to the entrance, a hospital worker came out carrying a black object about three feet long. It was a leg that had just been amputated from one of the soldiers. The worker made his way to a two-wheeled cart off to one side and lifted a tarp. Underneath were all manner of similarly colored body parts -- feet, arms, hands, even ears. Peter looked away, covering his nose with his hand to muffle the

175

nauseating smell. The doctor nudged his arm. "This way," he said, leading him into the hospital.

Once inside, Peter was aghast by what he saw and by the smell that permeated the whole first floor. Rows and rows of makeshift beds lined the walls and filled the center of a large room. Some of the men, recovering from amputations, lay groaning beneath bloody sheets. The collective din rivaled that of some artillery barrages. Others lay in wait for amputations, with their limbs and extremities as black as those Peter had seen outside. There was a smell of rotting flesh in the air, as gangrene was also a prominent malady.

Peter was taken upstairs to the second floor where men with illnesses like his were cared for. The moans and groans were still present but not nearly as loud as those from the amputees downstairs. The stench, however, still assaulted the nostrils. There were buckets for the men to throw up, but as often as not, the ill soldiers missed their target. An indoor outhouse was off to one corner, but many of the sick either couldn't get out of bed at all, or those who did couldn't quite make it. As a result, the smell of feces and urine was nearly unbearable, despite the efforts of several women assigned to clean up.

Peter was escorted to a bed about halfway down one row. "Lie down there and Doctor Bodo will take a look at you in a while," the camp doctor told him. Doctor Bodo was an older German fellow. He and his two sons, also doctors, were running the hospital. Peter did as instructed and quickly dozed off. It wasn't too long before someone was poking him in the side, and he opened his eyes to see an elderly man with a shock of white hair in a bloodstained white coat bending over him. Looking at a piece of paper that had been pinned to Peter's sheet by the camp doctor, the physician seemed to be pondering the information provided. "It says here that you have a bad cough, a high fever and trouble breathing, is that right?" the doctor inquired.

"Yes, sir," Peter said in a raspy, weak voice.

"Well, it's likely you have pneumonia. Don't worry. We'll take good care of you and send you back to duty in no time. Consider yourself lucky. Most of these men have come down with dysentery and typhus. For the life of me, I don't know why the men insist on relieving themselves upstream rather than downstream from the camp. I hear that the general has issued orders about proper sanitation, but looking around here, I'd say that's a horse that's already escaped the barn. Anyway, I'm sure you don't want to hear about that. You just rest easy and someone will be along with some hot soup. That will make you feel better." Peter lay there with his mind spinning. After all, he had always gotten his supply of drinking water from one of the streams, and the thought of what the doctor had just said was enough to make him sick, if he wasn't sick already. He lapsed into intermittent dozing while waiting for the soup.

A while later a woman came by with some clear broth of animal stock with a few pieces of turnips, onions and carrots. She held a spoonful to Peter's mouth, and he was glad that it didn't really taste too bad. And it was hot. The warmth spread throughout his chest as he swallowed the first of it, and that felt good. Too soon he had consumed the entire bowl, and the woman daubed at Peter's chin with her apron. She was reading the paper with information about the patient currently occupying this bed.

"It says here that you're Peter Francisco. Well, I wish this bed was another six inches longer because then you might just fit. My name is Thelma Jackson. I'll be looking after you under the doctor's orders. It says here that you are to get soup four times a day and extra blankets. I'll see to that right away." Not waiting for a response, the woman scurried off toward the far end of the room. By the time she returned, Peter was sound asleep. From the hospital stores she had retrieved a fairly thick blanket, which she gently laid across her patient and ever so carefully pulled up to his neck, touching his cheek as she did so. "Such brave lads must suffer so much," she said under her breath. "What a shame." Then she noticed that in pulling the blanket up to Peter's chin, she had exposed his feet, so she went to the foot of the bed and gave a gentle tug to cover his feet; when she did so, Peter's chest was hardly covered. After several useless attempts to get just the right coverage, she got another blanket.

Several days passed and Peter went through the same regimen of eating soup and sleeping. When he slept, his dreams were of Susannah -- of their first kiss, of her standing on her porch waving goodbye -- punctuated by nightmares of battles won and lost, of Brandywine, and of being almost buried in dirt and mud at Fort Mifflin. In a few weeks, the magic elixir of soup and rest in a warm bed had done its job, and Peter was allowed to report back to camp.

By mid-February he arrived back at Valley Forge and immediately began searching for the hut that had belonged to his friend Lafayette. He knew he must be in the general area but had been so ill the night of his only visit that he couldn't determine exactly which hut it was. And he didn't want to start disturbing any of the other officers. Somewhat confused, he noticed a tall man rounding the corner. It was

178

General George Washington. Peter snapped to attention as he had been taught to do when in the presence of an officer.

"You're Peter Francisco, aren't you?" acknowledged Washington.

"Yes, sir," Peter said with the appropriate decorum. Then the decorum broke. "How did you know?"

"Patrick Henry pointed you out to me in Richmond. Besides, at your size, you're a bit unmistakable. I've seen you on the battlefield, too. You're quite the warrior. Would that I had a thousand just like you -- I could kick the infernal British in their collective backsides all the way back to England." Peter almost laughed at the thought but caught himself as he remembered he was in the presence of the most important man alive. Seeing Peter's distress, the general asked, "Who are you looking for, young fellow?"

"I was hoping to find Major General Lafayette, but I can't remember which hut is his."

"You're standing right in front of it, my boy, but he's not here right now. He and several of my officers are meeting with Barron von Steuben. He's telling them about our new training for the soldiers. That meeting should be ending soon. I'm sure the Marquis wouldn't mind if you waited in his hut. In fact, he's told me that the two of you have become comrades and that you have inquired about a larger sword."

"Yes, sir. A larger sword would be much appreciated. With my God-given stature and strength, I know I could swing a five foot blade just fine," Peter said enthusiastically.

"Now, I can't make any promises. It's hard enough to get almost any supplies right now, but I will look into it. I must admit that

179

sometimes I, too, find my saber a bit on the small side, and you appear to be a good four or five inches taller than I am. Just wait inside this hut right here -- I'm sure that the Marquis will be along forthwith."

Peter further stiffened his back and snapped a salute to the general. Washington offered a more relaxed salute, turned and walked away. The young soldier stood there trying to grasp the moment. The thought crossed his mind, "General George Washington knows who I am. He thinks I'm a great fighter. He may even get me my sword. Wait till Susannah hears about this!"

Though having been told he could wait inside Lafayette's hut, Peter thought that might look a bit too presumptuous, so he waited outside for his friend. The weather wasn't so severe as before and the snow had melted. Besides, after so much time spent in that stench-riddled hospital, Peter was thankful for the fresh air that filled his healing lungs.

Presently General Lafayette approached. When he spotted Peter, he hurried to greet him in the traditional French way with a hug and two kisses, one on each cheek. "Peter, how great it is to see you. How are you? Are you feeling better? Come inside and let us talk." Words came in a torrent as the Frenchman opened the door to his hut. "What was it like at the hospital? Did they treat you well? Tell me, for if they did not, I'll have their heads on a pike."

"Well, I'm here, aren't I?" said Peter whimsically. "I guess they must have done something right, so I suppose their heads are safe for now," he chided.

Lafayette tilted his head back in laughter. "Peter, it is so good to see you. That day they took you to the hospital, I feared that it might be the last I saw of you." Almost immediately, Lafayette's mood turned solemn. "What was it like there? We have heard many stories about the conditions. Did you know that we've lost nearly 3000 men since this camp was established?"

"I'm not surprised," Peter said as he went on to describe what he had seen at the hospital. "They do the best they can under the conditions. Our casualties would be far greater, if it weren't for Doctor Bodo and his sons,"

"I'm sure that's true. Perhaps General Nathanael Green, Washington's new quartermaster, will help, also. He's only been at his post for a short time, but already supplies and food have begun to arrive. I have other good news as well. Word has come that my country and yours have signed an alliance. It still needs to be ratified by your -- what do they call it? Your congress, that's it. But it is a mere formality. We are now officially in this war together, *mon ami*. Is that not good news?"

"Well, if you ask me, we've been in this war together for some time now. At least that's what I thought when those lobster backs were trying to shoot us both."

For the second time in the past few minutes, Lafayette broke out in laughter. "But I almost forgot. I have even better news. I just came from a meeting with Baron von Steuben, who was an officer in the Prussian-German Army, and he has volunteered to conduct the training of our troops. Believe me when I tell you this, *mon ami,* I have seen the Germans in battle and I have heard of their exploits. Their training sets them apart from almost any army in the world. Just look at the Hessians. You have seen how well they make war. We are indeed fortunate to have him on our side. With his guidance, I truly believe that we can win this war."

"Well, that's a good thing," Peter piped in. "When do we begin to train?"

"Tomorrow. The Barron wants to start immediately so that we can all train before breaking camp in the spring."

After talking for a while longer, during which he related his encounter with Washington, Peter excused himself to go back to his own hut to see how his mountain men friends were doing. When he entered, John Allen looked up and greeted him enthusiastically. "Look who's here. The Virginia giant has finally come home. It's good to have you back, Peter. We were worried about you, especially for the first couple of days when we didn't know where you were."

"So how did you find out that I was sick in the hospital?" asked Peter.

"Oh, that was easy. They've started posting duty rosters every day, and your name showed up on it as being sick. I guess they want us to be a real army, what with the new rules and regulations and duty rosters."

"You don't even know the whole story," Peter said with a certain glee, knowing something that John Allen didn't.

"So tell us, or do we all have to sit here and guess?"

"No, no. I'll tell you," and Peter recounted to the group what he had just heard from Lafayette. Some of the mountain men just shook their heads. They weren't used to having someone direct their every movement and every moment. -- most of them were pretty independent fellows -- but John Allen spoke up. "Fellas, the sooner we win this war, the sooner we get to go back to the mountains. Now I don't know about any of you others, but I'm for anything that gets us back home as quick as possible. I'll train, Peter. I don't mind a bit."

"Well, that's good, because I didn't get the idea that any of us have a choice in the matter." Despite some groans from some of the mountain men, Peter was certain they'd all join, even if they weren't exactly in favor of it.

What von Steuben found was an army in total disarray, if it could even be called an army. Until recently, there had been no regular roll calls. Even the size of fighting units varied considerably, and many orders went totally ignored. Frequently, soldiers just left camp, never to return. Knowing that he couldn't train thousands of men at one time, he broke it down to a select group of about one hundred men. These men would be taught proper military bearing, attire and skills that would make a soldier out of a civilian, a proper soldier. The first group of one hundred, still under von Steuben's guidance, would then train other groups of soldiers.

The fact that von Steuben spoke very little English posed a problem. He had to enlist the aid of people like Lafayette, fluent in several languages, to interpret. At times this was almost comical, as von Steuben was a profane man with little patience. Translating his cursing and swearing became a joke among the soldiers throughout the spring. However, the troops began to see the value of his training and their cooperation, and they appreciated that von Steuben often participated in their drills, demanding that junior officers do so, as well. As a result, most of the men became fond of their drillmaster, without realizing that many of their own lives would be saved by this man's manual of

183

training. Before long, there was an obvious change in the morale and spirit of the men.

Meanwhile, the alliance with France had been ratified, and French-made uniforms and armaments began to arrive. Food became more plentiful, especially shad spawning in the Schuylkill River. Even a German baker from Philadelphia had arrived with about seventy employees. They began baking all sorts of goods, winning the soldiers with the camp favorite, gingerbread. Additional rations of rum were distributed, as well as the reward of an extra month's pay.

When the middle of June arrived, it was time to go back to war. The troops, under von Steuben, had been well trained. Under the new quartermaster, supplies had increased. The agreement with France produced, among other things, a navy capable of going against the British fleet. Only a few days before camp was to break, Lafayette sought out Peter at his hut. "Peter, I have just been given a letter meant for you. It is from your sweetheart, Susannah. Please, come to my hut, for I mistakenly left it there." Lafayette hadn't really made a mistake. He remembered that Peter couldn't read or write and knew that he was quite self-conscious about it, and he didn't want the others in the hut to know. As Lafayette walked toward his personal quarters, Peter raced ahead.

"Come on. Come on," Peter called back. "What's the matter, Lafayette? Has all this training tired you out?"

"Ah, the energy of youth and the zest of love," muttered Lafayette, as he picked up his own pace to catch up with his friend. Handing the letter to Peter, Lafayette watched him tear open the envelope quickly and carefully unfold the letter. Then he stared at it for a few moments.

"What's this? asked Lafayette. "Have you learned to read during our stay here?"

"No," replied Peter. "But I like looking at her writing."

Lafayette sighed. "Like I said, the zest of love. Give it to me and let me read it to you."

Peter handed over the letter and Lafayette began to read it out loud:

My Dear Sweetheart, Peter

I hope this finds you well. Word has come to us about the horrible conditions that all of you withstood at Valley Forge. I was hoping you might return for the winter, but I guess that was out of the question.

I continue to miss you terribly, and I pray for you every day. I think that Father has guessed well the nature of our relationship. He says I pine for you too much, but then he laughs and says he understands. I am not sure that he truly understands, for he had made arrangements for me to marry another even before you left for the army. He has not spoken a word of it since you left, though, so maybe he understands after all.

In any event, he has spoken of you frequently and how he would not be at all opposed should you return to our farm rather than Hunting Tower. I believe he has begun to accept that, if it be the will of God, you and I shall spend our lives together. I do know that is my wish, and I hope that it is your wish, as well.

Word from Hunting Tower is that they have done quite well with their hemp crop, and things are much better for Judge Winston. Late last summer he advertised some of his plantation for sale, but there was no buyer. That would appear to be just as well, considering how they prosper now.

The British have begun to invade Georgia and South Carolina, so Father is to leave today for his first command. I fear for him as I do for you, but I know that it is something we must all bear in our separate ways.

185

With that, I must close, my darling. Father is going to post this letter in Richmond tomorrow when he reports there for duty. Always remember that I love you with all my heart, and I remain here awaiting your safe return.

My love always,

Susannah.

"*Mon ami*," said Lafayette. "You are truly a lucky man to have a woman like that waiting for you. I envy you and your future."

"Thank you, my friend. But why would you envy me? You have a wonderful family and much wealth to return to one day."

"*Oui*, but sadly, all that I possess cannot possibly purchase what you already have found."

"Will you write my reply?"

"You need not have asked," replied Lafayette, reaching for a paper and quill pen. "I had already made the arrangements to take your dictation."

Peter wasn't entirely sure what the last word meant, but he knew that his friend would write the letter:

My Dearest Susannah

It is so good to hear from you. I cannot even begin to tell you how much your letters mean to me. Your love for me sustains me through the most difficult times.

I must say that the past few months have been some of the most difficult of my life and of everyone else's who spent the winter here at Valley Forge. For a time I was quite ill, but they took good care of me at the army hospital, and I am now fully recovered. Others, I'm afraid, have not fared so well.

186

The spring, however, has brought a renewed spirit and confidence that we can endure and succeed in this war. Supplies have begun to arrive, although the uniforms are all still too small for me. We have also had plentiful food. A German officer has taken over our training. His teaching has been very good, and we shall approach upcoming battles with the ability to defeat the British.

I suppose that you have heard of our treaty with France. I am told that this will give us an advantage in rescuing the capital of Philadelphia. It is everyone's hope that this will lead to a much quicker end to the war.

I met General Washington in person. You might recall that he was at the church in Richmond. He even knew my name and called me a good fighter. He has said that he will try to get me a larger sword.

Your father's offer gives me comfort in pondering our future. Although I feel a great gratitude toward Judge Winston, I fight this war for the freedom of this country as well as for myself. I will be free to choose my own destiny, which includes my very reason for living -- you, my dear Susannah.

Without the comfort of knowing you are waiting for me, I should have given up the struggle. My heart longs for your smile, your touch and your embrace, and these thoughts sustain me until I return again.

I shall also pray for the safety of your father and those under his command.

I remain forever yours,

Love, Peter

12

ANOTHER BATTLE, ANOTHER MUSKETBALL

The alliance with France and the arrival of their navy to form a blockade on the Delaware River did indeed have a large impact on the progression of the war. As a result, the British determined that their best course of action would be to abandon Philadelphia and move to New York. General Henry Clinton had relieved General Howe as commander of the British troops, and he began to evacuate Philadelphia on June 18, 1778. Having sent approximately 3000 troops by ship to Florida, Clinton was left with 11,000 soldiers, about 1000 loyalists, and a baggage and supply train that stretched nearly twelve miles long and could travel only forty-miles a day.

This was exactly the opportunity General Washington was hoping for. With no fortifications behind which to hide, and with their column stretched thinly, the British should be easy to attack and destroy by a few small elements at a time. Preparing to take the fight to the Redcoats, approximately 13,000 men broke camp at Valley Forge.

As for Peter, though six feet six inches tall and with an accommodating body frame, the von Steuben-inspired training had revealed a man surprisingly nimble and light on his feet. Toward the end of training, he was chosen to become a member of an elite force of Light Infantry that would serve as an advanced scouting group and the spearhead of future attacks. It was a task that Peter relished, but it also meant that he was to be separated from his mountain men friends. Although Peter and John Allen would participate in some of the same battles, their days of fighting side-by-side had come to an end.

While the British headed toward New York through New Jersey, Washington appointed General Charles Lee to shadow, harass and provide any obstacle possible to Clinton's force. Serving directly under the command of Colonel Daniel Morgan, Peter was among the troops assigned to this task. Unfortunately, General Lee was not nearly as enthusiastic about the plan as was Washington, thus his halfhearted efforts did not have as much effect as they might have. As a result, General Washington called a meeting of his staff for the morning of June 24, during which General Lee argued convincingly for prudence.

"Gentlemen," Lee said. "We must proceed with caution. Our troops have not the experience to defeat the British under these circumstances. Were we to launch an all-out attack and be defeated, surely it would mark the end of our efforts to win our freedom." Despite all the advanced training provided by von Steuben, Lee still felt that the Americans were no match for the professional soldiers the British put on the field. Several of the staff officers also agreed with Lee.

Washington, however, remained convinced that this action against the British rear guard had a great chance for success. Although he relented and held the main body of colonial troops in reserve, he ordered Lee to take command of 1500 troops and attack the rear flank of the British column. Then he turned to General Marquis de Lafayette.

"General, do you think you could circle behind the British rear guard and coordinate an attack on the other flank with the same measure of force as General Lee's?" Washington inquired.

"Yes, General," said Major General Lafayette. "And I believe that our troops shall prevail in such an action."

"Then it's settled. General Lee, you will attack from one side and Lafayette will attack from the other. Meanwhile, I will keep the main column in reserve to intercept Clinton at Monmouth. Are we all agreed?" Washington didn't wait for a response to his rhetorical question, instead standing, as did the others. As the men filed out of the command tent, Lafayette approached General Washington.

"General," he said, "I have but one request."

"Yes, what is it?"

"I would like for Peter Francisco to be assigned personally to me. I prefer a personal assistant that I can trust to carry out my commands and relay information to my other officers on the battlefield."

"So be it. The Virginia Giant is yours."

"*Merci*, General."

Lafayette sought out Peter as quickly as he could to give him the news. "And so it is that we shall be fighting together, at last," Lafayette concluded.

"It will be an honor and a privilege to serve with you, General," Peter responded.

"Peter, *mon ami*, please let us not be so formal. Let us go together and kill as many British as we possibly can. Then you can go back home to Susannah," he said wryly. "You will invite me to the wedding, will you not?"

"I suppose I have to. It wouldn't be fair if Susannah never met the man who wrote all my letters, would it?"

With that, the two men laughed.

As the sun rose in the sky, Peter, Lafayette and the balance of troops under Lafayette's command left to make a sweeping arc south of the British, after which they would circle back north and take up positions. Peter, as Lafayette's personal assistant, was issued a horse and rode alongside his friend. It made him wonder what had happened to Isabel. He had been told that she was to be used to pull field artillery into action, but he soon lost track of her whereabouts. She had been a good horse and companion during the ride to the Shenandoah Valley, and he hoped that she had fared well.

While Lafayette, with Peter at his side, and his men were maneuvering into position, Washington had decided to add an additional 2000 troops to the action against the British rear guard. Since these troops were added late in the plans, they were placed under Lee's command. Having so many more troops under his command than those of Lafayette, Lee requested that he be appointed as overall commander of the action.

"I shall grant your request," said Washington, "under the condition that if Lafayette has already engaged the enemy upon your arrival, you will not interfere with any orders the Marquis has already given." Lee agreed and set off with his force more than twice the size of Lafayette's.

However, unknown to Lee, on June 27, Washington had become so convinced that attacking the rear guard would ultimately lead to an overwhelming victory that he wheeled his column to support Lee and Lafayette at Englishtown. He sent orders to Lee to commence the attack as soon as possible.

On the morning of June 28, the British were just breaking camp as Lee's battle group neared them a few miles north of Monmouth Court House. While Lee's main body slowly approached without a specific plan of action in place, the British were alerted, and sporadic gunfire broke out.

Thinking theirs was to be a coordinated effort, the young Frenchman gave orders for a rapid advance. When the order was given, Peter, astride his horse next to the commander, remembered his pre-battle ritual -- he reached for the handkerchief-wrapped buckles from his satchel and recited his Portuguese prayer. Immediately, with a surge of adrenalin, the tingling sensation and the roar in his head returned.

The fire of muskets broke out, and colonial artillery sent a barrage of cannonfire into the British camp, inflicting heavy casualties. Lafayette turned to Peter and shouted, "We have caught them by surprise. The victory is ours for the taking!"

Peter nodded in impassioned agreement. Not used to sitting so far back from the action, he wanted nothing more than to dismount and join the battle taking place about 200 yards in front of them.

Then, without warning, Lafayette gave his horse a kick and sprinted off to the right to speak to one of his captains. Unaccustomed to having a personal assistant, the general had forgotten that was why Peter was there, to deliver messages. Just as the commander dismounted, Peter caught up with him and took the reins of both horses. When Lafayette finished the conversation with his subordinate officer, he turned to see Peter in control of both their animals.

"I thought this was my job," said Peter.

"You are correct. It is your job," Lafayette replied, "and you have performed your duty well." He had barely completed his sentence when British cannonfire landed near the two men – the enemy had swung around. The ground shook and spooked the horses, and it was all Peter could do to maintain control of their reins. Trees splintered all around them as the British began their counterattack. The crackle of musketfire grew louder and closer.

Peter looked directly at Lafayette. "I'm not so worried for my own safety as for yours. General Washington would be hard pressed to replace an officer like you. We should move to safety."

Noticing some of the Americans beginning to retreat, Lafayette would have none of that. "*Mon ami,* the time to withdraw to safety has passed. We must rally the troops. I shall stay here to encourage the men. You go to the left and do the same."

Peter remounted and drew his saber from its scabbard, waving it over his head as he had seen Lafayette do on more than one occasion. He yanked the reins to the left, jabbed his feet into the horse's ribs, and yelled at the retreating soldiers, "Turn and fight, men! Turn and fight! The British are not invincible. Turn and fight for your lives and for your

194

freedom!" Most of the soldiers did turn around and reload their muskets to face the British advance. A few did not. But Peter, maneuvering his horse and brandishing his sword, tried to block their way, screaming, "Turn and fight, or I swear to cut you down myself!" Luckily, he didn't have to make good on that threat. The remaining men turned around.

As the British troops moved closer, Peter rode directly toward the hand-to-hand combat. He leaped from his mount, grabbed his musket, took aim and fired once, eliminating a British officer from the battle. With no time to reload, Peter affixed his bayonet and pushed forward. One Redcoat lunged at him with his own bayonet, but Peter deftly parried the thrust, swung the butt of his weapon at the soldier's face, and took him to the ground. With his bayonet at the man's chest, he ended the enemy's life. It was cruel, but it was war.

Meanwhile, Lee's lack of planning was beginning to turn the tide in favor of the British. He was getting conflicting reports of what the British were doing; one said the British were in full retreat, another said they were attacking. Still wary of the colonial soldiers' fighting ability, Lee was unsure what to do. Finally, he issued orders for several units to move both to the left and to the right, with the intent to encircle about 2000 British troops and force them to surrender. But he had not clearly informed his subordinate officers of the plan, and once in position, they were unsure how to proceed.

In the meantime, British General Clinton realized that he was being attacked from behind, and he ordered his troops to turn back and support the rear guard. Simultaneously, British artillery was ordered to wheel about and provide cannon cover.

Assessing his position to no longer be viable, Lee ordered his command to retreat.

Back at Lafayette's command, the colonial troops were more than holding their own -- they were driving the British back. Remembering that his assignment was to be Lafayette's personal aid, Peter realized that he was unintentionally ignoring orders. When he turned his back on the battlefield to locate his horse, he made a mistake that would haunt and pain Peter Francisco for the rest of his life. Just as he was about to hoist himself into the saddle, a musketball tore into the highest point of his left thigh. With his foot already in the stirrup, his shoe caught and he tumbled to the ground. The horse bolted and for a few moments dragged the rider along the ground. Mercifully, the soon-loosened foot dumped Peter face up on the forest floor.

Though he had been shot in the thigh before – in fact, the same thigh -- this was far worse. This ball had not gone completely through the other side of his leg, and the pain was searing.

Meanwhile, General Lee had by now ordered a full retreat, including Lafayette's contingent.

Without warning, Peter felt himself being hoisted by his shoulders. A retreating soldier, struggling mightily under Peter's bulk, was able to help him back onto his retrieved horse. But the pain of putting that left foot back in the stirrup and the pressure on it as he swung his right leg over the mount brought an agonized scream from the Virginia giant.

Finally in the saddle, he glanced down at the face of the soldier who had come to his aid. It was the sentry Peter had relieved of guard duty at Valley Forge, the man who had been standing barefoot on his hat.

196

He had said he would repay the favor one day, and Peter was about to say a thank-you. But it was too late. A British musketball tore through the back of the soldier's head, lodging in Peter's saddle.

Time seemed to stand still as the growing circle of blood on the man's forehead began covering his face. He looked up at Peter with a blank expression, his hand on Peter's arm to steady him in the saddle slipping away as he fell backward. The soldier had repaid his debt of a small sacrifice with the sacrifice of his own life. Peter hadn't even known the soldier's name.

Regaining his senses, Peter could hear musketballs thwacking into the trees all around him. He yanked on the reins and joined in the retreat, although with every bounce, with every step his horse took, the burning in his leg turned to throbbing pain. He could feel himself passing out. Fighting the urge to let go of consciousness, he knew he had to do his best to survive -- for himself, for Susannah, for the soldier who had just sacrificed his own life so that Peter could live.

A cloud of unconsciousness began to overtake him. Vaguely he heard someone shouting his name and sensed his arm being grabbed. When he opened his eyes from the near faint, he saw Major General Lafayette.

"Peter, we must ride quickly to escape," he urged frantically. Grabbing the reins of Peter's horse, he drove both animals as fast as he could to the rapidly deteriorating lines.

On the other flank, Washington had arrived to find that General Lee had ordered a hasty retreat, an order that infuriated the commanding General. With his reinforcements, he was able to rally most of the troops and resume the offensive, but by mid-day, unseasonably high

197

temperatures reached in excess of 100 degrees, along with unbearable humidity, taking its toll. Both sides ceased organized attacks. That day more soldiers succumbed to the heat than fell in combat.

Relentlessly Washington set about the task of reorganizing his forces and prepared for British General Clinton's next move, but nothing happened. Night began to fall, preventing an attack. After a few hours of rest, Clinton ordered his column to rejoin the baggage train, and the British escaped into the darkness.

Meanwhile, the French patriot successfully guided his friend to a temporary hospital overflowing with wounded soldiers. Recalling his own leg wound from the battle at Brandywine, Lafayette carefully helped Peter from his horse and sat him down with his back against a large maple tree. With his leg throbbing terribly, Peter was grateful for the small respite from the intensity of pain. Lafayette then went in search of a doctor. "My friend has taken a musketball in the leg. He needs immediate attention," he pleaded.

The doctor, obviously harried by all that surrounded him, looked at the general in disbelief. "Don't you have eyes, man? Don't you see what's going on here? We can only take wounded men in the order that they arrive, and right now there are about twenty others ahead of your friend."

Lafayette's eyes narrowed to slits. His hand rested on a dagger that was always at his side, and the doctor took notice of this action.

"Go ahead and slit my throat," he said defiantly. "At least then I'll not have to witness any more death. I'll not have to cut off another man's limbs. I'll not see any more misery. Go ahead!"

With slumped shoulders but a compassionate heart, Lafayette returned to sit with his friend outside until morning, listening throughout the night to the screams of dying and mutilated men.

When the morning light shone early in the eastern sky, the very doctor Lafayette had spoken to and threatened appeared at the opening to the hospital tent and signaled that he would look at Francisco next. Lafayette roused Peter from a fitful sleep and helped him into the tent.

As the doctor examined the musket wound, the officer kept poking his face in to glimpse the progress of treatment. "It would be easier if I could see the wound rather than the back of your head," the doctor complained to Lafayette. He proceeded to clean the dried blood and wound where the ball had entered Peter's leg as well as he could. Then he sewed the wound closed, while the oversized soldier winced and grabbed the side of the table on which he rested with all his might.

"Doctor," Lafayette yelled. "What are you doing? Don't you see the ball is still in this man's leg?"

"I'm doing the only thing I can do," replied the doctor curtly. "I don't have anything to properly go digging into his leg to find that ball, and if I did, he'd probably lose the leg anyway. This is the best I can do for him under the circumstances."

Almost apologetically, Lafayette glanced at Peter. "It's all right," said the wounded man. "Let's just get it over with."

The general nodded at Peter, then looked at the doctor. "Proceed."

13

THE HERCULES OF THE REVOLUTION

The morning after Peter's 'surgery' to close the wound on his thigh, Lafayette came to visit at one of several recovery tents that had been set up for the wounded. As the Frenchman entered the tent, Peter looked up at him from his cot.

"You are looking much better than when last I saw you," commented the young general.

"I may look better, but my leg is sure sore," Peter bemoaned.

"I'm sure that it is, and it will likely remain so for some time to come. That is why I have made arrangements for you to recuperate at a private farmhouse called White Plains. It is somewhere in New York. I spoke personally to General Washington about you, and he is making sure that you get the proper care needed to recover and rejoin the struggle as soon as possible."

"I don't know what to say. You are a good friend."

"You need not say anything. It is what friends do for each other. But now, I must leave you. The general has given me a new assignment, and I leave within the hour. Rest well, recover quickly, and remain safe, *mon ami.*" He leaned over and gave Peter a kiss on the left cheek and then the right cheek.

"I'm not quite sure I'll ever get used to that," commented Peter. "Can't we just shake hands?"

"I shake hands with those I don't care about. I kiss my brother, and you are my brother. I look forward to kissing you again when next we meet."

With his friend's departure, Peter was left to contemplate Lafayette's words. Truly, although they shared not the same parents nor even the same country, he and Lafayette were brothers.

Later that day a wagon arrived, and Peter was taken to the White Plains home of William Dickenson. The man reminded Peter a little of Judge Winston when he greeted him. As Peter climbed down from the wagon using a makeshift crutch to steady his weakened left leg, his host offered his assistance. At five feet, three inches tall, Mr. Dickenson was only a little higher than Peter's waist, making it quite a challenge for him to really help Peter. "Come in, young man. We've been expecting you. My wife has busied herself preparing some delicious food to help you regain your strength."

Upon entering the house, Peter took a look around at his surroundings. Prior to seeing this, the main house on the Winston Plantation had been the nicest he had ever seen, but this place far exceeded the beauty of that dwelling. It was immaculate and furnished with the finest sofas, chairs and tables that Europe could offer. Mr. Dickinson was obviously a man of great prominence. Mrs. Dickenson appeared from the back of the house. "I see our house guest has finally arrived. It's so nice to have you visiting us," she said, welcoming the tall visitor. Peter was thankful for the warm welcome.

"My name is Peter Francisco," he said.

"Why, of course, you are," said Mrs. Dickenson. "Now, you just sit there for a minute," she said, indicating an overstuffed chair.

Looking at Mr. Dickenson she continued talking. "They didn't tell us he was so big. You'll need to put a bench at the bottom of the bed so the dear man's feet don't stick out."

"Yes, dear." William responded. "I already figured that out since I was the one who had to help this giant up the steps. You, my dear, should probably get to cooking some more food. I'll bet it takes a lot to fill up this big fellow."

The Dickensons left the room in opposite directions, he out the front door and she to the back of the house, and Peter was left sitting with his own ponderings. "What an odd couple," he thought to himself. "They spoke of me as though I wasn't even in the room. But they certainly seem nice enough."

Shortly, William returned carrying a bench about four feet wide and three feet in height. "Let me get this set up for you, and then I'll show you to your room." He walked toward the back of the house and returned just a few moments later. "Come with me and let's get you settled into bed. I'm sure you're tired after a long journey. Let me take your things."

The old farmer grabbed Peter's satchel, his musket and his sword and guided Peter down the dimly lit hallways. It was too narrow for Dickenson to offer any assistance, but Peter was able to manage on his crutch. The end of the hall opened into a kitchen where Mrs. Dickenson was preparing the next day's meal. There was so much food laid out on the kitchen table that it reminded Peter of some of the feasts and festivals back at Hunting Tower.

To his right was a door that led to the main bedroom. William directed Peter into that room and bade him to sit on the bed. "Normally, this is where the Mrs. and I sleep, but we want you to sleep here. Mrs. Dickenson and I will be right upstairs."

"But I don't want to put you out of your own bedroom," Peter said.

"Nonsense. You'll be more comfortable here. Besides, with that wound of yours, it wouldn't do to have you lumbering up and down the stairs. Why George...ah, Mr....General Washington would be sorely disappointed if anything bad were to happen to you. He must like you a lot. Anyway, you just lie back and rest now. There's a nightgown right behind you. I think you'll rest more comfortably in that. A bit later, my wife will bring you some food."

The thought of a little rest was comforting, and Peter reclined as Mr. Dickenson left the room and closed the door. Peter couldn't help but notice that the bed extension was indeed necessary; his feet would have been hanging over the end of the bed by a good eight inches but for the bench that had been piled high with extra quilts.

After only a few hours of sleep, Peter was awakened by the sound of the door being gently opened. Mrs. Dickenson entered the room followed by her husband and another gentleman.

"This is Dr. Dodge," William announced. "We've arranged for him to take a look at your wound and make sure it's healing properly."

"Good day, sir," greeted the doctor as he set a black leather bag on the side of the bed.

"Good day to you, too, sir," Peter replied.

The doctor started to lift the sheets, but he was on the wrong side of the bed. "It's the other leg," Peter said.

The doctor looked a bit embarrassed, though he couldn't have known which leg carried the musket ball. He walked around to the other side and lifted the sheet. Fortunately, Peter had put on the nightgown that the Dickenson's had given him, which provided easy access for the doctor to make his examination.

"We'll need to change this dressing," the doctor said as he carefully removed the bandage stuck with dried blood. "Now, let me take a closer look. Hmm. All things considered, this was rather well sewn. In a few days, we'll take the stitches out and see how well you're healing."

Turning to Mrs. Dickenson, the doctor continued, "You'll need to change the dressing twice a day to prevent infection. Other than that, just keep him comfortable, quiet and well fed."

Again, Peter thought it odd that people were talking about him as though he wasn't even in the room. No matter. It was clear that these folks genuinely cared about him, and for that Peter was grateful. It was also becoming more obvious that General Washington had had a personal hand in all this.

After applying a new bandage, the doctor left, but it wasn't long before Mrs. Dickenson returned with a bowl of soup. "The doctor says to start you out on this, but later tonight you'll feast on some of the meats and vegetables I've been preparing all day." The soup was delicious, far better than the soup he had been fed at the Yellow Springs hospital. Later in the evening, Peter enjoyed some of Mrs. Dickenson's more hearty offerings before settling back in the bed for a restful night's sleep.

This routine continued for the next few days. Mrs. Dickenson dutifully changed Peter's dressing twice a day, and she fed him so much food that he almost felt like he was a pig being fattened for slaughter. The doctor returned later in the week, removed the stitches and pronounced the wound to be healing as well as could be expected. Two months later, Peter was well enough to rejoin the army. The Dickensons had treated him well, and he had regained almost all of his strength. He no longer needed his crutch, although his leg did twinge him now and again, and he walked with a noticeable limp.

His good friend, Major General Lafayette, arranged for a horse to be delivered, and as Peter and the Dickensons stood on their front porch prior to his leaving, Peter couldn't resist the urge to kiss Mrs. Dickenson on both cheeks. She accepted politely that display of appreciation, but Mr. Dickenson was startled when the same expression was shown him. Seeing William Dickenson's surprise, Peter said, "Just ask a Frenchman. And thank you for all that you have done for me." He then mounted the horse, though his left leg tweaked when he hoisted himself up in the saddle, and aimed it south, headed for Middlebrook, New Jersey. He had been transferred from the 10th Virginia to the 6th Virginia Regiment. It didn't matter to Peter. Even though he would miss the friends he had made in his original unit, he was just happy to be getting back to the action.

When Peter reported to Middlebrook in October 1778, he was immediately selected for special training. Even though he had already been assigned to the Light Infantry, a select few of its soldiers were chosen for even more training as a reconnoitering and advanced party in missions that required a completely different style of combat. From fall to spring, Peter was exposed to all sorts of techniques that could be used to surprise the enemy in sneak attacks. In addition, these troops were shown methods to be used in night fighting, which was quite uncommon among organized militaries that preferred to fight by day in traditional confrontations and on typical battlefields.

During the fall training, Peter's leg was becoming stronger by the day. Again, his officers were completely surprised that a man of such size would be so quick and light on his feet. However, during the winter months, his left leg was often quite painful, especially on cold and damp days. The result was that there were times when he was clumsy and walked or ran still with a noticeable limp. Yet even when he was asked about it, Peter never once complained and never missed any drills or training exercises.

Spring was much kinder as temperatures and the overall climate began to moderate. Peter especially liked training for night fighting. Wearing dark clothing, the soldiers were taught to smudge their faces with dirt, secure all their weapons so that they didn't make any noise, walk quietly through any terrain, and use hand signals and animal sounds to communicate with fellow soldiers. Peter, though so tall and large, took special pride in being able to sneak up on just about anybody without being detected.

****

On May 1, 1779, most of the men who had been training at Middlebrook were assigned to West Point, where General Washington's army had spent the winter. This was certainly an improvement over the previous year's stay at Valley Forge.

In the meantime, the British, in an effort to cut off Washington's supply line along the Hudson River, had set about establishing fortifications slightly south of West Point on both sides of the river. In fact, one particular location, known as Stony Point, had come to be of keen interest to General Washington, and he observed its construction through a telescope from atop Buckberg Mountain.

In a further attempt to gain intelligence about the fort, its armaments and garrison strength, Washington had enlisted a number of civilians to visit the fort on the pretense of doing business there and report what they had seen. Those reports indicated that the so-called fort was manned by approximately 625 British soldiers under the command of Lt. Colonel Henry Johnson. Not entirely satisfied with or trusting of this intelligence gathering, Washington sought out a volunteer for a dangerous mission to gain further data about Stony Point. To that end, militia Captain Allen McClane stepped forward.

Two weeks later, near the first of July, McClane disguised himself as a local female farmer. As such, "she" told the British guards that she was there to visit her sons who were loyalists staying at the fort.

Once inside, McClane was able to determine that the fort wasn't really a fort in the traditional sense. Neither stone walls nor defensive walls of any type had been constructed, Instead, the British were relying on an extremely defensible terrain.

The land at Stony Point jutted about a half mile into the Hudson itself, the three sides being well protected by nearby British vessels and land- bound cannon. Outside the fort, immediately in front of the portion of land that connected this small peninsula to the mainland, there was a considerable marsh and swamp area. To further deter any attack from that direction, the British had constructed rows and rows of abatis, which were sharpened sticks and logs pointed directly toward any advancing army. These barriers, coupled with artillery and gun placements in two semi-circular lines, formed a seemingly impregnable position.

Nevertheless Washington and General Anthony Wayne came up with a plan to take the fort and ease the Hudson River blockade. It called for a three-pronged attack that included a diversion toward the center of the fort and a flanking movement by two other units to breach the "walls", well manned embankments fronted by the abatis. The plan was actually aided by short-sighted British engineers and the hand of Almighty God Himself. Although their use of the abatis had initially appeared ingenious, the engineers had failed to realize that at low tide, soldiers could approach the ends to that particular fortification, chop through a minimal amount of the spears, and allow following troops to flood in.

Thus it was that General Wayne's plan called for launching the attack on July 15/16, 1779 at midnight, when a low tide would occur. In addition, during the days leading up to the attack, any stray dogs within

209

two miles of the area were to be rounded up and killed so as not to raise alarm when the troops approached the fort in the dead of night.

At 8 o'clock on the night of the 15th, General Wayne gathered his troops at Springsteel's Farm and issued final orders. The smallest force, led by Major Hardy Murfree, would provide the diversion by approaching the center of the fort just outside the abatis. At the appointed time, they would begin firing on the British in the fort. Colonel Richard Butler would command a larger force that was to attempt to breach the British defenses on the north, while General Wayne himself would lead the largest group of about seven hundred in the assault on the south side of Stony Point.

Each of the north and south assault forces was further broken down into specialized groups. This advanced group, called the Forlorn Hope, was only twenty men each. The next to attack were one hundred and fifty riflemen. The balance of the troops would then overwhelm the remaining British and capture the fort.

As Wayne prepared the three groups to depart in separate columns, he issued some final orders. All muskets, with the exception of those used in the center diversionary assault, were to be unloaded for fear of an accidental discharge that might warn the British of the impending flanking attacks. In addition, if a column should encounter any civilians during the march to their positions, they were to be taken into custody in case they were British sympathizers who might sound the alarm.

Peter, having distinguished himself as a night fighter during training at Middlebrook, was assigned to the Forlorn Hope contingent in front of the northern assault group. He was especially pleased to have been given the task, and he could hardly contain himself during the night march.

As for God's part, He was quite cooperative in providing a thick cover of clouds such that the moon could not light up the swamp and marshland through which the Americans would make their way. He also provided just enough wind so that the British ships protecting the watersides of the fort were forced to seek a more sheltered portion of the Hudson. That also meant that they could not provide any covering fire for their fellow soldiers in the fort.

By midnight, all of the American forces had taken their positions. Wayne was to the south, Murfree was positioned in the center, and Butler's troops, including Peter Francisco's group of Forlorn Hope, were staring at the northern slope. Peter put his hand in the satchel and removed his ever present shoe buckles, still wrapped in Susannah Anderson's handkerchief. So as not to make a sound, he silently recited his Portuguese prayer and carefully returned the buckles to his satchel.

Murfree's troops began firing at the center of the fortification. Their goal was not so much to hit any of the British troops as it was to draw attention to that particular area. It was also the signal for the two Forlorn Hope groups to begin their silent assault.

Peter and his nineteen comrades began to trudge across the last bit of swamp and marshland. Even though it was low tide, the earth remained sodden, and the muck clung to their boots. Every time Peter tried to take another step, there was a sucking sound as he removed first one foot, then another, from the soaked dirt. It was especially difficult for him to move his left leg, as the pain reminded him that he was carrying a British musket ball high in his thigh.

211

The plan had called for the Forlorn Hope to use axes to cut through the abatis. The hope was that the diversionary fire and the British response would cover up any noise from the axes. But when Peter arrived first at the obstruction, he threw his axe away, lowered his shoulder, dug in his heels, and with all of his might and power pushed the pointed spears and logs out of the way. It took quite the effort but before long, Peter had cleared a path about ten feet wide.

Immediately Peter and the others in his advanced group began making their way up an exposed abatis point. He let out a muffled scream, but it was enough noise to alert the British troops above them. Withering musket fire rained down on them, and several of the men accompanying Peter fell. He took hold of his musket strapped across his back with its bayonet already attached as per instructions.

As the regiment reached the first perimeter of defense, one of the British soldiers had just finished reloading. Swinging the muzzle in Peter's direction, he failed to notice that the Portuguese, with his long legs, covered the last few paces more quickly than the soldier had anticipated. Peter stood above him and ruthlessly drove his bayonet completely though the man's neck. The soldier dropped his weapon and clutched at his throat, and his eyes grew wide. At the pace of his own racing heart, blood spurted from the wound that had severed his carotid artery. He lived only moments longer.

The hand-to-hand combat became even fiercer, and Peter waded in among the British soldiers wielding his sharp-pointed weapon, dealing death and ungodly wounds with every step he took.

Having eliminated most of the defenders of the first ring of British defense, Peter and the remainder of his commandoes continued to charge up toward the second embankment. Again, a fusillade of musket balls filled the air with deadly lead. More comrades fell all around Peter, but even though he was at the front of the attack, it was almost as if there was a guardian angel protecting him from the deadly fire.

Peter and a French nobleman by the name of Lt. Colonel Francois de Fleury were rapidly approaching the British upper works of the fort. Fleury and Francisco had met back at Middlebrook and had become friends because of the Virginian's relationship with Lafayette. Now the two of them were racing for a cash prize -- Washington had offered a bounty for the first soldier to breach the British upper defenses. The first man over the defense was to collect five hundred dollars. The second man would collect four hundred, the prize decreasing by a rate of one hundred dollars down to the fifth man.

As they reached the second line of defense, three soldiers jumped up and leveled their guns at Peter, Fleury and another man who was with them. Their effort wasn't very well coordinated, as all three musket balls cut down the third man in their advancing party. His reward would have to be collected in heaven.

Fleury chose the grenadier on the right and drove his bayonet deep into the man's chest. Peter had to contend with the remaining two soldiers. The first was dispatched with a bayonet thrust to the stomach. As Peter tried to remove his weapon, the blade ripped a gaping hole in the soldier and his entrails spilled to the ground. The other soldier turned his weapon toward Peter. Like the earlier British trooper, he had fired his weapon but had no time to reload, but his bayonet was ready. However, as he swung his weapon in a sweeping arc, the bayonet fell harmlessly to the ground, for in his haste the soldier had not attached it properly.

The two men, Peter and the soldier, were momentarily stunned, though it seemed like an eternity to both of them. Just before the grenadier could react, Peter brought the butt end of his musket around and caught his combatant square on the jaw. As the soldier's head spun by the force of the blow, Peter noticed small white objects spew from the grenadier's mouth, presumably teeth. The man crumpled to the ground writhing in pain, and then he lay still.

The extra time Peter had taken fighting the second Redcoat had cost him one hundred dollars in reward money, as Fleury had already scaled the last embankment. Yet the money had never been Peter's primary objective. In all the battles in which he had fought, Peter had always wanted to capture a British Union Jack.

Fleury was now engaged with another British trooper when Francisco spotted the British flagpole. His eyes drifted upwards in the night sky. He couldn't make out the flag in the darkness, but he could hear the distinctive sound of it flapping in the breeze as the howling winds picked up even more.

A lone sentry guarding the pole was looking in the other direction, while Wayne's men were now entering the fort from the opposite side. The sentry must have sensed Peter's advance, because at the last moment he turned and slashed at Peter with his bayonet. Unlike earlier, this bayonet was firmly attached and it caught Peter across the midsection, opening a nine-inch gash. Peter clutched at the wound for just a moment, then, being too close to use his own weapon, he dropped his musket, grabbed the man in a bear hug and literally squeezed the life out of him. Still ignoring his wound, he grabbed at the rope to which the flag was attached and lowered it from the pole. Once within his reach, he grabbed the flag and held it to his stomach that was bleeding profusely. He then dropped to his knees still clutching the flag. He could hear shouts of "The fort's our own!" a signal that was to indicate the success of the Americans.

As he lay there holding onto his prize, Peter spoke his last words before passing out, "Susannah…Susannah!"

Two days later, he awoke in the hospital ward of West Point. His friend, Lafayette, was standing next to his bed holding Peter's massive hand in his own. Behind him was General George Washington. There was a doctor on the opposite side of the bed looking at the wound that he had attended to when Peter was first brought there.

"*Mon ami,* you are truly a lucky man. You and Fleury were the only two from your group to make it out of Stony Point alive. I'm starting to wonder just how many angels are watching over you, *mon ami.* Rest well. Just like with all your other injuries, you'll be better soon, I'm sure."

Washington then addressed the doctor. "Make sure he gets the best of care. This man is the Hercules of the Revolution, and we can ill afford to lose such a great soldier."

Peter drifted back to sleep with Washington's words subtly ringing in his ears, "This man is the Hercules of the Revolution." The Union Jack, with his own blood still on it, lay across the foot of his bed.

14

A RETURN TO VIRGINIA

After a few weeks of bed rest at West Point, Peter was sent to Fishkill, New York to finish recuperating from his wounds. Later, he participated in a number of small battles throughout New York, and New Jersey, but, for all intents and purposes, the Battle at Stony Point ended the war in the north, and in December of 1779, Peter's enlistment of three years had come to an end.

Peter had served with distinction. He had become recognized as one of the very best soldiers ever in the Colonial Army. He had suffered and survived that horrible winter at Valley Forge, had seen some of his friends die terrible deaths, and had been wounded three times, still carrying a British musket ball in his left thigh. He had done his duty and had come to the decision that it was now the time for others to do the fighting. He longed for Virginia, and he ached for the sight and the touch of Susannah Anderson.

At his last posting in Morristown, Peter found his old friend and mountain man, John Allen. Since his enlistment was also completed, he had come to the same decision as Peter, and now he was headed home -- not to the sweeping valleys and rolling hills of eastern Virginia, but to the never-ending expanse of the Shenandoahs. Despite their vastly different destinations, however, the two determined that they would travel together down the east coast before John headed in a more westerly direction.

Before his departure, Peter also came across another old friend, the Marquis de Lafayette. Just one day before he and Allen were to leave, Peter was exiting his hut when he saw Lafayette riding toward him.

"*Mon ami, mon ami*," Lafayette shouted. "I was afraid you would leave before I could see you again. You are going home to Virginia, is that not right?"

"Yes, my friend," replied Peter. "I'm going home. I've fought for three years, and I've been wounded, and…"

Lafayette cut Peter off. "You need not explain anything to me. I shall miss you -- the army shall miss you -- but you have done your duty, and you need not apologize to me or make excuses to any man." There was a long pause and when Lafayette spoke again, his voice cracked. "I shall always be proud to call you my friend."

"Thank you. I had hoped that you would understand. I just feel guilty that the fighting is not finished."

"Of course, you do, but who among us can predict when that day will come? Next year? The year after? Who knows? But it is time for you to go home. Go home to lovely Susannah, and take her for your own. Just don't forget, you are to invite me to your wedding. Tell me when the glorious occasion is to take place and even if I am in pitch battle with the lobster backs, I shall break off the attack and rush to your side, *mon ami.*"

"I'll let you know as soon as I know," replied Peter. "Now, let's find a tavern, drink a couple of beers and talk about our adventures."

The two men laughed as they walked into town and spent the evening regaling each other with one tall story after another. By the time they had finished and dawn was breaking, they had both killed about twice as many British soldiers as had even been sent to the continent.

Overnight a fresh snow had fallen. Lafayette bent down, gathered up a quantity in his hand and formed a snowball that he immediately unleashed on an unsuspecting Peter. Peter, not to surrender so easily, did the same; soon the Frenchman and the Portuguese, who had become joined by a common conflict in a new world, were in a full blown snowball fight, laughing like a couple of teenagers, which wasn't very far from the truth.

With arms slung over each other's shoulders, the two strode into camp to find John Allen waiting for Peter. He had two horses saddled and ready to go. The army, in honor of all men completing their enlistment, gave each a horse for their respective journeys home. Peter's few belongings were secured to the saddle.

Acknowledging Lafayette, John said, "It's good to see you again, General."

To which Lafayette replied, "It's good to see you too, Mr. Allen."

Turning his attention to Peter, John continued. "You look awful."

"Think nothing of it," said Peter. "I think I probably feel worse than I look."

"Well, the road is long, and we ain't makin' any headway standin' here," said John, mounting his horse.

Peter turned to Lafayette. "I can't be sure when our paths will cross again, but know that I look forward to that day." He then took the Frenchman by the arms and gave him a kiss on each cheek.

Lafayette stood there speechless as Peter climbed aboard his mount. Peter looked down and said, "Goodbye, monami." He never had gotten the pronunciation quite right. "I shall miss you."

"Goodbye, *mon ami*. I feel in my heart that we shall be together again sooner than you think."

Peter and John yanked the reins of their horses and set off on a southerly course. After they had ridden only thirty yards, John looked over at his companion. "What in the world was that all about?"

"Whatever do you mean?" said Peter, faking ignorance.

"Well, unless my eyes have gone bad, you just up and kissed the general back there."

"Oh, did I? I guess you have to be French to understand."

Both men broke out laughing. Peter had laughed a lot over the past several hours, and the scar on his stomach began to hurt -- but it was a good hurt.

During the rest of the trip, John and Peter shared stories about their respective battles both won and lost. The December weather was miserable, and it brought back memories of Valley Forge for both of them. As they skirted west of Baltimore, a vicious snowstorm caught them, and they had to make camp for a couple of days before pushing on. As they crossed into Virginia, it was soon apparent that the time had come for the two men to go their separate ways.

"Peter Francisco," John said, "it's been an honor to know you. You're truly the Virginia Giant, and I'll always be grateful for knowin' you."

"The honor has been all mine. Stay well, my friend. Stay safe, and stay away from any of them Redcoats. But if you do see any, shoot them down like the cur dogs they are."

"I'll try to do my best. Goodbye, Peter."

"Goodbye, John...and good hunting in your mountains."

Peter sat astride his horse as he watched the first friend he had ever had in the army head west -- west to a country of mountains and streams, but a country that still wasn't really theirs.

****

The next couple of weeks couldn't pass quickly enough for Peter as he headed home. Initially he thought that he was obligated to stop at Hunting Tower first. At least that was what his mind was saying. His heart was telling him to head directly to the Anderson farm. As usual with most young men, the heart won the battle.

221

With the approach of mid-morning, Peter arrived at the front of the main house of the Anderson plantation and found himself all alone; not a soul was in sight. He dismounted, walked up the steps where he and Susannah had last embraced, and knocked on the door. Nobody answered. He went around to the back of the house where Susannah had been tending the garden on the day they last saw each other. Still, Peter could see no one. To his immediate left, he heard some noises coming from the barn. He walked to the open door, and there she was. Susannah was tending to the Anderson horses, four of them. She appeared to be giving them a ration of oats, and her attention was completely on her task. Using his training as an elite Forlorn Hope soldier, Peter walked silently up behind her. As she turned to retrieve more food for the horses, she bumped right into the tall figure. Looking up, she started to scream, "Pet…"

He didn't wait for her to finish the second syllable. He wrapped his strong arms around her, pulled her closer, leaned down to meet her lips and kissed her. The last time they had kissed, more than three years previously, he had been so gentle. Not this time. His kiss was hard and long. Susannah returned the kiss in equal strength. Peter felt as though he could feel her heart beating against his chest, and he hoped that she could feel his as well. It seemed a lifetime passed as they held the embrace and the kiss, and neither of them cared a bit. The world around them no longer existed. In the entire universe, they were alone with each other.

Finally, they could sustain the kiss and the embrace no longer, and ever so slightly, they pulled away from each other.

"Peter, my dear Peter. How I've longed for you," Susannah whispered. Then she stepped back to look up at him. "Peter, why did you

222

not write that you were coming home?" she almost scolded. Glancing down she continued without drawing a breath, "I must look a sight. You always seem to catch me at my worst." Trying to tidy herself, she brushed both dirt and wrinkles from her dress, but her attention was on him more than herself. "Oh, Peter, I've missed you so much." Her words were coming so fast that he thought he was listening to a female Lafayette. To Peter, she didn't look at all drab in her aproned blue dress with course shawl around her shoulders. Quite to the contrary, he couldn't remember that she had ever looked more beautiful.

"I have missed you too, my dear. Truly I have. You cannot possibly know how much I've thought of you, wanted to be able to touch you, to kiss you, to hold you in my arms. If there's anything right in this world, I will never have to leave your side again. I love you so much."

Susannah seemed to change the subject. "Come inside with me, Peter. I'm sure Father will want to see you. He's in the house."

"He is? I knocked on the door but no one came to answer. Is it possible that he didn't hear me?"

"No," she said slowly. "I'm sure he heard you. He has only recently returned from the fighting in Georgia, but he's changed...he's changed so much. He was wounded in the leg, which I know causes him considerable pain; now he walks with a limp. But I fear that is not the worst of it. He won't talk about it, but I fear he has seen things that no man should have to witness, just as I am sure you have, The poor man suffers so. There are nights when he actually screams until he awakens himself."

"What of your brothers? Where are they?"

223

"Thomas went with Father to fight in Georgia, and he remains there to this day. James, Jr. joined him when Father returned. The idea was that one of the menfolk would always remain here at the Mansion to keep the plantation running, but when James, Jr. left, Father seemed to sink deeper and deeper within himself. Look around. Our lovely farm has fallen into such disrepair…" Susannah's voice trailed off.

Peter glanced around him. When he had first arrived, he was so excited to see Susannah that he hadn't noticed the rundown condition of everything. The fields had been poorly kept. A wagon just to the side of the barn had not one but two broken wheels. Boards were falling from the sides of the barn as well as from the main house.

"And what of your mother?" Peter inquired.

"She's visiting the Morgan's farm just up the road. A number of our slaves have run off, and the Morgan's have more than they need. She's hoping to rent some for the spring planting season -- that is, if she can negotiate a reasonable price. I'm sure she'll be home directly."

Peter and Susannah began to walk toward the main house. He looked down to find that she had slipped her small, delicate hand in his rough, oversized one. "This is as it should be," he thought to himself.

When the two of them entered the house and scanned the parlor, James Anderson was nowhere in sight.

"Father," Susannah said in a loud voice. "Father, where are you?" There was no answer in return. "He must be in the kitchen," she commented. "He spends a lot of time there."

Susannah led Peter to the back of the house. She led Peter to the back of the house where, as she had predicted, they found James Anderson was sitting at the kitchen table drinking some tea. He gazed out the window appearing to be surveying his property but actually seeing nothing.

"Father, look who is here. Look who has come home."

The elderly gentleman turned his head. His eyes looked lifeless, but when he got a good look at Peter, the life came back into them, and he rose to his feet unsteadily, holding onto the back of the chair. "Peter. Peter, my boy. You've come home. It's great to see you. Oh, it is good to see you. We've heard a lot about your exploits in the northern army in behalf of our cause. I surely wish I had had someone like you in Georgia."

Peter walked over to Susannah's father and extended his hand. "It's good to see you, too, sir. Susannah says you have not been feeling well."

"Oh it's nothing, nothing at all. I just need to rest a bit." It was the same excuse that James Anderson had been giving ever since arriving back at The Mansion several months ago. Peter, I would like to talk more with you about the war, but for now, I think I need to lie down and rest a bit. You two go and enjoy each other's company."

As her father shuffled across the room, Susannah took Peter through the back door and hand-in-hand, gave him a guided tour of the plantation, showing him even more evidence of the decay that now visited the once proud farm. A small group of cattle wandered aimlessly in a pasture surrounded by a fence with posts tilted at all sorts of odd angles.

"It's just been so hard. We only have half the slaves that we did when the war began. Things are just falling apart here," Susannah mourned, looking up into Peter's eyes.

"Let me ask you something," Peter broke in. "Is your father's offer still good? Would he still want me to stay here rather than go back to Hunting Tower?"

"Oh, yes, Peter. Yes, I'm sure he would be ever most grateful."

"Then that's what I'll do. I'll go and inform Judge Winston immediately."

"Peter, must you leave so soon? Please stay the night. Mother would never forgive me if I were to let you leave before she saw you again and gave you something to eat. You look a sight. Why, I'll bet you haven't had a decent meal in weeks. And you and Father can talk tomorrow. I'm certain he'd be ever so appreciative having a man to talk to. Please say that you will stay. Please."

Convincing him wasn't difficult. The home-cooked meal sounded inviting, but being near to Susannah was the deciding factor. "I would be honored."

When Mrs. Anderson arrived, she was delighted to see Peter and gave him a welcoming, motherly kiss on the cheek, appropriate for any returning soldier. Peter's mind flashed back to the kisses he had received from Lafayette. "Show Peter where he can sit and relax, then come help me in the kitchen, Susannah. Tonight, we shall dine properly."

Susannah directed Peter back to the parlor, where he selected what appeared to be the most comfortable chair, and within moments he was fast asleep. Susannah went to join her mother in the kitchen.

Winter's early darkness had enveloped the plantation when someone's nudging him on the arm startled Peter. Waking with a start, his instinct was to reach for a weapon, but when he opened his eyes more fully, there stood Susannah leaning over him and smiling.

"Dinner is ready, my darling. Wait till you see. Mother has prepared quite a feast in honor of your homecoming. And Father...well, he seems quite refreshed. I told him that you would be staying with us, and that appears to have picked up his spirits."

The two of them walked into the dining room where, indeed, the pungent odors of a wonderful meal wafted toward them and an abundant meal lay before them. Mr. Anderson, seated at the head of the table, smiled when the couple entered the room. "Come and join us, Peter. I daresay that my wife is the best cook in Cumberland County. Let's eat. Then, you and I have much to talk about."

Feast they did, as the head of the household continually prompted his guest to tell them stories of his adventures with the northern army. Peter did so willingly, though he was hesitant to talk about any of his personal accomplishments and left out entirely some of the more harrowing moments.

After dinner, Peter and Mr. Anderson retired to the parlor for a few puffs of tobacco. The older man preferred a pipe while the younger settled for a hand-rolled Virginia cigar. Although Peter wanted to spend more time with Susannah, he knew that there would be time enough for that. For now, he sensed that the family patriarch needed to talk to someone -- a man who had seen what he had been through. They talked for hours, well past the normal bedtime in the Anderson household, but through it all, Mr. Anderson seemed to be renewed and reinvigorated. By the end of the conversation, Peter and he were talking about all the things that they could do to restore The Mansion to her days of pre-war glory.

Peter was grateful when Susannah finally came into the room, for his short nap had not been nearly long enough to relieve the weariness of his long journey home.

"Father," she said, rescuing their guest, "Peter has traveled a long way in the past few weeks. I'm sure he'd like some rest."

"Yes, yes. Of course," he concurred. "I've kept you up far too long. You go now and get some rest."

Peter got up from his chair, but not sure where he was to go, he looked at Susannah questioningly.

"Mother says you are to sleep in my brothers' room." Carrying a lamp, she led Peter up the stairs to the second floor, stopping at a closed door. "I'm sure you'll find this quite comfortable."

Peter bent down, looked at Susannah's sparkling blue eyes and was just about to kiss her when they both heard her father's awkward gait on the stairs. It reminded Peter of the one-legged pirate from so long ago.

They pulled away from each other as James reached the top of the stairs. He tugged at Susannah's sleeve. "Now you let young Peter get some rest. You'll have plenty of time to talk tomorrow."

Susannah followed her father on down the hall while Peter opened the door to Thomas' and James' room. It was totally dark, but as his eyes became accustomed to the dark, he could make out twin beds. He chose the closest one, laid down and fell into a dreamless sleep.

The next morning, Peter awoke to the glow of the sun breaking through the sheer curtains on the one window to this bedroom. At first he was momentarily disoriented. Could this be the room he had slept in at the Dickenson farm? Shaking his head, Peter recalled his surroundings.

His thoughts drifted back to the conversations he'd had with Susannah and her father just the day before, and he knew that his decision to live with the Andersons was the right one.

As he walked downstairs, Peter guessed he was probably the first one up, but he was quite surprised when he entered the kitchen to find Susannah and her mother preparing a breakfast of ham and eggs. James sat in the same chair where Peter had first seen him the day before, but his posture was indicative of the broken man he had encountered the day before.

Susannah was the first to notice Peter standing in the doorway. "Good morning, dear," she said, suddenly realizing that she had used a term of endearment in front of her parents. She hoped they hadn't noticed. "Ah... good morning, Peter," she repeated, trying to sound platonic. "I trust you slept well."

"Indeed, I did. It's been three years or more since I've slept as well."

Mr. Anderson looked toward the man joining them. "Peter, good morning. It's a new dawn for us all and a new dawn for The Mansion. We have much to talk about and plans to make."

"Yes, sir, I know. But today I must go to Hunting Tower and address Judge Winston. He treated me well, and he gave me my freedom, and he said I would always have a home at Hunting Tower. If I am to decline his offer, I must do it face-to-face, and the sooner the better."

"I understand, Peter. Judge Winston is a good man and a good friend, though we've had our differences in the past. You go to Hunting Tower after we have eaten and make known your plans. We can talk later."

After the delicious breakfast and engaging conversation, Peter went outside to saddle his horse and Susannah quickly followed. As he cinched the saddle, he turned toward her. "Do you really think your father understands about us...about..."

"I just don't know for sure. I think he understands our strong feelings for each other. Yet I also believe that he clings to the notion that I will marry George Carrington; that's the man I wrote you about. Our families have known each other for a long time, and I've known George since I was a little girl. He's a cavalry officer, you know."

"Do you love him?"

"No." The word was emphatic. "Father just wants me to marry him because he comes from a wealthy family, but I...I have feelings for you, my dear Peter," she said almost shyly yet confidently.

"Then I will return and make my case for your hand to your father. I love you, Susannah, and now I feel I have the right to say that."

"I love you, too, Peter. I truly do." Her face showed her concern when she added, "But Father will not be so easy to convince."

Peter lifted himself onto his horse and eased himself down on the saddle. "Don't worry," he assured her. "I have fought bigger battles." Then he tugged at the reins and headed his horse toward Buckingham County and Hunting Tower. Since he wasn't sure how the judge would react to his decision, he took his time and didn't hurry, letting his horse dictate the pace, allowing himself time to ponder the situation.

"Things look almost the same," he mused when he arrived at Hunting Tower, reflecting on its appearance when he had left, three years prior to this homecoming, He observed the barn, where he had spent so many hours with Arthur, and noticed Alfred coming through the doors.

He had returned as slave master, and perhaps that was why everything looked so normal.

Alfred walked over to offer a hearty handshake as the returning friend dismounted. "Peter Francisco. You've come home," he greeted with a sincere smile. "The judge will be happy to see you. We've all heard so much about you." That was the second time someone had said that, and Peter was a bit surprised. He had not realized what a hero he had become throughout the area.

At almost the same moment, Petunia, the trusted slave who had taught him to speak and understand English, came around the corner, the very same corner she had rounded when first she laid eyes on Peter. She broke into a run and flung herself at the Virginia Giant, landing in his arms with her feet dangling several inches off the ground. "Peter, Peter, Peter. You is back. You is back. The judge, he shore be happy to see you again."

"The judge is in town attending to some business, but I 'spect he'll be home soon," Alfred broke in.

"I'm supposin' you heard about Arthur?" Petunia inquired.

"Yes. Yes, I did," replied Peter softly. "Where did they bury him?"

"He be over yonder at the back of the hemp fields. Come on. I'll take you there. He shore loved you, Peter Francisco. When you left, it near broke his heart."

Peter followed Petunia as they walked through the now barren field awaiting the next year's planting of hemp. After several minutes, they arrived at a patch of grass with a solitary rock. Inscribed there were the words "Faithful slave and friend." Peter looked at Petunia.

"The judge had Richard carve them words on there." Petunia figured that Peter still hadn't learned to read, so she read them for him.

Turning to Petunia, Peter asked, "Would you wait here for just a minute."

"Sure, Peter, sure. What's you gonna do?

"This rock isn't finished." He walked back to the barn and returned with a hammer and chisel. Slowly and with the help of Petunia, he set about carving on the rock. When he finished, it read, "Faithful slave and friend and father." Laying his tools aside, he bent down again, reached out and touched the rock once more, and bowed his head. A single tear splashed on the word "father." Then, having closed that chapter of their lives, Peter and Petunia walked back to the barn in silence.

Not long after that, Judge Winton's carriage came rolling up. Peter walked out to open the door as he had done on so many occasions, and when the judge looked out the door, he was flabbergasted.

"Peter. Peter Francisco. Peter! When did you get here?" The judge was almost ecstatic. "Good Lord, boy, it's good to see you. How are you? Did you have a good trip? What was it like in the war?" Peter was a bit amused at how people always asked a string of questions without waiting for any answers. "Come into the house," the judge continued. "It's too cold to stand out here and talk."

Together the two men walked up the steps and entered the house. It struck Peter as strange that he had spent about ten years of his life on this plantation, yet he had been inside the main house only a few times. On the other hand, he had actually slept in the main house of the Anderson home, and it was only his second visit there. As they sat in the parlor, Peter tried his best to remember all the questions Judge Winston had asked. "I got to the Anderson home yesterday and spent the night with them," he volunteered.

The judge's eyes grew wary with suspicion. Were the Andersons, using their daughter as bait, trying to lure one of the best workers Hunting Tower had ever seen? Trying not to let his misgivings become obvious, the judge interrupted. "I'm sure you were tired by the time you got there, so you needed a rest before coming home. But you're home now, and that's all that matters." His voice was resolute.

Peter went on to tell the judge about the war. He told him about training in the Shenandoahs, fighting at Brandywine, Germantown, Valley Forge, and just about everything he could remember. Again, however, he declined to discuss his own heroics or provide some of the more gruesome details.

Finally, he could no longer avoid the subject that he sensed was going to upset the judge. "I know that when I went off to war, sir, you said I would always have a home here at Hunting Tower. I want you to know how much I appreciate that. But," he ventured, "the Andersons need me even more than you do. The two Anderson boys are off fighting in Georgia. Mr. Anderson is not well. Most of their slaves have run off, and the whole place is just falling apart. For these reasons, I've decided to return to The Mansion to help them in any way I can."

"What? You can't be serious. This is your home. Hunting Tower is your home," spoke the judge loudly. "I'll not hear of it." Then, getting control, he added more calmly, "And if it's that Anderson girl who has you thinking about this, I can tell you right now that James Anderson has his plans for her already made. She's to marry the Carrington boy. Now, let's stop all this foolish talk. Hunting Tower is your home, and here is where you'll stay...and that's my final decision."

"No sir. That's not your decision to make. When I left, you granted me my freedom. I just spent the last three years fighting for freedom, both yours and mine. The decision is mine to make and as much as I'm grateful for all the kindnesses you've shown me, I'll be moving to the Andersons."

The judge slammed his hand on the table. "Then get out. Get out! Get off this plantation and don't come back. You ingrate...after all I've done for you. I took you into my home. I treated you like a son. I never want to see you again. Get out, and take everything that belongs to you with you. Get out now, or I'll have Alfred escort you off the property."

Peter felt the mingling of hurt and anger over this unexpected rejection rising from deep inside him. He wanted to dispute that the judge had taken him into his home. He had slept in an attached shack, after all. And he surely was never treated like the judge's sons. But Peter managed to control his temper. "I'm sorry you feel that way, Judge Winston. I surely am, but this is something I must do."

Peter stood up, walked out the front door and strode behind the main house into the room that he and Arthur had made together for him so long ago. Looking around, it was exactly as he had left it, sparsely furnished with just a bed and dresser. Atop the dresser was the tri-corner hat that Mr. Anderson had given him for his act of gallantry. He rummaged through the dresser drawers. There were only a couple of shirts worth taking...that and his hat. Gathering up his few things, Peter walked around to the front of the main house. His horse stood there still saddled, since he had been there only a few hours.

Alfred came out of the barn and walked over to where Peter was just about to climb onto the animal. "The judge says I'm to throw you off the plantation," he said in a monotone, "though I don't know how in the world I'd do it." He paused, looked into Peter's deep, black eyes and added, "I'll miss you. I was looking forward to having you back. Good luck to you." Then he offered a farewell handshake.

"Thank you. I'm sorry the judge feels the way he does," Peter said, looking down at the ground. Then, responding to Alfred's gesture, he replied, "Good bye."

He rode away from the plantation with mixed emotions. All he had wanted was to return home from three years of fighting and hear his father say, "I'm so proud of you, son!" But that moment in time had been stolen by the pirates some fourteen years earlier. Now, he at least hoped that Judge Winston would be proud of his efforts toward freedom for the colonists, and that he would understand Peter's freedom to make his own decisions. The last thing he wanted to return to was a hornet's nest.

Although he anticipated the prospect of living with the Andersons, as well as the prospect of a future marriage, he was upset at how the judge had reacted. This had been his home for the majority of his life, and he would miss everything about it. He would also miss Judge Winston.

15

PETER AND SUSANNAH

As Peter directed his horse toward The Mansion, it started to snow. At first it was just a few flurries, then falling more thickly until the green blanket of forest floor began to take on a tone of white. Within just a few more miles, Peter could barely make out the trail. He protectively pulled his coat tighter, the one that Lafayette had purchased for him while he had recuperated at Yellow Springs Military Hospital in Valley Forge. He was also thankful that Susannah had given him one of Thomas's scarves, and he wound it tightly around his neck. The day had begun with moderate temperatures, but unsuspectingly the cold had come back with a vengeance, and with it came one of the most powerful snowstorms of the winter.

Though he was still miles away from the Anderson plantation, Peter could now hardly see the mane of the horse on which he was riding. Finally and regretfully, he knew he could go no farther. He found a clearing, much like the one where he had slept on the night he first set out to join the army. He had no hobbles for his horse, so he unsaddled her and wrapped her reins under a large, fallen tree. He cleared away a patch of snow until he reached a bed of pine needles, then, using the saddle as a pillow once again. He covered himself as well as he could with the needles, for insulation from the cold, and fell asleep, thinking for a few moments of that bitter winter at Valley Forge as well as all that had happened over the past two days. He knew that he loved Susannah, and he thought she felt just as deeply about him. Everything she had said, everything she had done, told him that. Susannah's father was another matter altogether. Judge Winston's reaction to Peter's news saddened him more deeply than he thought it would. He hoped that someday the judge would reconsider. Sleep finally came, and snow almost completely covered the giant who lay sleeping on the forest floor.

By early morning, Peter could barely lift himself underneath the blanket of new fallen, very wet snow. The forest was so quiet that, except for the rumblings of his empty stomach, the silence could almost ring in a man's ears. Since he had brought no provisions, he simply got his horse ready for the trip and was on his way again. The path had disappeared under the thick layer of white, but at least it had stopped snowing, and Peter was soon able to discern where the trail was. At around noon, he finally arrived at The Mansion. Before he could even bring his horse to a halt, Susannah was rushing out the door.

"Peter, Peter," she cried. "We were so worried about you. I stayed up all night waiting for you to return."

As Peter climbed down stiffly, Susannah continued on. "I was so afraid that Judge Winston had convinced you to stay on at Hunting Tower. Then, when it began to snow, I thought you might have gotten lost and froze to death."

"Calm down, Susannah," Peter said soothingly, seeing the distress in her blue eyes. "I told you I would be coming back, and here I am. The judge did expect me to stay, and he was furious when I told him of my decision to return here. In fact, he threw me off the plantation and said he never wants to see me again."

"Oh, Peter. I'm so sorry. I know you felt genuine appreciation and respect for the judge and loved Hunting Tower. I'm just so sorry it ended like that."

Peter, wanting to divert her comments, reassured her, "As for me getting lost and freezing to death, I found my way home from the war, didn't I? And I spent a lot colder nights at Valley Forge than the one last night."

Susannah sensed his annoyance, perhaps from the combination of cold and hunger, and said, "Never mind all that. I'm just glad that you're back. Have you had anything to eat?"

"I ate yesterday...you remember...at breakfast." A smile flashed across his face.

"Then you must be about half starved. Come on, let's get you something nice and hot." After taking his horse to the barn and tending to her care and feeding, Peter and Susannah headed for the main house. He found that his arm had slipped around her waist. It felt good.

At the end of that day, the whole of them, Peter and the Andersons, retired early as none of them had slept very well the previous

239

night. Once again, Susannah had escorted Peter to his bedroom door. This time, James Anderson was already in bed. She turned her face up to Peter, and the lantern light made her eyes look even bluer.

This time, Peter did not hesitate. He leaned forward, wrapped his long arms around her smallness and drew her closer. Their kiss was not nearly as innocent as it had been on the porch before he had left to fight. Nor was it as hard as when he had found her in the barn on his return. But this kiss had a passion all its own. Susannah's lips tasted so sweet and so tender, Peter secretly hoped that the moment would never end. Secretly, she hoped for the same. When they drew back at last, Peter just looked at the lovely young lady, and she at him.

Finally, Susannah broke the silence. "Sleep well, Peter."

"A kiss like that will find me dreaming the dreams of angels. Good night, my love."

The next morning, Susannah awoke early, but apparently not nearly early enough. Peering out the window, she could see the barn already lit with a lantern and two shadows playing around in the dim light. Wrapping herself in a large overcoat, she made her way through crunching snow to the barn and looked around the corner inside. Peter and her father were talking. Mr. Anderson also appeared to be writing on a small piece of paper. When Susannah entered, both men looked up.

She pretended to be angry. "And just what is it that the two of you are plotting out here in the near dead of night?" She even tapped her foot on the barn dirt to complete the picture of feigned irritation.

"Susannah," her father said. "What do you mean? Peter and I are making a list of materials we need. He says we need an anvil, and hammers and all sorts of things so that he can begin to make repairs around the place."

"Good morning, Susannah." It was Peter who spoke now.

"Good morning, Peter," she replied. "Alright, both of you. Finish your list and then come into the house. Mother and I will have breakfast for you in just a few minutes."

Of course, both men became fully engrossed in what they were doing and when breakfast had been prepared, Susannah had to yell for the men from the back door. As she watched her father and Peter head toward the house, she noticed her father, though still limping, had a renewed spring in his step. Looking at Peter, for the first time she noticed that he, too, limped, favoring his left leg. She made a mental note to ask him about it later.

As the four of them ate, James and Peter talked excitedly about plans for effecting repairs at the plantation. Later that day, the two men hitched up the one, good, remaining wagon and set off for town. If Susannah hadn't known better, she might have become jealous that her father was taking all of Peter's time. Deep inside, however, she knew it was for the best. The closer her father and Peter became, the easier it would be for James to accept Peter as her love.

Throughout the rest of the winter, Peter worked like a mad man on a mission, rising well before dawn and working well past dark. As had been the case at Hunting Tower, Peter was making fine music with his hammer and anvil. The broken wagon wheels had been repaired. In fact, all the wheels on wagons and carriages had been re-rimmed. The fence had been fixed as he worked side-by-side with the remaining slaves, who took well to Peter's instructions. Boards had been replaced on the main house as well as on the barn. He even made time to fix up the slave quarters, having always believed that the more comfortable they were, the harder they would work when the time came.

And when it came time for the spring planting, the slaves repaid Peter's humanitarian efforts. Although they were far fewer in number than before the war, they accomplished the work in a timely fashion, as they were anxious to show how much they had appreciated his kindnesses. As for Peter, he worked harder than any four men and was especially adept at plowing the fields with or without the assistance of a horse.

One morning in early May, Peter came downstairs to find that Susannah had actually awakened earlier than he had and was sitting at the kitchen table. He noticed a woven basket sitting there also.

"Susannah, what are you doing up so early?" Peter asked.

"You and I are going on a picnic today," she said matter-of-factly.

"I can't go. I have far too much to do today."

"Nonsense. You have worked seven days a week for the past three months. Today, you are taking me on a picnic, and there will be no more discussion about it." Her tone was decisive.

"But what about your father? We had plans to go into town for more supplies."

"My father knows of my plans, and he approves."

"But what about breakfast?" Peter was running out of excuses, although the thought of spending the day with Susannah sounded most appealing.

"I have made some biscuits and preserves for us to eat along the way."

Giving up on his half-hearted arguments, Peter had one more question. "Do you prefer an open carriage or an enclosed carriage?"

"If you think for one minute that I want to ride in back in an enclosed carriage while you drive us to a picnic, you are sadly mistaken," Susannah playfully protested.

As Peter went out the back door to get horses hitched to a carriage, he bent down and kissed Susannah on the top of the head. When he did, he took a deep breath, inhaling the sweet lilac scent of her hair. This was going to be a wonderful spring day.

When Peer had the carriage ready, Susannah walked over and Peter took the basket from her, placing it on the floor in the back. Momentarily, he held the door open, and Susannah glared at him. "I told you I wanted to sit up front with you."

"Indeed, you did." In a single motion, he swept her off her feet and deposited her ever so gently on the passenger's side of the seat.

"Peter, you could have thrown me clear to the other side."

"Yes, I could have...but I didn't," he joshed, and the two of them broke out in wide smiles. Indeed, it was going to be a great day. Peter headed the horses down the trail and away from The Mansion.

Traveling along, he came to a spot he recognized well. It was where he had sought refuge the night he had been caught in that brutal winter storm on the way back from Hunting Tower. He drew the horses to a halt and went around to the other side of the carriage, where he lifted Susannah out of her seat and softly set her down as though she were a feather in his hands. As he reached into the carriage to retrieve the picnic

243

basket, Susannah asked him how he had known about this spot. "Have you had another young lady here?" she teasingly questioned.

"No. This is where I slept that winter night when you were wondering where I was."

"Peter, I hope you didn't take me seriously. I was only kidding you."

"Oh," he said sheepishly.

He grabbed a blanket from under the carriage seat, laid it out across the pine straw, perhaps the very straw that had kept him warm just a few months earlier, and the two of them sat on it. Susannah began to remove items from the basket -- several types of meats, breads and some early vegetables. The two lovers ate, joked playfully and giggled. Light streaming through the trees accented the natural highlights of her hair, and Peter could not help but stare at her.

After several moments of silence, Susannah broke the awkwardness. "Whatever in the world are you looking at?"

"Just the most beautiful girl in the whole world."

Susannah's cheeks flushed as Peter reached over to touch her face. He drew her closer and closer. Once again their lips met. She opened her lips ever so slightly, and he could feel her breath in his own mouth. Sensations that Peter had never felt swept over him. He even felt a bit lightheaded. She pressed her mouth tighter to his and he pressed back. She leaned back on the blanket and Peter leaned over her, their lips still joined, their hands caressing each other.

After several minutes, Peter, with his hand still behind Susannah's back, rolled over and looked up at the sun through the branches of the surrounding trees. Susannah rolled slightly toward him and placed her hand on his chest. "Peter, my dear, I don't know what I would have done had you not come back to us. I do love you so much...I do, I do."

"I love you, too. All the time I was away, thinking of you is what made me go on. Had I not known that you were here waiting, I'm not sure I would have had the strength to continue."

Peter sat up and wenr over to the wagon. He returned carrying his satchel -- the one that had been with him every day of the war -- opened it and pulled out its meager contents. There were the letters Susannah had written to him, read to him with the enlisted aid of his friend Lafayette. There was also wrapped around his old shoe buckles the handkerchief that she had given him on the day he departed for war.

"Whenever I prepared for battle, I looked at these things, and that gave me strength."

"Why, Peter, it's so soiled. I must wash it for you."

"No, I don't want you to do that."

"Why not?"

"Because it means so much to me just the way it is. I always want to remember that."

"Oh, Peter," she said. And once again they found themselves locked in an embrace.

It really had been the wonderful day they anticipated, but it was now turning to eventide, and they hastened to gather up their picnic leftovers and other belongings and head back to The Mansion before it became dark. Traveling by horseback along the trail at night was difficult enough. Maneuvering in a carriage was next to impossible, but it wouldn't do for the two of them to spend the night in the forest together.

James Anderson may have been softening, but that would not be at all acceptable.

As June and July passed, the Anderson plantation came back to life. Peter, James, the slaves and even Susannah and her mother all worked long and hard days, but the effort was well worth it. By late summer, it was obvious to everyone that The Mansion would produce the most bountiful crop in several years.

Meanwhile, James and Peter had grown closer and closer. Working with Peter had been good for the elder Anderson physically and, more importantly, emotionally. He was back to his old self and looking forward to each day more than ever.

One particular evening, James came into the barn to find Peter caring for the horses. "Peter," he said. "I can't tell you how much you have come to mean to us...to all of us. I don't think we could have brought the farm back if it hadn't been for you."

"Thank you, sir. It's been a privilege to work at your side. You've treated me like a member of your family, and...and...well." Peter couldn't make his mouth work.

"What is it, my boy? What is it?"

"Mr. Anderson..."

"Please call me James. You've earned the right."

"Mr. Anderson." Peter may have earned the right, but he was uncomfortable accepting it. "Mr. Anderson, I wish to marry your daughter, Susannah. I am asking you for her hand in marriage."

"Well, Peter, I was afraid you would bring this up one day. I do regard you as a son, but Susannah's future is set for her. I told you that she is to marry George Carrington as soon as he returns from the war. He comes from a good and prominent family. Besides, what have you to offer her? You have almost no possessions. You own no land. You have no other work than here at the plantation. Why, you don't even know how to read or write."

"But I will have land. The government has promised 100 acres to all who served. And I am to get a pension. And I will learn to read and write -- I promise that I will."

"Peter, I'll not say absolutely no, at least not yet, but I don't see how you can make it work. I really don't. I know that Susannah has feelings for you, too. I may be old, but I'm not blind. And what I want most of all for her is that she will be happy in her life. For now, though, let's just leave things the way they are and see how the future unfolds."

"Yes, sir. You'll see. I'll do all that I have said I will...you'll see."

"Very well, Peter. Now let's go into the house. Dinner is ready."

James left the barn, while Peter took a few moments more to finish his chores. In one respect, he was crestfallen. He had anticipated that he and Mr. Anderson had become so close that Susannah's father couldn't possibly refuse his request. Yet he understood why there had been hesitation. Ever since he had been kidnapped from his family in the Azores Islands, nothing had been easy. But he had overcome every obstacle, and he would do everything in his power to overcome the obstacles that were now set before him.

Peter did not speak further on the subject with James Anderson, nor did he mention it to Susannah.

In July, he took a wagon to town to fetch some supplies that were badly needed at The Mansion. After he had made his purchases and loaded them on a wagon, he stopped at one of the local taverns, recalling pleasant times with the Marquis de Lafayette. As he entered, he noticed several patrons gathered around a man wearing a Continental Army uniform. It was obvious that they had all been drinking a goodly share of rum. Peter approached and listened from the back for a while. The soldier was obviously a recruiting sergeant trying to talk the patrons into signing up for militias to fight in the southern campaigns. Just then, the sergeant noticed Peter.

"You're Peter Francisco, aren't you?" he queried.

"Why, yes. Yes, I am. How did you know?"

"Mr. Francisco, we've never met, but you're a bit well known, especially at your size."

Chants of "Peter, Peter" rang out from the men who had gathered there.

"Then I guess my secret's out," Peter said with a twinkle in his eye. "You've found me out. I am Peter Francisco."

The sergeant continued. "I was just telling the lads here what an honor it is to serve, as well as some of the side benefits."

One of the others spoke up. "Peter, this guy says we'll get all the rum we want and women, too."

"Well," Peter responded, "you do get a ration of rum, though I doubt it's as much as you can consume, Tommy White." Peter had met this man on numerous trips into town, and it always appeared that he had been consuming great quantities of alcohol of some sort, no matter the time of day. "As for the women, some of the men bring their wives and sweethearts, and there are a few unattached women as well, but…"

Peter's voice was drowned out by a rallying cry of "huzzahs" from the men.

"Tell the lads about what a great life it is," the sergeant spoke up again.

Peter's loyalty to the Continental Army took over. He told the men of campfire tales and tall stories, of the friends made, while omitting the friends lost, of the bravery he had witnessed, while omitting the stories of men in retreat. The men listened intently as if to a Sunday sermon. When Peter finished, the sergeant spoke again.

"Men, General Gates is raising an army to fight in the Carolinas, for if we do not fight there, surely the British will bring the fight to us right here in Virginia. Now, I don't know about you, but I don't want our womenfolk, the fairest anywhere in the world, to be anywhere near the fighting. I'm going to South Carolina. Now who's going with me?"

Every man there began to hoot and howl. Even Peter got caught up in the moment. He thought about Susannah. How would she take it if he went back to the fighting? On the other hand, he thought about what the sergeant had just said, and about Susannah, and about The Mansion, even Hunting Tower. What would happen if the war came here?

As men began signing papers to join the militia, the sergeant clapped Peter on the back. "How about you, Mr. Francisco? Will you join us, too?"

Before he fully understood what was happening, Peter was making his "X" on another piece of paper.

As the late day sun started its slow descent in the west, Peter began the ride back to the Anderson plantation. He wasn't sure how he was going to break the news to Susannah, or to her father, for that matter.

When he arrived back at The Mansion, Susannah, as was her custom, burst out the front door. "Peter, Peter," she called. "Wait till you hear. Thomas has completed his duty. He's coming home. Isn't that the most wonderful news?"

"Why, yes, Susannah. That is wonderful news." In the back of his mind he was relieved to know that Mr. Anderson would have one of his son's back to help with the fall harvest. "I have some news, too."

"What is it?" Susannah asked suspiciously, not really sure she wanted to hear what it was.

"News has come that the British are concentrating their efforts in the Carolinas. I have just enlisted in the militia." Peter read the stunned look on Susannah's face. "I must go, Susannah. I just must. If we don't stop them there, we'll be fighting them right here in Virginia." He wanted to explain more of his decision, but Susannah interrupted.

"No, Peter, no. You can't go. Not now. Not when we are making all our plans. I won't hear of it. I won't hear you speak of it. No, no, no!" She whirled around and headed for the front door.

Peter went inside the house, but she had already gone upstairs, where she flung herself on her bed and wailed. He walked back to the kitchen and found her father sitting in his familiar spot at the table. He went over and sat down opposite of him.

"What is it, my boy?" Anderson inquired. "What is it that sends my daughter upstairs to cry?"

Peter explained what had happened in town and that he was joining the militia. He was to report the next day.

"Well, my boy, I understand. I know you feel duty bound, so I understand. You know I don't think much of your plans for a future with

250

my daughter. I also know that her heart is breaking at this very moment. I bid you go to her and comfort her the best you can. We shall miss you here at The Mansion. God knows what we would have done without you. Truly, you were heaven-sent, but my boy comes home any day now, and we shall try to get along the best we can. Now go, Peter. Go to Susannah."

Peter crept up the stairs and paused at the door to her room. The wailing had stopped, and now it was just soft sobbing that echoed through the hall. Peter knocked, but there was no answer. He knocked again, only to hear Susannah's voice order him, "Go away."

He persisted. He knocked once more, then opened the door and entered her room. It was the first time he had ever been in there, and it almost felt like he was standing in forbidden territory. She was lying on her stomach facing him when he first came in, but she rolled her head to look away. He walked over, sat on the edge of the bed, and placed his hand on the small of her back.

"Please don't cry, Susannah. Please don't."

She rolled back over and looked up at him. The rims of her eyes were red, and he could see the stains of tears on her cheeks.

"How can you do this to me, Peter Francisco? How can you do this to us?" She started to cry again.

"Susannah, listen to me. I'm not doing this *to* us. I'm doing this *for* us." He saw the perplexed look on her face. "I don't want to go to war. I don't want to fight anymore. But I'm not going to war. The war is coming to us, and I don't want you anywhere near it. If anything were to happen to you, my life would be over."

"But Peter, I feel the same way about you. All the while you were gone to war, I feared for the day when we would get a message saying you had been killed. I don't think I can stand that again."

"I promise you this, my love. I'll be gone no more than a year, just one year. If the conflict is not resolved by then, I'll come home anyway."

Susannah rolled over on her back, reached up and wrapped her arms around Peter's neck. "You promise? Do you really promise?"

"I promise."

Despite all the assurances, that evening's dinner was a rather solemn affair with few words spoken among the four at the table. As it was quite warm, Peter retired to the porch afterward to drink in some of the cooler evening breezes. James soon joined him. Peter was on the swing, while Mr. Anderson selected a chair and pulled out his pipe.

"Peter, you know we'll miss you, all of us, although I suspect Susannah will miss you the most. No, I *know* she will miss you the most. I really believe from all that I have been hearing that this awful war will end soon, though its outcome remains in doubt. I just don't think that either side has the stomach for much more bloodshed."

"And I believe you're right, sir. At least I hope so, because I have promised Susannah that I will remain away no more than one year."

"And when that year is over – sooner, God willing -- please believe that you will be welcomed back here with open arms. One way or the other, you are part of our family now." As James Anderson rose, he held out his hand. "Be safe, and be careful."

"Thank you, sir. I'll try to do just that."

As the elder man reached the door, he turned around. "I'm sure that Susannah will join you directly. Enjoy your evening together." He didn't wait for a reply as he entered the house.

Just a few moments later, his lovely daughter appeared in the doorway, wearing the same green dress that she had worn when Peter had left more than three years earlier. She sat down on the swing next to him, just as she had more than three years earlier. But there was something different this time.

This time, Susannah didn't wait for Peter. This time, she reached out for him, pulled his face to hers and kissed him. This kiss was very much like the kiss they had shared while on their picnic only a few months ago. Their lips burned with desire ands passion, and when it was over, they were both breathless. They shared many such kisses that night, and they talked of the future and of their plans with each other. They held nothing back in expressing their love for each other. They talked and kissed, and talked and held each other throughout the night. They were both surprised when the first shafts of sunlight began to bathe the easterly facing porch.

"I had best be going, my love. We leave for South Carolina no later than mid-morning."

Peter got up, went into the house and gathered the few things he would take with him. He had two satchels – one, the larger one, in which he carried his clothes, and the other smaller, though considerably more important one. Instantly, Susannah, who had waited on the porch, spotted it.

"You have my handkerchief and your buckles?" she asked.

"Of course, I do," he replied.

253

"I would give you a new handkerchief, but I think you were right back in the forest. I know they brought you good luck before, and I pray they do so again."

Peter descended the steps, went to the barn to get his horse, and returned to the front of the porch where Susannah waited. He gave her a long, deep kiss, then put his foot in the stirrup and settled onto the saddle. She reached for his arm, but before she could touch him, Peter leaned down, picked her up, kissed her one last time, and said, "I love you."

As he ever so gently placed her back on the ground, she looked at him with tears streaming down her face. "I love you, too, Peter Francisco. I love you with all my heart."

Peter could take no more. He jabbed the horse with his heels, and she bolted for the edge of the property. Once again he turned to look back at his one true love. Once again, he saw her standing there, waving good bye. Tears began to well in his eyes as well, as he headed toward town…and toward more bloody battles.

16

COLONEL MAYO AND THE CANNON

As Peter joined the Virginia Militia in Mid-July 1780, he recalled all the training that he and his fellow soldiers had been through under the watchful eye of Barron von Steuben. Until that point, the Continental Army had been little more than a rag tag collection of individuals who had not the slightest idea how to fight as a unit. Von Steuben had changed all that, and Peter was certain that the more disciplined mindset would be in place for these newly formed militias. Furthermore, the southern campaign would be led by none other than General Horatio Gates, who had garnered a good deal of well-deserved fame at the Battle of Saratoga.

Unfortunately, Peter was greatly disappointed when he saw his comrades drilling and preparing for battle. Like those he had met at the tavern where he had been convinced to re-enlist, most of these men barely knew one end of a musket from the other. They had no idea as to lines of authority. They had no idea of military discipline. They had no idea of what battle was all about. To them, this was a late summer lark.

Thinking back, Peter recalled the words of the recruiting sergeant, who had painted a totally different, less demanding and less threatening picture of war than was the truth. Peter had inadvertently joined in on the ploy. Now he wished the recruiter had painted a more accurate description of what war was really all about. If he had, perhaps some of the enlistees would have known that the waging of war is less about glory than it is gumption and blood and guts.

One good thing came out of it all, however. Peter got to renew an old acquaintance with John Allen, the western Virginia mountain man he had parted company with on the way home from the northern campaign. Their meeting was strictly by chance. Colonel William Mayo was to be Peter's commanding officer in the field. He was well respected as a field officer who took care of his men and was more than willing to fight right alongside his troops rather than ride his horse at the rear, shouting commands. Colonel Mayo had also been a friend to Major General Lafayette, who had related stories about a huge Virginian named Peter Francisco. Thus, when Peter reported for duty, Colonel Mayo immediately tapped him to be his personal aide. So it was that Peter was with the colonel when a group of buckskin-clothed men with long rifles rode into camp to report for duty. Heading the group was none other than John Allen.

Seeing Peter standing next to the colonel, Allen literally leaped off his horse and ran to greet him. "Peter Francisco, how are you, my old friend?"

256

"I'm fine, John, just fine. But what brings you from your cozy little home in the mountains? When I last saw you heading west, I thought you'd never leave the comfort of the Shenandoahs ever again."

"Aw, you know how it is, Peter. I'm sure it's the same thing that brought you here. We got word that if we didn't face off with the Redcoats here, we'd be fightin' 'em back home. Now, to tell you the truth, personally, I'd love to get these lobster backs to fightin' in the mountains. Why, we'd just pick 'em off by the dozens. But here I am, ready to fight. I shore am glad you're here, too."

The whole of this conversation took place while Colonel Mayo stood aside just listening. Peter then took Allen off to one side. "John, don't be so happy. This won't be easy," he cautioned. "I've been here a week now, and by the looks of our troops, we're in for some tough times. Why, they aren't even getting the training we got in the Shenandoah Valley. I'm in dreaded fear for the first time we go into battle. I truly am. The only good thing is that we've got some boys from Delaware and Maryland, and they've had some solid battle experience "

"That doesn't sound very good. Not good at all."

"It's not, my friend. Why, when some of these fellows showed up, they didn't even have a musket or much else, and the word is that we're to break camp and head for South Carolina any day now. I don't know when supplies will catch up with us."

The rumors that Peter had been hearing soon materialized, and the gathered militias broke camp a few days later, heading south through North Carolina and on to South Carolina. Ill equipped and poorly trained, they were surely, Peter thought, heading for disaster.

Of course, General Gates had fared well in a battle over a fixed fortification, but he was poorly suited for directing his troops over miles and miles of marching and maneuvering. As a result, his forces meandered all over the Carolinas to the point that they seldom had even enough to eat, other than a few ears of corn and some turnips. It reminded Peter of Valley Forge, when their diet had consisted of little more than firecakes. At least now they weren't cold. Then again, perhaps that would have been better, as General Gates, not very familiar with the southern terrain, would often camp his forces near swamps and marshes. Those areas were breeding grounds for mosquitoes, and they made life miserable for everyone. Poor diet and lack of sleep made many of the soldiers sick, and dysentery was not at all uncommon.

Gates also miscalculated his troop strength. Other militias and soldiers had joined Gates's forces along the way, which led the general to calculate that he had perhaps 7000 troops at his disposal. Actually, he had less than 5000, and some of those men simply left and went home, since army life was not at all what they had imagined or, in some cases, had been promised.

As for the British, having seen the northern campaign disintegrate into one disaster after another, they laid the rest of their chances of stamping out the rebellion in the south, where they felt they could depend on a stronghold of loyalists. Indeed, there was a large segment of the population that had remained loyal to British rule, but not in the numbers that the English had hoped would swell their ranks. However, the British had been successful in capturing Charleston earlier in the year, at the expense of a large number of American casualties.

Thus, the British, under the command of General Lord Charles Cornwallis, were now attempting to gain control of the South Carolina backcountry, and Camden had become a major base of operations where men and supplies were amassed. On August 14, Cornwallis received word that the Americans were approaching Camden, but rather than simply wait in a defensive position, he decided to take the fight to the Americans. Having sent out some advanced scouting parties, the British general would be sending the balance of his forces to meet Gates' army head-on.

On that same night, Colonel Mayo was grousing to Peter about the lack of even some essential supplies. "Peter," he said to his personal aide, "do you realize that we go into battle with the British within days, perhaps even hours, and we don't even have weapons or clothes for all the men?"

"Yes, sir, Colonel Mayo. Several of the boys will have to fight hand-to-hand if they are to fight at all."

"This is intolerable, absolutely intolerable. It's bad enough that these lads are not yet properly trained, but to send them to battle without muskets...it's intolerable, I tell you." Then, seeming to put the unchangeable behind him, he said, "Very well, Peter. That will be all. You go and get some rest now."

"Yes, sir. I'll do that."

Peter did not do as instructed, however. Rather, he wandered about the campfires until he found his friend, John Allen. As he approached the group of men, Peter asked John to come and speak with him privately. "John, you know we go into battle soon," he spoke gravely.

"Yes, of course I do," John responded.

"You know that a number of our boys don't even have muskets."

"Yes, I know. What are you gettin' at, Peter?"

"Well, we know that the Redcoats always send out some advanced scouts. Suppose we choose for ourselves a soldier who has had special training for sneaking around, and another soldier who's a crack shot to give him cover. And suppose those two fellows sneak into one of the enemy's camps and make off with some of their supplies. And suppose they brought those supplies back here to give to our boys."

"And, I'm supposin' you figure we are the two fellas to do that job?"

"Suppose I am."

"Then I guess we better get to it."

As Peter and John set out, it wasn't long before the glow of a distant campfire caught their eye. The British were camped just across a small stream, and the two men sat among some Palmetto scrub to watch. There they noticed that the British weren't being very attentive. By the number of horses that had been hobbled off to one side, Peter estimated that there were only ten troops among the party. They had pitched a few tents, and most of them must have been asleep, as there was only one sentry that Peter could see. Thinking that the stream provided a natural shield, this lone guard was concentrating his attention at the opposite side of the camp away from the scouts' position.

Peter looked over at John Allen and whispered, "I'm going to head back upstream and cross the river so that they can't hear me splashing around in the water. You stay here, and when you see me on the other side, you watch for any alarm in the camp. If they sound the alert, you pick off the sentry first. With any luck, I'll already have their guns, but I'll leave my musket with you in case you need a second shot."

"Peter," John said, "you must be crazy. You can't possibly sneak into the camp, get their guns, and get outta there without gettin' caught."

"Yes, I can, John. You just wait and see."

"Well, it's your funeral then. I can't help you much after my two shots."

"You won't be taking *any* shots…just watch."

It was absolutely astounding that a man as big as Peter Francisco could be so quiet. Sneaking stealthily among brush, twigs and all sorts of things that should have made noise, especially at night, he silently made his way upstream. When he figured he had gone far enough, he entered the water and made his way to the other side. The bank there was steeper, and, as there was no path, he decided to stay in the water until the last possible moment.

This marshland tributary was obviously full of critters, but the surreptitious scout preferred not to think about that, especially since he had taken off his boots before climbing down into the water. Mud and decaying debris oozed through his toes as he made his way along the embankment. A few yards before he reached the point where the stream lay next to the British camp, he reached down, grabbed a handful of mud, and smeared it all over his face.

The glow from the campfire danced on the water, revealing to John Allen his friend creeping ever closer to the encampment. The smell of burning wood filled the air. Once Peter arrived at just the right spot, he furtively pulled himself up the embankment little by little. Every once in a while he slipped backwards, but after five or so minutes, he was fully

261

out of the water and lying flat on his belly at the stream's edge of the camp. Fortunately, the British had decided to stack their muskets in a tripod arrangement right near the water's edge -- three with three muskets each. This accounted for the nine sleeping troops.

Peter was ever so careful in disassembling each of the tripods, making sure that none of the weapons fell, which would have made more than enough noise to rouse the sleeping troops and bring the plan to a disappointing, perhaps dangerous, conclusion. Each time he had gathered three more muskets, he eased them over to the bank of the stream. Once he had all nine, he became even more daring. Near one of the tents he spotted a small crate of musket balls.

Allen, stationed on the opposite bank, had kept his long rifle trained on the sentry the whole time, while Peter secured the muskets. Then he saw him making his way over toward one of the tents. "Peter, you fool, leave well enough alone," John muttered under his breath, out of his partner's hearing.

Francisco crawled on his belly until he neared the crate, then extended one of his long arms and grabbed hold of the rope used for a carrying handle. But the crate weighed nearly fifty pounds, and when he tried to drag it, it made a scraping noise in the dirt. Peter, nearly holding his breath, glanced up quickly to see if the sentry had noticed. John Allen leveled his rifle and took better aim. The moment seemed to hang frozen in the air as the sentry stood oblivious to the action behind him.

Satisfied that the sentry had not been alerted, Peter rose to a crouching position while keeping one eye fixed on the guard. Still the guard kept his back to the stream and Peter, who grabbed the rope with one hand, easily lifted it off the ground and made his way to his stash of weapons. Silently he slithered back into the water. The crate was in one hand and heavily sank below the water line. Then Peter, with his massive hands, gathered all nine muskets at one time and pulled them into the water.

Slowly, ever so slowly, he made his way back upstream. John Allen took a breath for the first time in what seemed like forever. He also started to make his way upstream, creeping along a parallel course with his partner. After about 100 yards of skulking about, Peter came back across the stream.

John Allen addressed Peter in a hushed voice. "There for a minute, I thought you'd be caught. That was too close for me, my friend. The next time you want to do this, forget that I'm in the same army with you."

Peter smiled. "We got what we needed, didn't we?"

The two of them stole back to the American camp, Peter carrying the crate of balls and six of the muskets, John Allen carrying the other three weapons. When they arrived, Colonel Mayo, who couldn't sleep, was standing next to the fire closest to his personal tent, watching as Peter and John approached. "What have you there?" the colonel asked.

"Oh, just a few supplies the British have decided to donate to the cause." Peter replied coolly.

The colonel stood in amazement as the two friends told him what they had done. "I thought I told you to get some rest." the colonel scolded Peter. "I should have you court-martialed for disobeying a direct order." He winked at Allen.

"Yes, sir." That was all Peter could muster in response. He thought he had done well.

"Good job, boys. Good job. Now, go get some rest with what little is left of this night. And that's an absolute, direct order."

"Yes, sir. We'll do that," Peter said. He would have liked to go back to that camp to see the look on the Redcoats' faces when they discovered that all their muskets and fifty pounds of balls had up and disappeared in the night. That might even be worth a court martial, but Peter thought better of it.

The next day, when Colonel Mayo had the stolen weapons distributed, men kept coming up to Peter and congratulating him. He kept insisting that Allen had played a major role, too, but everyone knew who the hero of the hour was. It was Peter Francisco.

That evening the word went out to prepare for a march. Camp had been struck, and at midnight General Gates and his forces marched toward Camden. At almost the same time, British General Cornwallis ordered his troops to do the same. Since the two armies were marching directly toward each other, advanced columns ran into each other at about two-thirty in the morning. There were a few small skirmishes, but both commands withdrew to await the dawn.

When the sun rose, the respective armies realized that their battlefield would be much smaller than anticipated. The killing ground was flanked by marshland that was nearly impossible for a man to stand in, let alone fight in. This was a huge advantage for the British, for, even though they had less than half the men of the American forces, this was much like the Spartans hundreds of years earlier at the Battle of Thermopylae. Defending their position would be far easier than anyone would have anticipated.

Unfortunately, General Gates proved not to be a very good tactician on the open field of battle. When he deployed his troops, he had the rawest and least experienced men on the front lines, directly facing the guns and bayonets of the well-trained British soldiers. To the flanks, he stationed somewhat more experienced soldiers such as Peter Francisco's group. The last line of Gates's force was by far the most experienced -- Maryland regulars.

On the other hand, Cornwallis's men were all battle-hardened veterans, backed up by the cavalry led by Colonel Banastre Tarleton's Legion, a unit of bloodthirsty men with an equally bloodthirsty leader.

The front line Americans were told to get off at least two volleys of fire before withdrawing rearward, where they would join the troops from Maryland. In fact, they were threatened with being shot if they disobeyed the order. But it was no use.

Peter was sitting on his horse next to Colonel Mayo. Hastily, he reached inside his satchel and took out the handkerchief-wrapped buckles. Quickly, he recited his Portuguese prayer and returned the buckles to their place of safety, for he knew the battle would soon begin.

The British first attacked the left flank, where Peter was still stationed alongside Colonel Mayo. Most of the Virginians had no stomach for the fight. As the first British volley rained down upon them, they turned and ran, many of them throwing their weapons down while fleeing. The colonel and Peter did their best to rally the troops, both of them waving swords over their heads as they rode their horses up and down the lines. A few of the men turned around to fire at the British, but they weren't really aiming at anyone, and most of them didn't hit a thing. When the fleeing soldiers reached a secondary line of North Carolinians, it got even worse. The North Carolina boys joined the retreat rather than stand their ground.

Peter and the colonel were left with very few troops as the British advanced for close-up combat. The Virginian slashed at a British trooper and opened a wide gash in the man's neck, but at that moment his horse took a musket ball in the dead center of his chest. The horse's front legs buckled, catapulting Peter head first onto the ground and causing him to lose his sword in the process. He reached around and grabbed his musket strapped to his back. A grenadier rushed forward intending to bayonet him, but Peter firmly planted his right foot on the ground and deftly stepped to his left. The soldier passed right by before losing his balance in the lunge. Peter drove his own bayonet deep into the man's back.

Amidst the chaos of combat, Colonel Mayo was shouting something that Peter couldn't hear. Ignoring his own safety, he turned his head in Mayo's direction so that he could hear what the colonel was shouting. "The artillery! We must save the cannon!" screamed Mayo.

Seven pieces of artillery had been spread among the front lines. Two of those cannon were assigned to the Virginians, but the soldiers in charge of them had joined the retreat, and the horses that had pulled the cannon into position had been shot dead.

With cat-like quickness, Peter sprinted to the artillery pieces. Instantly, seeing that both of their sets of wheels had sunk into the soft earth bordering the swamp, he cut loose the leather straps that lashed one of the cannon to its barrel. Then, in a show of unbelievable strength, Peter Francisco lifted the weapon out of its cradle, all 1100 pounds of it, and hoisted it upon his shoulders. Colonel Mayo couldn't believe his eyes, nor could anyone else who witnessed the event. Even the British soldiers stopped charging, in awe of the feat.

Colonel Mayo rode alongside Peter as he carried the cannon to a wagon near the rear lines. There, at least, the men of Maryland were fighting valiantly along with their brothers from Delaware. Placing the cannon securely in the back of the wagon, Peter turned around to find that Tarleton's legion had been unleashed and were about to join the fray. Meanwhile, all around were advancing grenadiers, one of whom aimed a bayonet thrust directly at Mayo's midsection. Not having fired his weapon as yet, Peter brought his musket to bear and put a ball and three pellets into the British soldier's body.

Smoke and gunfire filled the air. A musket ball found its home in the left flank of Mayo's horse, collapsing the animal. Peter ran to assist his superior officer, who obviously was shaken.

"Come on, Colonel, we must join the others in retreat," Peter yelled, to be heard over all the battle sounds. The colonel nodded in agreement, and the two men set off toward safety. However, in the fall from his horse, Colonel Mayo had twisted his ankle, and he couldn't run fast. Behind him, Peter could hear the sound of hoofs fall, and he turned around to see one of Tarleton's men bearing down on them on horseback. In order to give the colonel more time to get away, the Virginian stood his ground and faced the charging legionnaire. The enemy closed in and swung wildly with his sword, a move that Peter was able to sidestep. The man wheeled his horse back toward Peter, charging again. But Peter was ready. Once more he sidestepped, at the same time bringing his musket, with bayonet firmly attached, up toward the trooper's stomach. The blade sank clear to the hilt. As the horse continued its run, Peter was left standing there with a British soldier fully impaled, dangling from the end of his weapon. The man wriggled about for just a few more seconds and then went limp.

The legionnaire's horse only continued a few paces before she stopped. Peter went over and took hold of her reins, mounted, and returned to the fallen soldier to grab his rather distinctive headgear. Placing it on his own head, the Virginian prodded the horse into a gallop, all the while encouraging the British to give chase, yelling and screaming for all he was worth. "After them, boys. Don't let the rebels escape!" It was a self-protective ploy. At least they wouldn't shoot at him if he made them think he was one of their own.

He had ridden about a half-mile when he spied Colonel Mayo taking refuge among some trees. Peter rode over to his superior and looked down from atop the horse. "Colonel Mayo? Are you alright, sir?"

"Peter, I'm afraid that I am not. I can't go on. I just can't. Now you get out of here before they catch up to both of us. That's an order."

"Well, it's another order I must disobey," Peter confessed, as he dismounted. "Take the horse and ride to safety as fast as you can. Tarleton's Legion is fast on my heels."

The colonel, struggling to stand, allowed Peter to assist him into the saddle. "I should have you court-martialed for this, for disobeying another order. That or I shall be privileged to pin a medal on your chest. I shall never forget this, Peter...never."

"Ride!" Francisco ordered as if in command. "I'll be close behind." As fast as he was, he couldn't keep up with the horse Mayo was riding. He was fast enough, however, to escape Tarleton's cavalry.

The battle ended in a major defeat. If there was anything that General Gates could have done wrong, he did it in this battle, and in the process lost almost half his men. For Peter, this was a signal that he should never, ever go to battle with so many untrained soldiers. He had also come to another conclusion. He preferred going to battle sitting on a horse.

17

BURYING A FRIEND

When Peter finally made it to the rear lines, he saw a group of men standing around Colonel Mayo, who was telling them about how Peter had rescued one of the cannon. As Mayo saw Peter approaching, he pointed out the oversized soldier to the listeners. For several seconds they just stared at him. Compared to the average young soldier, he was obviously huge, but to have picked up an 1100-pound cannon was beyond their imagination.

On the heels of a defeat, one of the men began to shout, "Hooray for Peter Francisco!" Others joined in until it almost became a chant. The group surrounded him and targeted him with a good many backslaps. As he continued into camp, he couldn't help but notice several of the distinctively clad mountain men gathered around one of the hospital tents. He approached with cautious curiosity.

"Is somebody hurt?" Peter inquired.

"It's John Allen," one of the men spoke up. "You're friends with him, ain't you?"

"Yes. Yes, I am. Is it bad?"

"Ol' John took a ball to the chest. It don't look good."

Immediately, Peter pulled back the flap of the tent. Allen, lying in a crimson-stained shirt and appearing to be unconscious, was stretched across several boards, waiting to be seen by a doctor. Peter approached and touched his friend's hand.

The wounded soldier opened his eyes slightly, looking directly at Peter. "You were right, big fella,' We weren't even a little bit ready for battle." He coughed, grimaced in pain, and a curl of blood rolled down his chin. Finding it almost too difficult to talk, and in a voice little more than a whisper, he breathed, "Come 'ere, Peter. I got a favor to ask." Peter took John's hand in his and bent down close to his face.

"Peter," he spoke haltingly, "take me home...promise me... you'll take me home. I want to... go back... to the mountains."

Peter looked at his friend. "Hey, mountain man, you'll be taking yourself home in no time. These doctors will fix you right up, and you can ride back to your glorious mountains."

"Not this time, Peter. Not this time." John's voice was growing weaker. "I know the boys...they would take me back....but you're 'bout the best friend I got....Peter...please promise me...you'll take me home...promise me." The belabored pleading reached the giant man's soft heart.

"I'll take you home, John. I promise...I promise."

Those were the last words John Allen would ever hear. He rolled his head to the side and a gurgling noise escaped his throat. Just then a doctor came over, took hold of his wrist and felt for a pulse. Looking at Peter, not callously as one who had seen so many deaths in this war but sorrowfully, he said, "If this man was your friend, he's gone."

As the doctor walked away, Peter bent low and gave his companion a kiss on each cheek. "I'll take you home, monami. I'll take you home and bury you in the mountains that call out your name." Peter exited the tent and the other mountain men gathered around him.

"Is he going to be alright?" one of them asked.

"No," Peter said, walking away. Spying Colonel Mayo, Peter headed over to him to tell him of his plans.

"You don't look like you're taking to your role as a hero, Peter," the colonel intoned.

"Being a hero doesn't mean much when you lose a good friend," was his response. He went on to explain what had happened to John Allen.

"I'm sorry about your friend, Peter. I didn't know him, but what you two did the other night was pretty amazing."

"Colonel, I need to tell you something else. I'm going to take John's body back to the Shenandoahs to bury him. I promised him that I'd do that, so I'll be needing a wagon and a couple of horses."

"Peter, with what you've done, you've earned at least that privilege. I'll make the arrangements."

"There's something else, Colonel."

"What is it, my boy?"

"I hear that they've been organizing cavalry units, and I'll be joining up with one of those. I don't ever want to fight a battle like I fought today, so I won't be coming back to this militia."

"I understand, Peter. I really do, though I'll miss you. What you did for me today, I can never repay. I'll have the wagon sent over to the hospital tent directly."

Peter and the colonel shook hands. Within the hour, Peter had gathered up his few belongings, loaded the wrapped body of his friend in the back of the wagon, and pointed the team of horses north. Even though it would be dark soon, he wanted to leave the camp as soon as possible. In all the battles he had fought, never had the Americans been so thoroughly routed. It was a taste in his mouth that this soldier would not soon forget.

At first Peter had thought about stopping at the Anderson's plantation before heading deep into the mountains of Virginia, but that would have extended his task by many days. He also knew that the body would soon decompose, and he didn't want to subject the Andersons to that. Initially, the journey itself wasn't unpleasant. The land was fairly flat, and Peter made good time for the first few days, during which he found his mind wandering to all that had happened --battles won and battles lost....friends found and friends also lost...Susannah. Always his thoughts came back to Susannah. He reached into his satchel and fingered her handkerchief wrapped around the buckles. Just the touch of material gave him comfort.

At night, Peter secured the horses, bedded down and thought about what the future might hold.

Several days of heading northwest brought the funeral procession, as it were, to where foothills began and the mountains of western North Carolina lay beyond. The horses began to strain and the wagon creaked louder and louder with every step the animals took. Peter decided that he might be better off to detour a bit east before the animals wore out and the wagon fell apart. This went on for several days as he kept the mountain peaks on his left and guided the wagon up towards the Shenandoah Valley.

Eventually, he crossed over into Virginia. Peter could sense that his last journey with his friend John was coming to an end. He even began to recognize, from his original journey to join the army, where he was. He knew he was getting close now, but the ride was getting more difficult and the wagon strained. Peter could no longer keep the team from traveling a much more perilous course, not if he was to do as promised and take his friend home to the mountains. A trip that would have taken a man on horseback a few days was taking weeks.

Finally, the wagon could take no more. Peter had aimed the team up a rocky incline. The horses were straining, and their breathing had become labored. As for the wagon, it was tilting from one side to the next. Boards began to shake loose. When the wooden wheels could no longer take the pounding of the rocks, the two at the back of the wagon just splintered. The front end tilted up into the air as the back end no longer had any support, and Peter was nearly thrown from his seat. Allen's body slid out the back and rolled down some rocks before finally coming to a rest against an outcropping.

Peter panicked and ran down to check on his friend. As he reached the wrapped body, he was actually a bit amused at his own reaction. John probably would have been laughing, too, he thought. After all, it wasn't as if John could feel any of this. Picking the body up, Peter walked the fairly short distance to the collapsed wagon and, laying the body down in a secure place, he took a look at the two broken wheels. If he had been back at Hunting Tower or The Mansion, he could have repaired the damage. As it was, the wagon had now been rendered useless. With dusk settling in, Peter decided to call it a day and make camp right where the wagon had broken down. As he tried his best to sleep, a singular wolf sang its night song.

The next morning, Peter tied John Allen's body to one of the horses. Fortunately, he'd had the good sense to bring a saddle and bridle for himself. A rope around the neck of the second horse allowed Peter to lead it up an ever-increasing incline, but even without the wagon to pull, the horses found the going quite difficult, and both labored mightily under their loads.

Despite the stress, Peter looked up at some of the most beautiful scenery he had ever beheld. The sky was as blue as Susannah's eyes, punctuated by majestic peaks carved by the hand of God Himself. Then there were the trees. Peter had seen tall trees before, but none that could match the ones in the distance. Straight ahead he spotted a mountain peak that seemed to beckon as if it would be just the spot to lay his friend to rest. The horses, however, could not traverse the last several hundred yards, so Peter stopped the animals, got down from his horse and rested for about an hour. He refreshed himself with water from a rushing stream that culminated in a waterfall, drank his fill and took the rest back to the horses. During the journey, he had let them graze on whatever vegetation was available, but both animals had lost quite a bit of weight, almost to the point of emaciation.

Taking John's stiff body on his shoulder, much as he had the cannon in Camden, the Virginia giant began the climb up a jagged rock face. Even for a man as strong as Peter, it was a backbreaking task, and he had to stop and catch his breath several times. Upon reaching the summit, he saw there was a lone pine tree that occupied the tallest portion of the peak. Fortunately, there was a heavy layer of dirt, since Peter had not given any thought about trying to dig through solid rock. He had remembered to bring his bayonet, though, which would prove quite useful.

Putting the body next to the tree, Peter set about loosening the soil with his blade. Then he scooped out dirt with his bare hands. Even though the temperature was quite brisk at this elevation, he broke out in a sweat, and before long his shirt and trousers were soaked through. Six inches at a time he scraped with his bayonet, and six inches at a time he scooped the loosened dirt by hand. It took hours. Having reached a depth of about four feet, he felt secure that this was deep enough to prevent the mountain animals from disturbing his friend's grave. He walked over to the body, carefully lifted it in his arms, and gently placed his fellow soldier in the bottom of the grave. One last time, he reached out to touch the mountain man, then began the task of filling the dirt back into the grave. When he was finished, he wasn't sure what to do next. Then it came to him. Softly he said, "Com Jesus me deito (With Jesus I go to sleep), Com a grac'a de Deus (With the grace of God), Edo Espirito Santo (and of the Holy Spirit). Rest well, my friend. Rest well."

Peter's strength was completely spent and darkness was upon him by now, so he stretched out next to the grave and fell soundly, dreamlessly asleep.

Very early the next morning, the sounds of birds alerted him that a new day had begun. Looking at John Allen's grave one last time, Peter started his descent to where he had tied the horses. They seemed somewhat better after the night's rest, and after saddling up, he began the next leg of his travel -- home to the Anderson plantation, home to Susannah.

****

Far less arduous, this leg of Peter's journey and its end were something to look forward to rather than dread. After several days instead of weeks, he laid eyes once again on The Mansion. As he rode toward the main house, he anticipated seeing his beloved Susannah, and he didn't have to wait long. It was almost as if she had a sixth sense that she was to see her dear Peter, for as he brought his two horses to a halt, she burst through the door.

"Peter," she screamed. "Peter, Peter, Peter, Peter!"

Descending from his mount, Peter barely had his feet on the ground when Susannah flung herself at him, leaping in the air so that she could wrap her arms around his neck.

"Peter, I had no idea that you would return so soon. Is the war over? We've had no news that the war is over."

"No, my love," he said, kissing her once more, while holding her up with her feet dangling above the ground. As he slowly set her down, he confessed, "It's not over yet. If our battle at Camden is taken into account, the war is far from over."

"Does that mean…" and then there was a painful pause, "does that mean you're going back?"

"Yes, Susannah, it does." He could see the disappointment in her face and hear it in her voice.

"But, Peter, you promised.…"

"I promised that I wouldn't be gone more than a year, and I've only been gone a few months," he corrected.

"But…, Peter…"

"Susannah, I love you. You know I love you. But I've just spent some of the most miserable months of my life. We were routed at our battle at Camden. Then I had to take a good friend home to be buried." He didn't want to get into the details. "Right now, I just really need some rest."

"Alright. We can talk about it later. Have you had anything to eat today?"

"I haven't really had a decent meal in weeks."

"Then let's go in. You've arrived just in time for dinner. Mother and Father will be so glad to see you."

After some warm welcomes, the Andersons, including Thomas, and Peter sat down to eat. But for poor Peter, hungry as he was, the enjoyment of food and company could barely keep him awake. As soon as he finished eating, he went to sit on the porch swing while Mrs. Anderson and Susannah cleaned up, but by the time she joined him, he was sound asleep. With some considerable shaking, Thomas was scarcely able to rouse him and assist him up the stairs to bed.

279

The next morning, after uninterrupted sleep in a real bed, Peter woke up quite refreshed. Downstairs in the kitchen, he found everyone was ready for the day. Thomas and Mr. Anderson were naturally eager to hear what he had to say about the southern campaign. Unfortunately, he wasn't able to paint a pretty picture.

"Do you think that Cornwallis is headed this way?" James asked.

"I do believe that will be his next move," Peter replied. "It's the only thing that makes sense."

"Susannah says you're going back to fight."

"Yes, sir, I am. I rejoined the army because I wanted to stop Cornwallis before he got to Virginia, and if there is any possible way to do that, I want to help." Peter darted a glance toward Susannah to see what her reaction was, and the look on her face revealed what he expected.

"Maybe I should go with you," Thomas pondered aloud.

Mrs. Anderson turned around now. "You listen to me, Thomas Anderson. You've already done your part, and your brother James, Jr. is still in Georgia."

"She's right," Peter chimed in. "Besides, you're needed here at the plantation."

"We need *you* here, too." Susannah's pleading comment was directed squarely at Peter.

"Don't think for one minute that I look forward to meeting up against the British again. Believe me, I would prefer to stay right here and tend to the farm. But not long ago I saw a British soldier named Tarleton. He's as mean as they come, and he needs to be stopped because if he gets the chance, he'll kill every patriot he can, and he'll lay waste to

280

every farm and plantation in sight. There's a coldness and ruthlessness about that man that has to be stopped."

"Peter is right, Susannah." said James. "The men back at camp have spoke about this fellow, Tarleton. He's the worst and most ruthless the Redcoats have."

"But Peter," Susannah pleaded. "After what you just told us about Camden and all those soldiers who ran away, why would you want to go back and fight another battle with them?"

"I'm not. I'm joining a cavalry unit that Thomas Watkins is getting together. It's made up of only experienced soldiers, so that should make a difference." Peter didn't bother to say that new soldiers would also be on the battlefield.

"I don't care! Let the British take it all…let them take it all back. I want you to stay!" Not waiting for any response, she bolted out the back door, followed immediately by Peter.

"Let her go, Peter. Let her go," said her mother. "She just needs to pout for a while. She was always like that, even as a little girl. Just let her be for a while. She'll be all right. You'll see." Mrs. Anderson seemed less defensive and more understanding of her than he expected.

Peter spent the rest of the day in the barn with Thomas, talking about what Thomas had been doing since he returned. He still wasn't quite sure how to use all the tools that Peter and his father had purchased while he was away in Georgia, but he was a quick student.

Late that afternoon, Susannah came to the barn. She shot a look at her brother -- a look he had seen before -- so he relinquished the barn to Peter and his sister. Susannah walked directly over to Peter and tried her very best to look up at him defiantly. It didn't work. She stretched her arms around his waist and nuzzled her head as near to his chest as she could reach. Once more, the scent of her hair intoxicated him.

"I'm so sorry I spoke to you that way," she said softly. "I do so love you, and I fear for you, but Father says you have to do this. But...how long can you stay with us?"

"Well, when we were fighting up north, it was the strangest thing I ever saw. The armies took the whole winter off. Now down here where it doesn't snow nearly as much, I'm not sure what they'll do, so I'll stay until I hear otherwise."

And stay he did. As winter set in, Peter and Susannah did their best to make the most of what time they had together. He also spent a good deal of time with Thomas, and the two of them made an efficient team in keeping up with the never-ending needs around the plantation as well as the preparations for the next season's planting. Following the lead of Judge Winston, the Andersons also devoted a vast majority of their acreage to planting hemp that could be made into rope and used on American ships.

As anticipated, news arrived that Lord Cornwallis was raiding across the Carolinas, wreaking havoc and destruction. The utter defeat of the Colonials at Camden had set the war effort back a good deal. In fact, the Continental Congress was so upset by the loss that they authorized General Washington to appoint a new commander to lead the army in the south. This was good news for Peter, for although he admired what General Gates had done at Saratoga, he viewed what took place at Camden as simply inexcusable. In Gates' place came General Nathanael Greene, who was a New England Quaker.

Word eventually came that Captain Watkins was ready to put his unit in the field, so Peter once again bid a sad goodbye to Susannah and her family and set off for war. On January 17, 1781, the Virginia giant was back in South Carolina for the Battle of Cowpens. His cavalry unit, among dozens of others, would be facing the Legion of Banastre Tarleton. However, this time the outcome was vastly different than that of Camden.

Lord Cornwallis had learned that American troops, under the command of General Daniel Morgan, were traveling in the western part of the state. His plan was to lure the colonials into a trap by having Tarleton and his troops either crush the patriots or push them toward his army stationed at King's Mountain.

But Morgan was a marvelous tactician, skillfully luring Tarleton into a trap of his own.

Each of the armies had about 1000 men. Peter was among eighty cavalrymen in this battle that began at seven in the morning, but it wasn't much of a battle. In a little less than an hour, over 100 of Tarleton's men had been killed and most of the rest had been captured.

At one point during the battle, Peter spied Lt. Colonel William Washington, a relative of the great general, dueling on horseback with Tarleton himself. The continental defender drove his horse as hard as he could and charged the animal right into Tarleton's mount, just as he was about to land a blow to Washington. Tarleton's steed regained its balance, and the British colonel slashed back at Peter. Their swords met in midair and sparks flashed as the two blades gleamed in the sunlight. As was his custom, Peter looked directly into the eyes of his opponent's lifeless eyes, as black and hardened as coal. Spittle flew from Tarleton's mouth.

Peter knew Tarleton's reputation. This was a man who, by all accounts, had ordered the slaughter of surrendering Americans at other battles. This was the man Peter most wanted to keep from ever getting to Virginia or anywhere near his dear Susannah. This was the man he wanted to kill right here and right now. Again, their swords flashed, each man's parrying the other's attempted blow. Suddenly both men threw all their strength into a last attempt to kill one another. But as their swords met violently, each snapped at the hilt. The two men glared at each other with antagonized hatred.

"There'll be another day, another time, another battlefield, giant," Tarleton spewed his vitriol. "I'll not rest until I have you and everyone who ever meant anything to you at the end of my sword." Tarleton immediately turned his horse and fled.

Peter, still on his horse, was filled with regret at his failure to end Tarleton's life. In his head, he heard the roar again, an unmistakable sound, the roar he heard every time he went into battle. This time, it was the roar of disappointment.

Despite Tarleton's successful escape, the Americans, having lost only twelve men, were rewarded with a resounding victory. This ultimately led to the battle that essentially decided the war in the south, a battle in which Peter Francisco would play a major role. And he would come face-to-face with death.

18

A GIFT FROM WASHINGTON

After the Battle of Cowpens, Peter was attached as the personal aide to Lt. Colonel William Washington, the second cousin of General George Washington.

Both the British and American armies were quite low on supplies as they played a cat and mouse game throughout North Carolina. General Nathanael Greene faced the never-ending dilemma that had haunted colonial forces since the war began -- not enough supplies and, more importantly, not enough men. On the British side, Lord Cornwallis wanted to seek out and destroy the Americans before his supplies were completely gone.

After Cowpens, Cornwallis had been furious. He became absolutely bent on razing the army that had inflicted such a painful loss on his forces. Greene, on the other hand, knew he had to somehow resupply both troops and necessities. In order to further thwart Cornwallis' efforts, he decided to split his forces between himself and General Daniel Morgan, who had masterminded the Cowpens victory.

Cornwallis became so frustrated with American tactics that he decided to make his army even lighter and faster, so even though he was short on materiel, he ordered his supply wagons burned, along with many of the badly needed stores that they carried.

Meanwhile, Greene had his armies crossing back and forth over the border between North Carolina and Virginia. Once again, the call went out for men to volunteer for local militias, and the call was met. After a few weeks, hundreds of militia from both North Carolina and Virginia helped swell Greene's strength to nearly 4500 men, although the exact number was never known, since volunteers could come and go as they pleased. Many of them did just that. There was, however, a core of 1600 Continental Army regulars, as well as members of the militia, who had seen extensive action in other campaigns. Among those regulars was Peter Francisco.

All of this casting about soon came to an abrupt end at a place called Guilford Courthouse in North Carolina. On March 12, 1781, General Greene marched his troops to within twenty miles of the fateful battleground, having heard that Cornwallis had withdrawn his army to a location near there. A new camp was set up, but everyone knew that they would not be there long. That evening, among the myriad campfires and tents, each man prepared in his own way for the events that were about to unfold. Some of the soldiers bedded down early to get some extra rest. Others sat around the warming fires and told stories and jokes.

Peter put the training he received under Baron von Steuben to good use as he prepared for battle. He made sure that his musket was clean and ready for action, that the barrel was dirt free, and that the firing mechanism was in good working condition. Then he set about shining and polishing his bayonet. Long ago he had noticed how the British troops, with their bayonets gleaming in the sunlight, could be so intimidating, especially to those colonials who had never seen battle before. Although he hated the British, he admired their tactics, right down to the last detail. He, therefore, put a high sheen on his saber. He figured he would soon be using it to cut down enemy soldiers from his position on horseback alongside Colonel Washington. Additionally, Peter checked his ammunition satchel to make sure that he had plenty of musket balls and pellets. He wasn't anticipating that he would use his musket much, but it was always best to be prepared because in his experience, battles seldom went exactly as planned.

As the evening wore on, the men sought shelter and warmth as well as they could, since the nights remained chilly at that time of year.

The next morning, everyone in camp was surprised and thankful to see that General George Washington had sent a supply wagon train to General Greene's camp. Among the supplies were food and clothing, for which the men were most grateful, because many were barefoot and shirtless.

One item was of particular interest. It was a crate, small in every dimension except length -- it was nearly seven-feet long -- and was addressed to Lt. Colonel William Washington. He was in his tent when the item was delivered to him, and several men gathered around to see what it was. Before long, Colonel Washington came out joined them.

287

"What's in the crate?" one of the men asked.

"Yeah, what did you get, Colonel?" another inquired.

Colonel Washington didn't respond but instead inquired as to the whereabouts of one Private Peter Francisco.

"After he helped unload the supply wagons, I think I saw him go up to the horse pen. You know how Peter loves his horses," one of the men acknowledged.

Colonel Washington headed off in the direction of the horse pen, and, sure enough, there was the Virginia Giant, now weighing almost 280 pounds, currying his horse and talking gently in one of her ears.

"Peter," the Colonel hollered as he approached. "Peter, I need you to come with me. I have something I'd like you to see."

Peter left the horse pen, taking care to replace the rail through which he had gained entrance. "What is it, Colonel? Have I done something wrong?"

"No Peter, you've not done anything wrong. It's just something I'd like to show you. I need your opinion."

As the two men walked back to Colonel Washington's tent, Peter kept firing questions in an effort to find out what it was he needed so desperately to see. The colonel provided no clues.

When they arrived back at the colonel's tent, Washington pulled the flap back to allow Peter to enter. This was unusual since officers always entered first, especially before privates. Being full daylight, it took a few moments for Peter's eyes to become accustomed to the dark shade, which the tent provided.

There it was, lying on Colonel Washington's cot. It was six feet in length with a five-foot blade. It was the sword that Peter and Lafayette had spoken about when they were both recovering from their wounds at Brandywine. General George Washington had finally seen to it that Peter had a proper fighting weapon. Never again would his sword shatter as it had in the duel against Tarleton. Peter was speechless.

"What do you think, Peter?" Colonel Washington asked, breaking the silence. "My cousin, the general, had this especially made for you."

Almost awestruck, Francisco blurted, "Oh, she's a beauty." Then, with more respect and commitment than awe, he continued, "Colonel, I'll use this weapon to eliminate our enemies. I'll carry it into battle proudly. I swear by all that's holy, I look forward to meeting Colonel Tarleton on the battlefield, where he'll taste my steel. And I'm so grateful that General Washington would take the time to have this made for me, a lowly private."

"That's something else I wanted to talk to you about, Peter. General Greene has seen fit to offer you a battlefield commission. You are to be an officer, Peter. What do you think of that?"

"It is a great honor, truly it is. But," Francisco spoke with a twinge of regret, "I must decline, sir."

"But why, Peter?"

"I know that officers need to read and write reports, but I have the skills for neither. I can't read or write."

"Peter, I didn't know. I'm so sorry. I just didn't know. What I do know is that you have served our new country well. You have been valiant in every respect. You have won the admiration of everyone with whom you have served, and your name shall be recorded in the annals as a true patriot. As I've heard my cousin say on more than one occasion, you really are the Hercules of the Revolution, and now you have the sword to prove it."

"Thank you, sir. Your words mean a great deal to me. I have sought no honor, only freedom from tyranny and protection for my family and friends. And now with this sword, I'll no longer be waving a toothpick at my enemies." His smile was almost sinister as he ran his hand carefully, admiringly over the gleaming blade and the well-crafted handle.

The colonel and Peter exchanged handshakes. When he opened the tent flap to go outside, a large crowd of men had gathered who still wanted to know what was in the crate. Peter, so proud of his sword, held it high above his head. His combined height with the length of the sword seemed to reach up and touch the sun that was reflected in a flash of light off the blade. The brilliance danced off it so that almost everyone assembled saw it.

"Good Lord, do you see the size of that thing?" one man was heard to say.

"This must be a sign from God that victory is ahead," gloated another.

"Hooray for Peter Francisco!" The chant, just as at Camden, started with one man, but soon there were hundreds, all cheering simultaneously. "Hooray for Peter Francisco! Hooray for Peter Francisco!"

For the remainder of the day, soldiers from all around camp kept approaching Peter, wanting to look at the sword. It was by far the biggest that any of them had ever seen, and they marveled at how easily he could wield it. He practiced repeatedly for the time when he could use it on the British and, in particular, on Colonel Banastre Tarleton.

That night Peter slept with his new sword at his side, waking the next morning with a new purpose. He asked one of the mountain men, whom he had met through John Allen, to help him make a scabbard to strap across his back for his prized piece of steel. He shined and shined the sword, all the better to blind his opponents just before they met their demise at the end of it. And he honed it and honed it, all in the hope that someday soon it would be the instrument of execution for the hated Tarleton.

The next day -- the fateful day -- the two enemies prepared to face off in one of the bloodiest battles of the entire war. The Americans, newly supplied, bolstered their strength and endurance by eating a hearty breakfast. Additionally, each soldier received a quantity of rum. With a heavy frost on the ground, the sound of crunching could be heard from beneath the men's feet and horses' hoofs as they took their places for battle, and the breath of both men and equines could be seen in the chilled morning air. General Greene deployed his forces in three lines that stretched across New Garden Road, which ran through the center of the battlefield.

For the Americans, the first line consisted of North Carolina militia. These men found some protection behind a rail fence from which to fire upon the advancing British. On their flanks were the mountain men with their long rifles, as well as the cavalry units, including Peter Francisco and Colonel William Washington on the right. Two six-pound cannon sat on either side of the road.

The second line of colonials -- about 350 yards behind the first -- was made up of the Virginia militia as well as some Continental army veterans. The most seasoned troops, some 1400 of them, from Virginia, Delaware and Maryland, were the third and last line. This line also had two more cannon.

The plan was to have the mountain men use their long guns to pick off at a distance the advancing British, a tactic that the British could not counter. Then, once the English were in range, the first line would fire two volleys and fall back in an orderly fashion. As before at the battle at Camden, these troops were told to fire twice and hold their ground until the retreat was called or they would be shot by the defenders in the second line. Although the threat had not been taken seriously at Camden, most of the front line soldiers were convinced that the orders would be carried out this time. The cavalry would remain in reserve unless needed. They, too, were to fall back with the first line, thus supporting the second and eventually the third line of defenders.

As General Greene took note of his troop placements, he was quite pleased and secure in his battle plan. One other aspect gave the general cause for confidence, and that was that the terrain offered an unexpected advantage. Each of his lines was at a slightly higher elevation than the one preceding. Therefore, the British would have an uphill battle every inch of the way.

As for Cornwallis, even though his forces were far inferior in numbers, he was confident that his trained and experienced professional soldiers would carry the day. With information that his opponent was just ten miles away, the British general ordered his troops to begin their march at 5:30 in the morning. Unlike the Americans, they had little food for breakfast. At about noon, Cornwallis arrived to take stock of the battlefield. He could see the rail fence behind which Greene's first line was hiding. He saw the wooded area on either side where the mountain men and cavalries were lying in wait.

Peter, donning his new sword strapped across his back and sitting astride his horse next to Colonel Washington, reached into his satchel and took out the buckles that were wrapped in Susannah's handkerchief.

"Com Jesus me deito (With Jesus I go to sleep),

Com Jesus me levasto (With Jesus I awake),

Com a grac'a de Deus (With the grace of God),

E do Espirito Santo (and of the Holy Spirit),

Eu vou para a batalha (I go into battle.)"

Placing the items back in his pouch, Peter could hear the familiar roar in his head and feel the tingling in his arms. He was ready.

It was one o'clock in the afternoon. Cornwallis, in an attempt to draw some fire so that he could better determine exactly where the Americans were, brought up his artillery, but the Americans beat them to the punch and fired their cannon first. The British responded in kind and the earth shook with resounding thuds. Cornwallis' men formed their ranks and began their traditional "attack", marching in step as they moved toward the American front lines. As these troops drew within 150 yards of the fence, shots rang out from both flanks as the mountain men took careful aim and drew down on their targets. British soldiers, pawns in the cruel game of battle, began to fall. The front line of Americans used the fence rails to steady their aim and cut loose with a fusillade of musket fire. Wide gaps began appearing in the British line, but still they kept coming.

As the 33rd Regiment of Foot neared to within thirty yards, they fired on the Americans with their own volley. Smoke and musket balls filled the air. Some of Greene's troops fell under the withering fire. Unlike in the past, however, most of the militia stood fast, reloaded and got another volley off at the enemy with deadly accuracy.

Then, unfazed by the number of their fellow soldiers who had already fallen, the British regiment initiated its classic bayonet charge, a most formidable sight. Much to General Greene's dismay, the center of his first line disintegrated in fear and cowardice and made a mad dash rearward. The riflemen and cavalry on the flanks, including Peter's unit, were far more orderly in the planned retreat and also provided deadly covering fire for those troops heading for the second line of defense.

The British, under the command of Colonel James Webster, were suffering terrible casualties, but they continued their forward advance. As the infantry approached the second of Greene's lines, they quickly realized that they would be facing a far more defiant foe. The Virginia militia was considerably different than the first line North Carolinians. Many of them had been regulars, and there was a smattering of long-riflemen sprinkled among them.

As before, the long rifles spoke first as the English came within range. The Redcoats continued to see their ranks thinning, but they were powerless to remedy the loss. Some, both on the far left and right, sought shelter in the woods. That's when Colonel Washington, Peter Francisco and the cavalry sprang into action.

As was his custom, Washington led the charge with Peter to his immediate right, who had unsheathed his massive broadsword. Within only moments, he had cut down two of the British troopers with crashed blows. A few of the lobster backs, seeing the massive sword, did their very best not to confront the giant Portuguese, preferring instead to choose lesser targets to fight.

As seconds grew into minutes, the fighting was so intense that the soldiers on either side, confused in the fray, could scarcely tell exactly what was going on. The second line kept firing. There was none of the "fire two shots and run" that had characterized most of the first line. Men were shooting, reloading and shooting again as fast as they could, some as many as ten, twelve and even fourteen times, obscuring the field and their view with thick smoke. When visibility became impossible, Greene ordered the orderly retreat that would meld his second line with his third.

Peter's cavalry withdrew as ordered, but not until the six-foot sword had eliminated yet two more of the enemy. As they reached the third of General Greene's lines, the cavalry pulled their horses about and prepared to clash once again with the advancing British. One trooper charged at Peter with his bayonet raised. Peter brought his sword down and shattered the man's musket. Then with a swift backhand motion, the steel in his hand cruelly removed the soldier's head. The man's body fell onto Peter's horse, leaving a blood trail down the side of the animal.

Another of the enemy charged at Peter's horse, causing the animal to rear up and throw its rider to the ground. With unimaginable reflexes, Peter was on his feet before the soldier could finish him off. As the Redcoat charged at him, the Virginian brandished his weapon and pulled it through a wide arc; the blade cut entirely through the man at mid-torso. His upper body fell to the ground, before his legs, in ghostly fashion, took a few more steps.

Observing a number of British infantry crowded around Colonel Washington, Peter sprinted to protect the officer for whom he felt great personal responsibility. His blade rose and fell, swirling through the thickened gun smoke as he charged across the battlefield on foot. One blow removed the arm, shoulder and a portion of the upper chest of his opponent. Another was not quite as well aimed, and the sharp blade was off its target. It didn't matter. The mass of the blade itself, having been swung with such ferocity by such a large man, seemed to break every bone in the soldier's upper body. Anyone nearby could hear the bones crunch.

Seeing that his colonel was at least temporarily out of harm's way, Peter found his horse and mounted in order to more effectively fight and chase the British. Just as he fastened his seat into his saddle, a grenadier appeared out the smoke and drove his bayonet deep into Peter's left calf, to the point that Peter was actually pinned to his horse. Fearing that a sudden move would cost him his leg, he cognitively motioned for the Redcoat to step back. But the soldier had not seen the fearsome weapon held on the other side of the horse, which his nemesis had already dexterously used to dispatch eight of his compatriots. As the British soldier withdrew his blade, he stepped back and steadied himself to make another thrust. Peter's sword, however, caught a stray flash of sunlight, and for the briefest of seconds, the Redcoat looked up and spied that which would end his life. Peter, using just one hand operated by the power of his huge forceps, brought the sword down with such force that it struck the soldier on the crown of his head, splitting the skull open and continuing into the shoulder region. When he lifted it away, the man's body, like his compatriot's, actually took several steps before collapsing.

Through the haze, Peter could see that the British cavalry had been ordered into the battle, no doubt led by the bloodthirsty Colonel Banastre Tarleton. As well as he could, peering and squinting through the smoke, Peter scanned the scene, searching for the man he most wanted to kill. In the distance he spotted his target wearing his legion's distinctive headgear and officer's coat. Peter's eyes narrowed. He could hear the roar in his head, but again it had nothing to do with the din around him. He could feel the tingling in his arms. He became singularly focused on nothing but the British officer. Ending Tarleton's life became Peter's only goal, and he charged his horse in that direction.

That focus nearly cost the Portuguese his life, as two of Tarleton's men saw where he was heading and together charged him from the side. Their horses rammed his steed. Peter grasped his sword with two hands and brought it around, cutting through the air so deftly that it made an eerie hum. In that one flash of steel, the Virginia giant cut the heads off both of the attacking members of Tarleton's legion.

Remembering his objective, Peter suddenly realized that he couldn't see Tarleton anymore. In a panic, he sought sight of him. Then, just as quickly as he had disappeared, Tarleton came back into view, challenging Peter to a duel, a dare which Peter was more than ready to accept. He jammed his heels into the sides of his horse and goaded the animal on toward the British colonel. Being so focused on his intended target, however, he hadn't noticed a group of British infantry with bayonets pointed upward, forming a traditional square of defense between Peter and Tarleton. As Peter reached them, one lunged forward, driving his bayonet into Peter's flesh just above the right knee, and the momentum of his horse drove the blade up his leg near the hip. His horse toppled, and Peter was thrown to the ground.

Though the battle raged, time for Peter reached a standstill. The offending trooper was looming over him ready to make a final thrust into the massive chest of the Portuguese. Under his breath, Tarleton muttered, "Kill him. Kill him." Mentally, Peter prepared to die. But as the man lifted his weapon for the last plunge, the guardsman's chest exploded.

Cornwallis, seeing that his forces were being badly slaughtered, had ordered his cannon loaded with grapeshot and fired into the midst of the fiercest fighting. His own officers had argued against this action, but the general thought it was the only way to put an end to the carnage. Americans and British alike were horrifically cut down and mutilated by the onslaught, but the British rearguard was able to retreat, including Tarleton, who was still determined to eliminate all those for whom Peter ever cared.

General Greene decided to abandon the field rather than risk losing any more of his forces. With such serious injuries, Peter was left to die. In and out of consciousness, he intermittently felt the overwhelming pain in his leg. There was nothing to compare it to -- not the musket ball at Germantown, not the ball that he still carried in his thigh as a result of action at Monmouth, not the nine-inch slash that had cut his belly open, not the bayonet by the grenadier that he had taken in his left calf while on the horse. None of those wounds compared to this one. The slightest stir of the breeze against the open wound was enough to make Peter to cry out, yet he could not find the voice or strength to do so. After a while, he mustered what strength he could when he noticed a large oak tree several yards away. He slowly, inch-by-inch, dragged himself over to it and leaned against its trunk to await death. As he sat there, the sounds of battle receded. The haze still lingered and hung like a cloud over the scene. The smell of sulphur was gagging.

Both of the armies had given up the field, though the British remained in close proximity. Technically, the British were the victors, but Cornwallis had lost better than a quarter of his men. The reality was that the conflict would serve to signal the beginning of the end, as Cornwallis would embark on a course that would lead to the closing stages of British occupation of the colonies.

Sitting and bleeding next to that oak tree, Peter could not possibly know this. All he knew was that death was all around him. Bodies were strewn across the field. In some places they were stacked atop one another. In the distance, he could hear moaning and crying as some tried to stay alive and others simply gave in to encroaching death.

As the cries became louder due to the absence of any battle, Peter could take it no longer. In his exceedingly weakened condition, he crawled in the direction of the loudest moans, reaching one of his fellow cavalrymen. With his long arm, he reached out and fumbled to grab some material of the man's uniform. Finally, he got a fistful of shirt and slowly, painfully pulled the man over to the oak. He was just about spent, but the groans and cries kept reaching his ears. He repeated this maneuver, this rescue mission, three more times, and each time, he returned to his tree with another brave soldier.

The afternoon wore on until dusk began to settle over the hundreds of dead and dying bodies. Peter drifted in and out of consciousness. His thoughts floated back to when he was just a little boy in the Azores Islands and of his momma and papa; to Edna Watkins, the kind lady who had fed and clothed him when he was abandoned on a Virginia dock; to Arthur, who had become a father figure to him; to Judge Winston, who had given him a home for almost a decade; to John Allen, the mountain man who had become his friend; to the Marquis de Lafayette, who was almost like a brother. Most of all, he thought of Susannah, who had captured his very heart and soul. What would become of her now?

The showers began so softly, as though they were the very tears from God's eyes. Then the rain came. Peter's head slumped on his chest, and the gurgling sound that had signaled the end for John Allen escaped from his own mouth.

19

LEFT FOR DEAD

Although it was true that at the end of the day the British maintained control of the battlefield, it was a hollow victory. At a later date, Charles James Fox, a vocal critic of the war, would proclaim, "Another such victory would ruin the British army." It was a classic example of winning the battle and losing the war, and eventually, with Greene's forces in pursuit, Cornwallis would retreat all the way to Wilmington, North Carolina.

In the meantime, General Greene had been aware that there was a large number of Quakers, much like himself, who were living in the area. From his own upbringing, he knew that those of his faith were widely recognized as caring and empathetic and well skilled in caring for the ill and injured. He sent out a request that those nearby farmers search the battlefield and offer aid and comfort to any wounded soldiers, regardless of their affiliation in the conflict. They did so by the hundreds. Almost every nearby farmhouse, in addition to the Guilford Courthouse, was converted into a hospital of sorts.

One Quaker, by the name of John Robinson, came across an especially gruesome sight. A giant of a man lay propped up against an old oak tree. His left leg had an oozing wound, but it was not very large. His right leg, however, was laid bare to the bone. Around him were the bodies of four men. Robinson checked on the four smaller soldiers, and then turned his attention toward Peter. As Robinson shook him by the shoulder, Peter was deep in unconsciousness. He felt the hand on his shoulder and wondered if God was waking him in order to introduce him to Heaven, to allow him to be greeted by his friend John Allen and other friends he had seen fall, perhaps to reunite him with one or both of his parents. The shaking continued and eventually he opened his eyes to see a man peering down at him. Robinson spoke words that Peter would never -- could never -- forget. "My name is Robinson, and I have come to comfort thee."

Peter could not speak. Even if he had been able, he had no words to say. He felt several men lift him and carry him to a nearby wagon. Peter wanted to ask about the men he had gathered. He wanted to ask about his sword. But he couldn't find the strength. He drifted, instead, to a world of darkness and pain.

Robinson transported him to a nearby farm where Martha Robinson was preparing to receive the wounded. She had cut bed linens to serve as bandages, and she had boiled water atop the wood stove to use for cleansing wounds and washing the wounded. Several barrels had been brought in from the barn, which were spanned by heavy wooden planks laid atop for makeshift beds. As several men entered carrying Peter, Mrs. Robinson was aghast at his size. Quickly she grabbed a couple more planks and laid them on top of another pair in order to further strengthen their ability to hold up under the strain of this huge man's weight.

Looking at Peter's leg, she frowned. She said to no one in particular, "I know not if I have the skills to stem the blood from a wound of this size." Despite her misgivings, she set about to cleaning the wound with cloths dipped in hot water so as to limit the possibility of infection. Though she did so as gently as she possibly could, with each touch to the gaping gash, he cried softly in his stupor. Mrs. Robinson instructed two men to hold the Virginia giant still, and she covered his face with a cloth for fear that he might fully wake and go into shock. Working feverishly, she ignored lesser-wounded men to attend to Peter. She tried her best to move muscle and tissue into their proper places. Every now and again, she would use simple needle and thread to secure vital parts back to where they belonged. Once she was satisfied with the progress she had made, she began to sew the entire wound closed, again using dressmaker's needle and thread and little more than the skills she had acquired making clothing for her family. She had also attended to the less serious calf wound in his other leg. Before she was finished, Martha Robinson had spent almost as much time on this one patient as the battle itself had taken.

Again, it took several men to lift Peter's bulk and move him to a bedroom in the rear of the house. Lying on that bed, which once more had to be artificially lengthened to accommodate his height, Peter fell deeper and deeper into a slumber. It was a sleep that would last for three days, although Mrs. Robinson regularly checked on her patient.

Since taking care of him, John Robinson's wife had tended to all sorts of wounds and had sewn other gashes, though none as serious as Peter's. She had dug musket balls from the bodies of soldiers, both American and British, but none of their wounds had been as challenging as Peter's had been. As a result, she had taken a special interest in the Portuguese.

By mid-afternoon on the third day, Peter started to rouse. Martha noticed this and kept checking on him even more frequently. At long last, he struggled to open his eyes, and he saw yet another strange face looking at his. Attempting to speak, he felt as though his throat was full of sawdust. Martha pulled a chair near the edge of the bed to listen and put a gentle hand on his arm. "Speak not, for thou has suffered a great wound. Thou needs all thy strength to heal rather than speak, so rest back if thou wouldst."

But Peter could not resist. His head was full of questions. "Where am I? What happened? What of the soldiers I dragged from the battlefield? Where is my sword? How is my horse?"

"I can see that thou art not in the habit of following instructions, so I shall answer thy questions, but thou must promise to rest and not become excited."

"I promise," Peter spoke hoarsely.

"Thou art at the farm of my husband, John. Thou was brought here three, perhaps now four, nights ago. I seem to have lost track of time. Thou had a leg wound, one of the worst I have ever seen. With the grace and guidance of God, I pray I have been able to provide the proper care to help thee heal. As for the soldiers whom my husband found gathered around thee, none survived. Thy horse, I cannot answer to, but a goodly many were dead on the field. Even to this day, men are gathering their remains for proper disposal before they completely rot and decay. As to the sword, one of our neighbors found one that was taller than he. He brought it here thinking that thou art the only man large enough to carry it. I shall have it brought to thee, but now I ask thee to recall our agreement. Rest for now, and I shall bring thee some soup."

Peter did as instructed and rested his wounded body. He couldn't help thinking, "Soup? Soup again. After this, if I never have soup again, it'll be fine with me."

In only a few minutes Martha returned with a bowl of steaming broth, tastier than some others Peter had sampled. He shifted himself into a nearly seated position, but Mrs. Robinson insisted on spoon-feeding him. She was obviously quite skilled in the practice, for she spilled not a single drop. Just as she finished, a man came in. Peter recognized the face as that of the man who had found him leaning against the oak tree on the battlefield.

"I believe this belongs to thee," James Robinson said as he carried Peter's broadsword and laid it next to the bed. "I have taken the time to clean its blade of all the blood which rested upon it."

The effort of eating had expended what little energy Peter could muster. All he could say was a weak, "Thank you." Sliding back down in the bed, he again fell sound asleep.

Over the next several weeks, Martha Robinson nursed her patient back to health. After nearly a month of bed rest, he started to walk around the Robinson farm, slowly regaining his strength. A month later, after saying his goodbyes and thank-yous to the family that had taken him in and compassionately cared for him, Peter set out on a 200-mile journey back to Virginia, back to The Mansion, back to the Andersons -- back to Susannah. Walking all the way, Peter was able to gain strength in both legs, which had been so horribly wounded and terribly scarred in so many battles. His pace was steady but measured, and it took weeks.

In the meantime, the war continued. Cornwallis, after retreating to Wilmington, determined that his best course of action was to march his remaining troops up the East Coast of North Carolina and into Virginia. He had also given Tarleton orders to go in advance of the main body of troops. Specifically, Tarleton's instructions were to destroy food stores but leave enough food so that the civilians could continue to at least feed themselves. The point of the directive was to deny the American forces of food and supplies that could be used to strengthen the colonials.

However, Tarleton had always had his own way of interpreting orders. He had shown such a bent in the past when he ignored flags of surrender and truce and allowed his men to indiscriminately kill those who were unarmed. To say that Tarleton and his legion were savages does the word little justice.

Thus it was that Tarleton and his men set about to ravage the Virginia countryside. Six weeks after the Battle of Guilford Courthouse, Tarleton and his men swept down on Cumberland County. He had not forgotten the Virginia Giant and had learned that Peter lived on a plantation called The Mansion. After a few days of searching, Tarleton was satisfied that he knew the location of The Mansion, and he recalled his threat of a long ago battle. His intent now was to destroy his hated opponent as well as all those he cared about.

Arriving at The Mansion in the early evening hours, he personally conducted a search of the plantation. He and his men crept up the stairs, looked in every room, opened every door, and turned every mattress. The house, barn, and slave cabins were completely empty. They had been for two days.

Tarleton was livid. His prey had escaped his sword, but he had no knowledge that Peter Francisco had not even been at The Mansion for months and that he was only now making his way there from North Carolina. Finally satisfying himself that the plantation was vacant, Tarleton ordered it put to the torch.

The night sky grew bright with the orange glow cast by the flames as every building was burned to the ground. Fires were also set throughout the fields so as to render the first shoots of crops useless and singed. Tarleton sat astride his horse at the very spot where Peter had waved goodbye to his dear Susannah. He was not pleased that his personal objective had not been met, but there was a certain satisfaction as he watched the conflagration with a sinister smile on his face.

Turning his troops north and westward, Tarleton continued his raids through the countryside, exacting a mean-spirited revenge for a war that even he had already concluded was lost.

A few days after the burning of The Mansion, Peter arrived to see what destruction had been visited upon the place he now called home. Everything lay in ruin. Peter hurriedly ran up the path that led straight to where the main house once stood. Feverishly, he tore at timber and boards that were, even now, warm to the touch. He was frantically looking for Susannah and her family, hoping beyond hope that he would find no sign of a charred body. Instead, smoldering ashes were all that remained. Continuing to survey the destruction, Peter was naturally drawn to where the barn once stood. The only thing recognizable was the anvil that he and James Anderson had purchased together. The smell of the still-smoking lumber was becoming oppressive. He reached inside his pouch and touched Susannah's handkerchief. For the moment, it was his only connection to the woman he loved so much.

Not knowing where to turn next, he set a course for Hunting Tower, unsure of how he might be greeted, wondering if that, too, had been destroyed. Nevertheless, he was more than willing to swallow his pride in search of any information as to the whereabouts and safety of the Andersons.

Two days later he arrived at Hunting Tower, the house where he had spent the formative years of his life. Hesitating a bit to approach the door or even move toward the steps, he stood there for about fifteen minutes recalling the way he and Judge Winston had last parted, when he had been ordered off the property. Just then the front door opened and Judge Winston came out onto the porch.

The judge was momentarily stunned to see Peter, the once-little boy he had purchased at an orphanage -- now a weary and worn defender of freedom – standing and facing him. Finally, the judge cleared his throat and spoke. "Peter? My God, Peter. Where did you come from? Where have you been?"

"Judge...sir...I...I just came from the Anderson's farm. The Mansion has been burned to the ground. There's nobody there. I can't find...I can't find Susannah or her family," said Peter, in purposeful control of his emotions.

But the judge could see that Peter was visibly shaken. "Calm down, Peter. Calm down. As far as I know, all of the Andersons, including your Susannah, are alright. I received word that some British cavalry officer by the name of Tar..."

"Tarleton!" Peter broke in. "Tarleton! He's an animal! He's worse than an animal! I hate him with every fiber of my body. He's here in Virginia? He's here in the area?"

"He was, but I don't know where he is now. He was looking for you, Peter. You have made a real enemy in that man. Anyway, when I heard he was looking for you, I thought he might go to the Anderson plantation, so I sent Alfred to warn them."

Judge Winston, through his nephew, Patrick Henry, had learned what Tarleton had planned. When Alfred had arrived with his warning, the Andersons gathered up as many belongings as had value, loaded them into wagons and carriages, and made good their escape.

"I do thank you for warning them. I know we have not always seen eye-to-eye. As for Tarleton, it is *he* who has made an enemy of *me*...more than just once. I swear, I'll hunt him down, and I'll kill him." Instinctively, Peter reached above his head and touched his broadsword.

"What have you there, Peter?"

"It's a sword. General George Washington himself had it made for me."

"From everything I have heard, you deserve it and much more. Word of how you have fought has reached all around these parts. Everybody says you're a war hero, and they speak of you as the Virginia

Giant and the Hercules of the Revolution." The judge stepped back as if to go into the house, then turned again toward the tall man on his lawn and spoke words Peter had not expected to hear...ever. "I'm so proud of you, Peter. I really am. But where do you go now?"

Trying to absorb what he had just heard, he responded, "I'm not sure. I need to find Susannah, but I don't even know where to begin to look. I also owe that cursed Tarleton a visit."

"Now hold on, Peter. I'm told that Tarleton has as many as 400 troops in his command. I don't think that even you and that sword can match those odds."

"You may be right, judge, but I have to make my plans."

"Well, in the meantime, my boy, I recall telling you that you would always have a home here at Hunting Tower."

Peter refused tones of anger or rejection when he reminded the judge, "And I recall you telling Alfred to escort me from the plantation."

"You're absolutely right, Peter. I did. But those were the ravings of a bitter and jealous man. Your room behind the main house is still empty. You are welcome to use it for as long as you want, and to come and go as you please."

The judge offered his hand. Peter hugged him instead. "My life would not be what it has become were it not for you. For that, I am forever grateful."

"It is I, and all who may one day be free of the English yoke, who should be grateful to you, Peter Francisco."

An embarrassed look swept across Peter's face, for since he did not look for praise, neither did he accept it well. He viewed himself as just another man doing what he knew in his heart needed to be done.

He did stay at Hunting Tower for several weeks and even took to his old blacksmith duties to help out. Occasionally, he would go to town and spend time exchanging stories with the very people who held him in such high regard. On one of these excursions, Peter spent the night at a tavern owned by Ben Ward.

Early in the morning, he and Ward were eating and talking. Ward had always been an affable fellow, although Peter did not trust the man because he seemed much like a willow tree that bent in whatever way the wind was blowing. He could be a loyalist one minute and a revolutionary the next. As the two chatted, they heard some riders approach and looked out the window.

It was a party of Tarleton's legion numbering nine in strength. Having left his sword upstairs in his room, Peter had no choice but to attempt an escape out a side door, but when he opened it, there stood one of the Dragoons with his sword drawn and ready.

Sensing that this was a fight he could not win, Peter threw up his hands and surrendered. However, to his good fortune, none of the raiding party realized that they had the very man their leader, Colonel Banastre Tarleton, so desperately wanted to kill. The rest of the Dragoons, looking to quench their thirst, walked into the tavern and ordered up gills of rum. In the meantime, the one who stood guard over Peter eyed him up and down.

"You don't look all that prosperous, but I'll be asking you to empty your pockets and give me all you have."

Carrying nothing of real value, Peter gave the soldier the little money he had and a pocket watch. Then the soldier spotted Peter's britches. Since returning to Hunting Tower, Peter had asked Petunia to sew his old shoe buckles to his britches so that he could buckle them just below the knee. Those buckles, shining in the sun, were what drew the Dragoon's attention now.

"Hand over those knee buckles. I'll bet they may have some value in trade." said the soldier.

The familiar roar returned to Peter, as did the tingling sensation. "These buckles hold great sentimental value to me, and I'm not handing them over to anybody. So if you want them, you'll have to take them."

In spite of his captive's size, the guard naively sensed no particular danger, especially since his fellow troopers were just inside the tavern, so he set about removing the buckles from Peter's britches. As he did so, he placed his saber under his right arm with the handle and hilt extending toward Peter.

Just as the man reached out to remove the buckle shaped like a "P," Peter grabbed the handle of the sword. With not a wasted motion, he raised the weapon and brought it down on the Dragoon's head. Though the death was quick, he managed to call out to his friends inside the tavern.

Peter took up a position right next to the door. As a hand holding a pistol aimed outward toward him, Peter brought the sword down again. Both hand and pistol fell to the ground. The troopers realized that they were trapped by a large party of colonialists, and they ran for the other door. Peter sprinted around the side of the building just as one of them mounted his horse and, aiming a musket at him, pulled the trigger. Nothing happened. The soldier re-cocked his weapon and fired again, but his carelessness in attending to his musket and not keeping the firing mechanism clean would cost him his life. The flint failed to provide a spark, and the musket failed once again to fire.

Seeing his opening, Peter charged the mounted soldier, deftly plunged his saber just beneath the man's ribcage, and lifted him off the horse.

The remaining Dragoons were in a panic trying to mount their horses, but the animals themselves were panicked. At the same time, Tarleton's men sensed that they were under attack by a superior force. When Peter realized that these soldiers were looking at the woods as much as they were paying attention to him, he seized on an idea.

"Come on boys. Help me finish them off," Peter shouted to no one. "Don't let them get away." In fear for their very lives, the remaining Dragoons abandoned all hope of remounting and started to escape on foot, but unknown to Peter, a much larger force of Tarleton's men were just a quarter mile away. When he finally saw dust in the distance behind the running men, he knew he needed to make a hasty retreat himself.

Standing near the nine horses that were still tethered, he found it easy to draw together the reins and mount one particularly handsome white stallion. With no time to waste, Peter goaded the horse and galloped off in the opposite direction from the approaching column of men being led by Tarleton himself.

Seeing that the American's head start could not be matched, Tarleton drew his horse to a halt and dismounted. As the vanquished troopers later recounted their story, Tarleton soon realized that just one man had defeated nine of his Dragoons, and to make matters worse, that one man had been Peter Francisco.

"Have none of you even the courage of a river rat?" he shouted. "I should hang you all." In a fit of rage, Tarleton drew his pistol, aimed it at the face of one of the soldiers and pulled the trigger. While reaching for his own saber and intending to take down the rest, he was pulled away by some of the Dragoons. It took several minutes for him to regain any sense of composure after being humiliated by the escape of the one opponent he hated so much.

Assuming that Tarleton's men were in pursuit, Peter ran the group of horses as fast as he could deep into the forest. After a time of meandering to cover his trail, he circled back to the tavern to see what had happened, leaving the horses behind in the woods. When he was sure that Tarleton and his men had moved on, he rode up to the tavern, wanting to retrieve his sword. Cautiously he walked in to find Ben Ward standing next to the bar. It was obvious that he had wet his pants.

"I see the excitement was a bit too much for you, old man," Peter laughed heartily.

"Peter, thank God you're alright. I told them British that you would head straight north, and they believed me! I even watched as they rode off in that direction."

"Yes, I'm sure you did. I'm sure you did just that," Peter said. Then glancing around, he added, "I'm here for my sword and belongings."

"Sure, Peter. But don't you think I'm due something for my trouble? After all, I sent them in the wrong direction, didn't I?"

Peter didn't believe a word that Ward was saying. On the other hand, it might be worth something to keep the man quiet. After all, should Tarleton's men return, Peter didn't want old man Ward pointing out the direction to Hunting Tower.

"Would two of the horses be enough to satisfy you and purchase your continued loyalty?" Peter asked.

"Absolutely. You can trust me," he answered disingenuously.

"I'm sure I can," Peter replied, not buying the commitment. "But if I learn otherwise, I'll return and our conversation will be a bit less friendly, as it will be my broadsword that'll lead the discussion." Then he wasted no time gathering up his things and returned to the woods to head the remaining horses toward the Winston plantation. When he arrived, Judge Winston was just coming out of the barn.

"My word, Peter, where did you get all those horses?" the judge queried.

"Just a little donation from Tarleton's men," Peter answered, recalling the response he and John Allen had given Colonel Mayo in answer to a similar question.

"Well, what are you going to do with them?"

"I thought you might like to buy them, since some of your Canadians have died."

"Indeed, I would, Peter, and I'll give you a fair price for them."

"I never once thought that you wouldn't, Judge. But this one," Peter said, indicating the steed he rode, "This one is not for sale. He seems a sturdy mount, and I'll name him Tarleton. If somehow my destiny is not to kill him, than I'll surely ride on his back."

20

THE END IS NEAR

The summer pressed on, and Peter was quick to jump back into a variety of duties at Hunting Tower. He was no longer looked at as a slave, or as an indentured servant, or as owned property. In fact, Judge Winston, in addition to allowing him to stay in his old room, even paid him a small sum for the work he did.

On one particularly sun-filled day, Peter knocked on the door at the main house, and Mrs. Winston answered. From the very first day, she had not taken kindly to her husband's purchase at the orphanage over fifteen years earlier. Those feelings had not really changed, though she couldn't help but admire the reputation Peter had gained from his action in the war.

"Peter, what brings you here?" Mrs. Winston said, gazing up at the man standing at her door.

"I've come to fetch the judge, but I'd also like the rest of the family to see what I have to show him."

"Come in, then. Come in. I'll go see where everybody is."

"If it's alright, I'll just wait here on the porch." Peter knew how Mrs. Winston felt, and he preferred not to come into the house. A few moments later, the entire Winston family including the children, none of whom were children anymore, gathered on the front porch.

The eldest, Sarah, had married, but her husband had been killed in the southern campaign at Charleston. After his death, she had moved back home. Anthony, Jr. had also been at Charleston where he lost an arm when the cannon he was manning exploded. Alice and Martha had grown into handsome young women but had not as yet found husbands, since most able-bodied men had gone off to fight.

Judge Winston was the last to come out onto the porch. "What's this all about, Peter? My wife says you have something to show us."

"Yes, sir, I do. I'd like you all to follow me to the barn."

The family followed him, but when they got to the barn, they saw nothing out of the ordinary.

"I don't see anything different," Sarah said.

Without saying a word, Peter pointed to the barn roof about thirty feet over them. There at the zenith of the barn's peak was attached the most magnificent and largest weather vane any of them had ever seen.

As the little group gazed into the sky, Peter broke the silence. "I don't know how long I'll be staying at Hunting Tower, but I wanted to give you something to remember me by."

Judge Winston finally spoke up. "Why, it's wonderful, Peter, just wonderful. I've always wanted a weather vane. I just never got around to having one made. Thank you, Peter. I can assure you that whenever I look up at that barn, I shall always remember the scared little boy I brought here and the fine man he has become. Thank you." The rest of the family also congratulated Peter on his work, and even the judge's wife offered some kind words.

That evening, as had become his custom since reestablishing residence at the Winston plantation, Peter visited Arthur's rock. During these visits, he poured his heart out to the old Negro who had meant so much to him. He spoke of some of the men he had fought beside in the war and of some of the battles. In the end, however, these 'discussions' always got around to Susannah.

"You would like her, Arthur. You really would. She's the one person on this earth who completes me. She makes me whole. She's the sunrise of my day, and I love her truly. But now, I don't even know where she is. I don't know if she's safe or not."

He paused for a long time. Then his conversation turned to God, about whom he had learned as a little boy. "Please, God, if there are angels in Heaven, could you ask them to look out for her and keep her from any harm? Even though You've given me great strength, I'm powerless right now, and I don't know what Tarleton's men may have done to my Susannah. Please protect her...I beg of you."

In late August, word came to Hunting Tower that Cornwallis had marched his troops toward Yorktown. His latest strategy called not for defeating the colonialists in the north, nor for defeating them in the south. His goal was to sweep across Virginia and split the colonies in two.

In the meantime, Lafayette had been harassing British fighting forces wherever and whenever he could find them. Most of these troops, however, had withdrawn with Cornwallis, who was amassing his army in Yorktown. General Washington saw an opportunity to bottle Cornwallis up and perhaps even drive the British into the sea. Thus, on August 19, he and more than 7000 of the Continental Army began their march to the south. Other colonial militia and regular forces were also told to rally there, and their strength eventually numbered nearly 20,000.

Somehow, Lafayette was able to find out that his old friend, Peter Francisco, was at Hunting Tower. Sensing that this was to be the last action, he sent a messenger to the Winston plantation to ask Peter to join him in what he was certain would be victory.

So after saying another goodbye to the Winstons, Peter mounted Tarleton, the horse, and headed toward Yorktown, arriving there on September 6, 1781. He was a bit concerned when he rode into the American camp, for he could only estimate some 4000 troops, not nearly enough to finish off Cornwallis and his men. Reaching Lafayette's tent, Peter climbed down from Tarleton just as the general was coming out of his quarters.

"*Mon ami,*" Lafayette shouted. "Peter! I cannot tell you how good it is to lay eyes on you at last. Victory is in the air, and I didn't want you to miss it."

"Victory? Did you say victory? You must have had far too many gills of rum to be claiming victory. Why, you haven't even the troop strength to put up a good fight."

"Ah, you worry too much. General Washington should arrive within the week. He has a magnificent plan to bottle up the English and put an end to them. Trust me, *mon ami*. We shall drive Cornwallis into the ocean. But how have you been? I heard about your little adventure with Tarleton's men. How is your lady friend? Are there plans for marriage yet? Remember, I am to be invited." As usual, Lafayette fired his questions like a musket volley, so happy to see his Portuguese friend.

"Lafayette, my brother, I don't know of Susannah or her whereabouts. Her family was warned about a raid by Tarleton, and they left their home only a couple of days before he arrived and burned it to the ground. Sadly, they also left before I could reach home."

Lafayette could see that his friend was quite upset, so he changed the subject while at the same time noticing the sword strapped to Peter's back. "So that's the sword the good general had made for you?"

"I almost forgot," replied Peter, drawing the sword from its scabbard to show it off.

"Oh, my God. It is even more magnificent than I had imagined. I know it took a while to get it to you, but I hear you took the lives of a good many Redcoats down at Guilford."

"Indeed. She has served me well, and I pray to use her next to put an end to Tarleton before this war comes to an end."

"Perhaps you shall. I hear that he is here with Cornwallis, so perhaps you shall. Now, come," said Lafayette as he reached up slightly and dropped an arm around Peter's shoulder. "Come tell me all that I ask."

The two of them retired to Lafayette's tent and talked the evening and night away, reminiscing about their shared adventures and bringing each other up to date on what they had done since Lafayette had waved goodbye to Peter so long ago. Lafayette had ordered an extra cot placed in his personal tent so that Peter could stay with him that night.

During one conversation, Peter told Lafayette that he had turned down the offer of a commission because he still could neither read nor write.

"There will be time for that once this war has concluded. For now, however, I wish to name you as my personal aide. Will you accept that responsibility?"

"I've served many in the same role -- Colonel Mayo, Colonel Washington and others. I would consider it the highest honor to serve as such with you, General Lafayette."

"Call me general one more time when we are alone together, *mon ami,* and I shall have you executed for insubordination." The subsequent guffaws coming from the tent compelled several high-ranking officers to look in to see what was going on.

Nearby where the war continued, a few remote skirmishes occurred on a daily basis, but none were of any consequence, and Peter and Lafayette did not participate. True to Lafayette's prediction, on September 29, reinforcements led by General George Washington arrived, having spent three days in Williamsburg. Cornwallis, sensing the Americans' intentions, had pulled his troops ever closer to Yorktown proper in order to further concentrate the strength of his defenses.

As Cornwallis continued to draw his men into a tighter circle, they were abandoning defensive trenches that they had previously dug. Washington ordered artillery placed there, his plan being to lay siege on Cornwallis and bombard the British general into submission. However,

Lord Cornwallis had left a number of redoubts to remain on the flanks of the entrenchment, so that they might harass the Americans as they prepared their cannon emplacements. At one of these redoubts, Peter Francisco would see his final action of the war.

Realizing that those British positions had to be eliminated, Washington asked for volunteers to overrun the English outposts. Lafayette was quick to accept the challenge, so Peter and his sword entered one last battle. It was to be a night attack, similar to Stony Point, and guns were not to be loaded. Lafayette's group totaled about 400 men. A similarly sized force of French troops was assigned to take a nearby redoubt.

There wasn't much action, as Lafayette's men easily stormed the position and took it at bayonet point with almost no resistance. Peter's participation was primarily to stand by Lafayette and serve as his bodyguard, and that proved to be a wise decision. As Lafayette entered the redoubt, a wounded officer lay on the ground and brought his pistol to bear on the Frenchman. Peter saw what was coming and deftly stepped between Lafayette and harm's way and drove his sword into the British officer's chest.

"*Mon ami*," Lafayette said from behind Peter's massive shoulders. "I see that I shall owe you an eternity of favors. I hate owing favors, but in this case, I shall make the exception." Peter turned around to catch the grin on Lafayette's face.

The general then sent a message to the leader of the French group, which had been assigned to take the other redoubt. It said: "I am in my redoubt. Where are you?" It took several minutes, but the French also reported that they had completed their mission.

After still more maneuvering and digging new trenches, even closer to Cornwallis and his forces, the bombardment began on October 9 and intensified on October 16 by yet more cannon. The British were taking a terrible pounding, and French ships had closed off their potential escape by sea.

On the morning of October 17, Peter and Lafayette were sitting horseback on a hilltop overlooking the trenches, cannon and the city. Without warning, out of the early morning mist came a drummer and a British officer waving a white flag. Lafayette, in somewhat disbelief, reached over and gave Peter a hard slap on the arm. "Do you see, *mon ami*? Do you see that? They are giving up. Cornwallis is surrendering. We have won. We have won. We have won!"

While that should have been Peter's most satisfying moment, the very moment he was fighting for, the surrender did not bring celebration. His mind quickly shifted to Susannah. Was she dead or alive? Where could she possibly be, and how was he going to find her? He was also greatly disappointed that he would never have the opportunity to meet Tarleton on the battlefield.

"Peter, you hardly look like a man should on such a victorious day. What is it that dulls your celebration?"

"I was just thinking about Susannah. I *am* glad the war is over, but freedom spent without the love of my life would be a hollow life, indeed."

"This I promise you, *mon ami*. We shall find her. You and I -- together. I shall not retire from these shores until we do. I owe you at least that much."

The negotiations for surrender went on for two days until, on the afternoon of October 19, the victorious troops lined both sides of the road leading from Yorktown to a makeshift table where the papers of capitulation were signed. The French were on one side of the road, the colonials on the other. In the distance, everyone could hear British drums begin to roll. Then their band started to play a somber tune called "The World Turned Upside Down" -- appropriate for the defeated English.

Surprisingly, General Lord Charles Cornwallis did not lead the British. Rather, at the head of the column came General Charles O'Hara, as Cornwallis claimed to be too ill to attend the ceremony. Also conspicuously absent was Colonel Banastre Tarleton. Perhaps the British realized that the Virginia marauder would stir up such sentiment that a riot might ensue.

The British troops declined to look directly at the Americans, preferring instead to focus their attention on the finely uniformed French. Interpreting this as an insult, Lafayette sent instructions for the American band to strike up a rendition of "Yankee Doodle." This was originally a song of mockery directed by the British troops toward the Americans in long ago and far away Boston. American soldiers up and down the lines now snickered at the turnabout.

At the conclusion of the treaty signing, the British soldiers withdrew. General George Washington mounted his horse and rode along the columns of men to review his troops. When he arrived at the point where Lafayette and Peter Francisco were sitting on their mounts, the general stopped and approached Lafayette. He nodded toward Peter, then spoke directly to Lafayette. "Without him," he said, tilting his head in Peter's direction, "we would have lost two crucial battles, perhaps the war and with it our freedom. He was truly a one-man army."

As Washington left, Lafayette, with a smile of "well done" on his face, looked over at Peter. This time Peter was smiling, too.

EPILOGUE

A man of his word, Lafayette joined Peter and the two of them set out to find Peter's lost love, Susannah Anderson. They even stopped at Hunting Tower for an evening, where Lafayette regaled the entire Winston family with tales from the war, always making sure they fully understood what a hero Peter Francisco had been. They were invited to spend the night, and when the evening drew near, Peter began to proceed to his old sleeping quarters. General Lafayette was expected to stay in the main house.

"Where are you going, *mon ami*?" Lafayette asked.

"To my room out back," Peter replied.

"Then I shall sleep there as well."

"Now wait just a minute," Judge Winston insisted "My wife has set up a room to accommodate both of you. No one is expected to sleep behind the house tonight." That was the very first time Peter had been welcomed to sleep in the main house at Hunting Tower, and it felt good.

The next morning, he and Lafayette stopped by Arthur's rock. Peter climbed down from Tarleton and spent a few moments in quiet contemplation. As he remounted, Lafayette noticed that his friend had tears in his eyes.

"He must have been quite a man," Lafayette commented.

"He was. He most certainly was," replied Peter.

"Well, he raised a fine son, and he would be proud of you, Peter Francisco." Lafayette had read the inscription Peter had put on the rock.

After stopping by what remained of The Mansion and the Anderson plantation, Peter and Lafayette scoured the countryside for any word on where Susannah might have gone. In mid-December, they spoke with a merchant who had had several business dealings with James Anderson, and he told the pair he had heard that the family had kin in Richmond. Peter and Lafayette rode as quickly as they could toward Richmond.

Arriving late at night, they took up residence at the very same hotel where Peter and Judge Winston had stayed years earlier when they went to St. John's Parish Church. Richmond had grown a great deal since then, almost tripling its population to nearly two thousand. Not knowing where to start, the two spent days going door-to-door, but still there was no word of Susannah. The days turned bitter cold, and a wet snow covered the streets as Peter and his friend approached the St. John's Church early one evening.

"Look there," said Peter pointing toward the church. "That's where I heard Patrick Henry. That's where I knew I was to fight for this country's freedom."

"That was most certainly a fateful day, Peter," Lafayette responded.

With the conclusion of the worship service, the church door was opened and people began to file out, wrapping scarves around their faces in protection against the miserable weather. This made it difficult to see where they were walking or anything else, for that matter.

Just as Peter and Lafayette arrived at the steps, a young lady slipped on a patch of ice and began to stumble. As she was about to topple into the street, Peter reached out and deftly caught her before she landed in harm's way.

The young lady looked up into the eyes of her rescuer. An awkward moment hung frozen in the winter air.

"Peter Francisco!" she uttered in astonishment. The young lady was Susannah Anderson.

Peter spoke with equal astonishment, "Susannah! I have been looking for you for so long, my love." The two held their pose, and Peter flashed his eyes at Lafayette. "We have found her, Lafayette. We have found her!"

Once again the Marquis broke into a smile. "*Mon ami.* I do not believe I have ever seen two people fall in love so...so literally. This is providence. Surely, this is the hand of God."

Peter, looking down at Susannah, smiled in agreement -- and she smiled up at him -- then pulled her closer until their lips met. That moment felt just like the night when they had first sat together on her front porch swing. Not a sound could be heard as the couple stood in that embrace with snow falling gently all around them.